For the mediaeval mystical traditions, the Christian soul meets God in a 'cloud of unknowing', a divine darkness of ignorance. This meeting with God is beyond all knowing and beyond all experiencing. Mysticisms of the modern period, on the contrary, place 'mystical experience' at the centre, and contemporary readers are inclined to misunderstand the mediaeval tradition in 'experientialist' terms. Denys Turner argues that the distinctiveness and contemporary relevance of mediaeval mysticism lies precisely in its rejection of 'mystical experience', and locates the mystical firmly within the grasp of the ordinary and the everyday. The argument covers some central authorities in the period from Augustine to John of the Cross.

THE DARKNESS OF GOD

THE DARKNESS OF GOD

Negativity in Christian mysticism

DENYS TURNER

Senior Lecturer in Theology,
University of Bristol

CAMBRIDGE
UNIVERSITY PRESS

Published by the Press Syndicate of the University of Cambridge
The Pitt Building, Trumpington Street, Cambridge CB2 1RP
40 West 20th Street, New York, NY 10011–4211, USA
10 Stamford Road, Oakleigh, Melbourne 3166, Australia

© Cambridge University Press 1995

First published 1995

Printed in Great Britain at the University Press, Cambridge

A catalogue record for this book is available from the British Library

Library of Congress cataloguing in publication data

Turner, Denys, 1942–
The darkness of God: negativity in Western mysticism / Denys Turner.
p.   cm.
Half title: The darkness of God
Includes bibliographical references (p.   ) and index.
ISBN 0 521 45317 8 (hardback.)
1. Mysticism – History – Middle Ages, 600–1500. 2. Language and languages – Religious
aspects – Christianity. 3. Negativity (Philosophy) 4. Neoplatonism. 5. Psychology, Religious.
I. Title. II. Title: The darkness of God.
BV5083.T87   1995
248.2′2′0902 – DC20 94 – 49980   CIP

ISBN 0 521 45317 8 hardback

TAG

Contents

Acknowledgements

My interest in writing this book arose out of a final year seminar course on mediaeval mysticism in the Department of Theology and Religious Studies at Bristol University. I am grateful for the enthusiasm and insight of eight generations of undergraduates who have contributed much to the formation of my ideas as well as to the formation of their own, often very different, interpretations. I wrote the whole of the text while on study-leave during the first term of the academic year 1993/4 in the Department of Theology at Durham University, in the shadow of Europe's finest Romanesque cathedral. The opportunity to engage in full-time writing in Durham was provided by my appointment to the Alan Richardson Fellowship. I owe much to my wife, Marie, for her encouragement and support and for bearing the brunt of things at home in my absence for three months. I am deeply grateful to the staff at the Durham University Library at Palace Green for their courtesy and efficiency in dealing with my somewhat unusual requests for books; and in particular to Dr Jan Rhodes of the Library at Ushaw College for personally shipping heavy folio volumes on more than one occasion by bicycle into Palace Green for my inspection.

But it is to my temporary colleagues in that fine Department in Durham that I owe the greatest academic debt. They provided me with ideal conditions, of work, friendship and hospitality, in which to write and they seemed unable to resent my self-centred exploitation of their many kindnesses. They patiently discussed many aspects of my work with me as if my work mattered as much as their own. This book is dedicated to all of them in gratitude: to Dr Robert Hayward, the Chairman of the Department; to Professors David Brown, James Dunn and Peter Selby, to Doctors Stephen Barton, Colin Crowder, Fr. George Dragas, Alan Ford, Tony

Gelston, Sheridan Gilley, Carol Harrison, Ann Loades, Walter Moberly, Alan Suggate and Sandy Wedderburn; to Sheila Robson, Margaret Parkinson and Ann Parker, the Departmental Secretarial staff; and, above all, to Mrs Phyllis Richardson, after whose late husband, Alan Richardson, the Fellowship I was so privileged to hold is named. I am also grateful to Alex Wright of Cambridge University Press for skilled advice, encouragement and much patience at every stage of the production of this book. I am indebted to Joanna Palmer of Cambridge University Press for her meticulous and sensitive copy-editing.

Introduction

This book is an essay in the philosophical history of some theological metaphors. The metaphors – of 'interiority', of 'ascent', of 'light and darkness' and of 'oneness with God' – appear to have occupied a central role in the description of the Christian ways of spirituality for as long as Christians have attempted to give one. And they still do. There are many other metaphors – in particular, there are many metaphors of Christian love – whose role is equally crucial, but I have chosen to study the particular metaphors I have mentioned, and not others, for a number of reasons, among which the following are perhaps the most important.

First, because the metaphors of inwardness, ascent and light–darkness form a closely related cluster; secondly, because taken together they have an impact on the description of the Christian way of life which is distinctively 'negative' or 'apophatic', for which reason I have called them 'metaphors of negativity'; thirdly, because they are metaphors characteristic of a Neoplatonic style of Christian theology, so that the study of them opens up lines of enquiry into an important aspect of the influence of Neoplatonism on Christian spirituality; fourthly, because they are metaphors which retain a currency still, and so it seemed that the study of them could also shed some light on what they do for us, by way of an account of the traditions from which we inherited them; and finally, this last reason seemed important to me because I suspected when I embarked on this study that the purposes which these metaphors serve for Christians today are very different from the purposes which they served within the ancient and mediaeval traditions of Christianity in the West, and that therefore it might be useful to know what those differences are. The evidence I have considered in the course of writing this book has, on the whole, confirmed this suspicion.

It takes much exposition and some argument to clarify what this suspicion amounts to, which is why it is not until the last chapter that I attempt any formal statement of it. Any explanation of my hypothesis ahead of that exposition and argument must therefore be tentative and heuristic. What I can say is that I began by wondering whether or not there was any such thing as 'mystical experience'. And I wondered about this question because on the one hand there seemed to be a common, informal view around that the 'mystical' had something to do with the having of very uncommon, privileged 'experiences'; and, on the other, because when I read any of the Christian writers who were said to be mystics I found that many of them – like Eckhart or the Author of *The Cloud of Unknowing* – made no mention at all of any such experiences and most of the rest who, like John of the Cross or Teresa of Avila, did make mention of 'experiences', attached little or no importance to them and certainly did not think the having of them to be definitive of 'the mystical'.

Then almost immediately I found myself wondering whether that was a very good question at all. For it seemed very unclear what the question was being asked about. What is 'mysticism'? What is 'experience'? The latter question seemed to me to be too difficult; the former, to be a blind alley, for I do not know of any discussions which shed less light on the subject of 'mysticism' than those many which attempt *definitional* answers to the question 'what is mysticism?' For it seems that answers generally fall into two categories: those which are merely *stipulative* and whose relation with actual mysticisms is at best contingent; and those which are merely *descriptive* of the varieties of actual mysticisms, the question of which varieties are included in the canon being left to convention or intuition. Neither way of answering the question seems very satisfactory in principle, nor do they shed much light on the subject in practice.

Hence, I set the problem as stated in that very a priori form on one side, though it seemed to me that there was *some* problem about 'experience' which did need clarification. And so I embarked upon the study of a group of 'mystical' writers within the late Patristic and mediaeval traditions of Latin Christianity: a group characterised by their explicit reception of the influence of Neoplatonism and by their systematic exploitation of these metaphors. My hope was to clarify what that problem was. Very quickly I began to observe a puzzling fact which did seem to have some bearing on the question of 'mystical experience' not in its limited form of 'special' or 'ecstatic' experiences, but in the most general form of the role of religious experience as such within the understanding of 'the mystical'.

I began by supposing that it would be fruitful to look at some elements of the metaphorical lingua franca of Western Christian writing about 'spirituality' and 'mysticism' – or what Bonaventure rather more engagingly called 'the journey of the soul into God'. It seemed that there was common agreement among these 'Neoplatonists', from Augustine to John of the Cross, in the description of that *itinerarium mentis* as an *itinerarium intus*, a journey of 'inwardness'; it was commonly agreed, moreover, that the journey of 'inwardness' could also be described as an 'ascent', whether of a ladder or of a mountain. And it was commonly agreed that as the soul ascended to God it would approach a source of light which, being too bright for its powers of reception, would cause in it profound darkness.

Now all these metaphors seem, as I have said, still to be in current usage when Christians, following ancient traditions, seek to describe the ways of prayer, spirituality and mysticism. I do not think we would know how to describe what it is that Christians are to do, or how they are to do it, without some appeal to the language of 'inwardness' and that of 'ascent', for those metaphors are built in to our psychological and epistemological language so intimately that we have, I suspect, quite literally *embodied* them. Christians, in the West, quite spontaneously close their eyes when they want to pray with concentration, in tribute, perhaps, to the need for inwardness. And though verticality is no longer, as it was once in the Middle Ages, the spontaneous communal architecture of the divine, it remains, I think, the natural metaphor of the individual, as against the communal, relationship with God: as when today some complain of excessively social forms of Christianity that they neglect the 'vertical' for the sake of the 'horizontal'.

But from my study of the mediaeval mystical tradition, I began to see that not only would it be dangerous to assume that the similarities of language entailed a similarity of purpose, but that it would be actually wrong to suppose this. For the purposes being served by this cluster of metaphors in the mediaeval traditions began to seem very different from those it is serving today and, in one important respect, it looked as if it is serving an opposed purpose. Moreover, that difference of purpose seemed to have to do with − and at the same time seemed to clarify − the problem about the role of 'experience' within 'the mystical'.

Put very bluntly, the difference seemed to be this: that whereas our employment of the metaphors of 'inwardness' and 'ascent' appears to be tied in with the achievement and the cultivation of a certain kind of experience − such as those recommended within the practice of what is called, nowadays, 'centring' or 'contemplative' prayer − the mediaeval employment of them was tied in with a 'critique' of such religious experiences and practices. Whereas we appear to have 'psychologized' the metaphors, the Neoplatonic mediaeval writer used the metaphors in an 'apophatic' spirit to play down the value of the 'experiential'; and that, therefore, whereas it would come naturally to the contemporary, 'psychologising' mind to think of 'the mystical' in terms of its characterizing *experiences*, the mediaeval mind thought of the 'mystical', that is to say, the 'hidden' or 'secret', wisdom as being what the Author of *The Cloud of Unknowing* called a 'divinity' which is 'hidden' precisely *from* experience. It is impossible, in advance of telling the long and complex story of mediaeval Neoplatonic mysticism, to state this opposition between the mediaeval and the modern employment of the common language otherwise than thus bluntly and crudely. But it is necessary to do so in advance, even if crudely, because, in the last resort, that is what the story as I tell it is about.

It is, after all, a story about the meaning of the word 'mystical'; and it is therefore a story about what the practice of 'mysticism' consists in. I have drawn the conclusion from my study that in so far as the word 'mysticism' has a contemporary meaning; and that in so far as that contemporary meaning links 'mysticism' to the cultivation of certain kinds of experience − of 'inwardness', 'ascent' and 'union' − then the mediaeval 'mystic' offers an *anti-mysticism*. For though the mediaeval Christian neoplatonist used that same language of interiority, ascent and 'oneness', he or she did so precisely in order to deny that they were terms descriptive of 'experiences'. And the central metaphor of this negativity, of this restraint of 'experience', was the apophatic metaphor of 'light' and 'darkness', of the 'cloud of unknowing'.

My suspicion being thus far clarified, it was obviously important to discover what accounted for this very radical shift of purpose to which that language had been submitted. And, again paraphrasing a complex answer, what is distinctive about the employment of these metaphors within the mediaeval traditions of 'mystical theology' is the Neoplatonic dialectical epistemology – its apophaticism – within which those metaphors are set and by which their employment is governed. What differentiates the mediaeval employment of those metaphors from ours is the fact that we have retained the metaphors, evacuated them of their dialectics and refilled them with the stuff of 'experience'. This modern development I call 'experientialism'. And for all I know it is a development to be welcomed. Some, no doubt, will say so, though I do not agree. But what matters from the point of view of the argument of this book is the quite different consideration that if we read the mediaeval Neoplatonic mystics – and increasingly they are being read – from within the perspectives of a contemporary 'experientialism' we will very grossly misread them, for we will find in them allies for a position which, in truth, they reject.

An ultimate purpose of this book is, therefore, to be an essay in the retrieval of the mediaeval tradition of apophatic, or 'negative' mysticism. The retrieval I have in mind is their rescue from a contemporary 'experientialist' misreading and therefore to make them more valuable to us, paradoxically not by making them easier to read but by making them more difficult. For as read adequately, they challenge much in contemporary thought and spirituality, in particular they challenge a certain positivism of religious experience. The mystics I discuss may seem to acquire, as a result, a rather more austere, spare, 'reduced' physiognomy than they appeared, formerly, to possess. But I am afraid I think it more important to dislike these authors, if we must, for what they are than to like them for what they are not.

That, more or less, was the programme I discovered for myself in the course of researching for this book. In the course of writing it, however, another important problem began to emerge which, like the first, brought into play the difficult matter of how to relate our contemporary conceptions with those of a long tract of a very different historical period. And that problem was the problem of 'the self'. I do not think that I became fully conscious of the scale of this problem until I began to write about the fourteenth-century masters, in particular about Meister Eckhart. But with Eckhart, with the *Cloud* Author and with John of the Cross, the problem became inescapable of what significance their practical strictures of a 'self-denial' and a detachment had for what we think of, if there is any one thing that we think of, as being 'the self'.

For in these authors may be found what I have called an 'apophatic anthropology' as radical as their apophatic theology, the one intimately connected with the other. All three in *some* sense deny that I am 'a self'; or at least, they appear to say that whatever may be the proper description of the fullest union of the human self with God, there is no distinction which we are able to make *between* that 'self' and the God it is one with. Nor are they alone in this, Julian of Norwich, Catherine of Genoa and Teresa of Avila being three others who say the same.

But in *what* sense do I, when 'one' with God, cease to be a 'self-other-than-God'? In some sense in which *we* think of 'selfhood'? Do they deny something which in our modern culture we think it important to assert – our identities as *individual* selves? Or is the mediaeval denial of 'the self' consistent with whatever it is that we wish to assert about the self? And what do *we* wish to assert about the self? For any given contemporary conception of the self, who are the 'we' who assert it? These questions made me uneasy. They seemed to create an immense and new agenda, altogether too vast in scope to be contained within the limits of the essay I had envisaged. And yet they were also inescapable questions, for they arose inevitably out of that original agenda; in fact, from Augustine to John of the Cross, the question of 'interiority' *is* the question of what 'I' am; for in this tradition 'I' am in the last resort what I am in my deepest 'interiority'. And if, in my deepest inwardness, I and God meet in a union beyond description and beyond experience, then an apophaticism of language about God and an apophaticism of language about the 'self' are obviously intimately connected. What is more, if that is the case then the same question of interpretation must be raised about the apophatic concepts of 'self' as about theological apophaticism: do we think about the 'self' so differently from our mediaeval forebears that perforce we misinterpret them in reading what they say about it against the background of our own preoccupations?

No one, least of all I, could regard the brief attempts I make to discuss these questions as being sufficient. It could be said that I attempt to bite off more than I can chew. That would be unfair. I attempt no such thing. Intentionally I only nibble. In particular, the historical hypothesis outlined in the last chapter is meant to be no more than a sketch of some late mediaeval developments which anticipate the emergence, perhaps in the nineteenth century, perhaps earlier (I do not know when) of a distinct, esoteric essence of the 'mystical', a thing in itself; and the sketch is intended only to be sufficient to indicate the plausibility of a rash hypothesis, having a bearing on both parts of my argument about mediaeval Neoplatonic mysticism; that is to say, both on the question of 'experience' and on that of 'the self'.

The hypothesis is that there is too much discontinuity between what the mediaeval Neoplatonic apophaticist meant by the 'mystical' element in theology and life and what modern people have come to mean by 'mysticism', to permit of the common assumption that Western Christianity possesses a single 'mystical tradition' embracing them both. For sure there is sequence and historical causation, often direct 'influence'. And there is a common vocabulary and imagery. But mere sequence and even common causation does not entail common purpose; common language and imagery do not entail a shared significance. At its boldest, my hypothesis is that modern interpretation has invented 'mysticism' and that we persist in reading back the terms of that conception upon a stock of mediaeval authorities who knew of no such thing – or, when they knew of it, decisively rejected it.

The outline of this hypothesis is so lightly sketched that true as I think it is, it is evidently falsifiable as it stands. I do not identify when, where or how this conception of 'mysticism' emerges – though I am inclined towards McGinn's suggestion that it is a product of nineteenth-century scholarship. Nor do I offer any account of what this 'mysticism' is, except in so far as I detect its emergence within developments in late mediaeval theology. My case rests on three factors mainly: first, and indicatively, that perhaps from the late fourteenth century, the canon of those now called 'mystics' ceases to include theologians of repute and, *e converso*, from that time to our own the canon of theologians includes no mystics. This generalization is surprisingly exceptionless. Secondly, and more substantively, in the classical period of mediaeval theology, the *metaphors* of negativity are interpenetrated by a high Neoplatonic *dialectics* of negativity; that late mediaeval voluntarisms begin to lose their grip on this dialectics at about the same time, and that, in modern times, the grip is lost entirely. Thirdly, and again at the same time, the problem of what I call 'experientialism' emerges. It is harder to doubt that these things happen than that they are linked, still less is it easily demonstrated that they are so linked as to put in question the continuity of 'the Western Christian mystical tradition'. For, of course, proof of connectedness is no more guaranteed by synchronicity than by sequence. But my claim is one of the plausibility of an hypothesis, not, as I say, of a certainty warranted by sufficient evidence.

Finally, it has been no purpose of mine to demonstrate, nor do I think it the inevitable consequence of what I do demonstrate, that we must despair of being able to read the mediaeval apophaticists without profitless misinterpretation. On the contrary, though I do believe that we have been misreading them equally within the recent traditions of comparative scholarship and within the rather closed, anti-intellectual world of Christian 'spiritualities', the concluding remarks of the last chapter hint at the possibility that certain quite contemporary developments in Western thought, associated with 'post-modernism', contain a revival of that awareness of the 'deconstructive' potential of human thought and language which so characterized classical mediaeval apophaticism. Those remarks contain the agenda of another book as much as the conclusion of this one. But it might be noted that if there are points of intellectual convergence in our times between mediaeval and contemporary apophaticisms, there is this at least in which those two cultures differ: that in the Middle Ages, apophaticism was no mere intellectual critique of discourse, but was in addition a practice which was expected to be embodied in a life. For us, the disarray of our cultural decentredness is often perceived as the bewildering consequence of a fact. Perhaps there is something to be learned from that Christian theological tradition which consciously *organized* a strategy of disarrangement as a way of life, as being that in which alone God is to be found.

PART ONE

Two sources and a synthesis

CHAPTER I

The Allegory and Exodus

I

It is necessary to begin the story-line of our enquiry somewhere. And though it is always possible to take the story back historically beyond a chosen starting point, the primary interest of this study is systematic and conceptual, rather than historical. When I say, therefore, that a source for the Western Christian employment of the metaphors of darkness and light and of ascent and descent may be found in the impact of converging Greek and Hebraic influences on Western Christian thought, I have primarily in mind a deductive possibility, designed to shed light on an historical claim. I maintain, that is to say, that you *could* extract the main linguistic building blocks of the Western Christian tradition from the quarry of this convergence, and, even more particularly, that you could extract those building blocks from two stories, each foundational in the intellectual and religious cultures of its respective tradition: the 'Allegory of the Cave' in Book 7 of Plato's *Republic*, and the story in Exodus of Moses' encounter with Yahweh on Mount Sinai. You *could* do this: that is to say, with those two stories as premisses, you could satisfactorily derive much of the distinctiveness of the language of the Western Christian mystical tradition as conclusion.

Nevertheless, it is perfectly reasonable to go beyond a point merely in explanatory logic. There is little doubt that, whether it was the Greek cast of mind picking up the religious significance of Exodus in Platonic terms, or an Hebraic mind which seized upon the philosophical opportunities to be explored in Plato, this convergence *did* happen and was consciously acknowledged to have happened by theologians both of Greek and Latin traditions. Thus for once, did logic and history coincide. What those theologians thought they were doing explains what they did. They wanted to bring Plato and Exodus together. The effect of their doing so was a seismic shock which was still registering tremors twelve hundred years later –

θ though in our time the earth no longer moves, and what we perceive is the fixed metaphoric topography into which the landscape has settled. Today most of us are no more aware of the geological origins of that landscape in the ancient upheaval than we are conscious of the geological origins of the Cambrian mountains we walk on.

From the standpoint we intend to occupy, three Greek theologians principally embody this convergence: Gregory of Nyssa, Denys the Areopagite[1] and Maximus the Confessor. Of these, the second is pivotal from the point of view of the Western mystical tradition. For from within the perspectives of the mediaeval Western mystic, Gregory's importance lay chiefly in his influence on Denys[2] and, though his work was known and studied in the mediaeval West, Maximus was best known as a commentator on Denys. The ranking of these three looks very different, of course, from the standpoint of Greek Christianity; for the Greek tradition Gregory and Maximus tower above Denys, who has never enjoyed in the Greek Church the prestige he was once accorded in the Latin.

Moreover, even in the Latin Church, the impact of Denys was slow to make its presence felt. Modern scholars assume Denys to have written at the end of the fifth or early in the sixth century, but he was not translated into intelligible Latin, by John Scottus, until the ninth century.[3] And a further qualification: enthusiasm for Denys was never universal even in the Latin West, for he found little favour with the majority of the monastic theologians,[4] his impact being felt mainly in the theological schools of the urban

---

[1] Throughout this essay I have preferred the archaism 'Denys' to the more modern appellations, 'the Pseudo-Dionysius' or 'Pseudo-Denys'. We do not know who he was; and what he was – a Greek speaking Syrian monk – is only probable. Our best efforts at dating suggest that he was writing towards the end of the fifth century and the early years of the sixth. He wrote as if he were the Denys mentioned in Acts 17, 34 as having been one of Paul's few successes in the Areopagus at Athens. This, of course, is untrue, but his credentials were not seriously or widely doubted until the sixteenth century. In the meantime he was credited with sub-apostolic authority in the High and Late Middle Ages.

[2] Though today, one has to add that there is in the West an increasing interest in Gregory's 'mystical' theology in its own right. Of course, as one of the three 'Cappadocian Fathers', Gregory of Nyssa's contribution to the development of Trinitarian orthodoxy has always been acknowledged, in the West as in the East.

[3] In fact the first Latin translation of Denys was made by Abbot Hilduin of St Denis for the Emperor Michael II, who sent a copy as a present to Louis the Pious in 827. But the translation was thought unreadably obscure and Charles II, the Bald, asked John Scottus to redo the translation in 860–62.

[4] Leclerq puts Denys' relative unpopularity with the monks down to a combination of the very great obscurity of his style and the 'little basis' of his ideas 'in sacred scripture'. See: Jean Leclerq, 'Influence and Non-influence of Dionysius in the Western Middle Ages', in, *Pseudo-Dionysius, The Complete Works*, trans. Colm Luibheid, New Jersey: Paulist Press, 1987, p. 31.

universities and in the circles of the 'mystical theologians'. Consequently, one has to say that the influence of Denys was principally felt within Western Christianity in the four hundred years from the twelfth century to the sixteenth, and then chiefly within the formation of its systematic and mystical theologies.

But when that has been said, it remains true that 'mystical theology' in the West is in itself unintelligible except against the background of Denys' writings, and in the same degree the course of its historical development would be inexplicable without them. More than that, if and insofar as 'mystical theology' is the product of the convergence of sources in Plato and in Exodus – or can be summarily construed that way – then it is scarcely an exaggeration to say that Denys invented the genre for the Latin Church; and for sure, he forged the language, or a good part of it, and he made a theology out of those central metaphors without which there could not have been the mystical tradition that there has been: 'light' and 'darkness', 'ascent' and 'descent', the love of God as *eros*. This is the vocabulary of our mysticism: historically we owe it to Denys; and he owed it, as he saw it, to Plato and Moses.

Here is how he combines the epistemological interests of Plato with the theological emphases of the Exodus narrative:

It is not for nothing that the blessed Moses is commanded to submit first to purification and then to depart from those who have not undergone this. When every purification is complete, he hears the many voiced trumpets. He sees the many lights, pure and with rays streaming abundantly. Then, standing apart from the crowds and accompanied by chosen priests, he pushes ahead to the summit of the divine ascents. And yet he does not meet God himself, but contemplates, not him who is invisible, but rather where he dwells. This means, I presume, that the holiest and highest of the things perceived with the eye of the body or the mind are but the rationale which presupposes all that lies below the Transcendent One. Through them, however, his unimaginable presence is shown, walking the heights of those holy places to which the mind at least can rise. But then he [Moses] breaks free of them, away from what sees and is seen, and he plunges into the truly mysterious darkness of unknowing. Here, renouncing all that the mind may conceive, wrapped entirely in the intangible and the invisible, he belongs completely to him who is beyond everything. Here, being neither oneself nor someone else, one is supremely united by a completely unknowing inactivity of all knowledge, and knows beyond the mind by knowing nothing.[5]

[5] *Mystical Theology* (*MT*), 1000C–1001A, in *Pseudo-Dionysius, The Complete Works*, trans. Colm Luibheid, New Jersey: Paulist Press, 1987.

II

This retelling of Moses' ascent of Mount Sinai is a pastiche of both the Exodus narrative and Platonic imagery. As to the imagery, the source is Plato's allegory of the philosopher's ascent to wisdom in *Republic* 7. Picture men, Socrates asks, who are imprisoned deep in a cave facing its back wall, unable to move their heads or any other parts of their bodies; imagine that, above and behind them, there is a low wall, behind which again is a fire casting the shadows of puppets representing all kinds of objects upon the back wall the prisoners face. The prisoners are able to see no more than the shadows of these puppets and hear nothing but the echoes of their operators' voices and, significantly, they cannot see even themselves but only their own shadows, for they cannot turn their faces to each other or to their own bodies. Would not such prisoners, Socrates asks, 'deem reality to be nothing else than the shadows of the artificial objects?'.[6]

Suppose further that one of the prisoners is released and turned to face the light which throws the shadows, will he not 'feel pain and because of the dazzle and glitter of the light' be 'unable to discern the objects whose shadows he formerly saw?'[7] Disoriented, his conversion has gained for him the worst of both worlds, for dazzled by the excess of light he derives no profit from that, and worse, as a result he is unable to see even in his former twilight world, to whose undemanding security he pines to return.

The prisoner, then, will not willingly proceed further 'up the ascent', for it is 'rough and steep';[8] and so he will have to be dragged forcibly out of the cave into the light of the sun, where 'his eyes will be filled with its beams, so that he would not be able to see even one of the things which we call real'.[9]

Once again, the excess of light is distress to the eyes which for a second time are plunged into darkness, now even deeper than the first. Gradually, however, as his eyes become stronger and more used to the new light, the prisoner feebly glimpses first in shadows and in reflections in pools the objects outside the cave, and then sees the things themselves: 'and from these he would go on to contemplate the appearances in the heavens and heaven itself, more

[6] *Republic*, 515C. All quotations from the *Republic* are given in the translation by Paul Shorey, Cambridge Mass.: Loeb Classical Library, 1956, 2 vols.

[7] Ibid., 515C.   [8] Ibid., 515E.   [9] Ibid., 516A.

easily by night, looking at the light of the stars and the moon, than by day the sun and the sun's light'.[10]

Finally, his eyes being at last fully habituated to the light, the prisoner will, Socrates says, 'be able to look upon the sun itself and see its true nature, not by reflections in water or phantasms of it in an alien setting, but in and by itself in its own place'.[11] And in contemplating the sun, the emancipated prisoner sees not only the highest and most luminous of all things, but also that which is 'the cause of all these things that they had seen'.[12]

Now the philosopher will pity his one-time fellow prisoners who, he sees, at best compete with one another in an absurd game of precedence in the perception of shadows and appearances, mistaking them for reality; they remain trapped in a world of lived unreality. Having seen it for what it is, the philosopher 'would choose to endure anything rather than such a life',[13] and in his pity he returns to the cave with the hope of persuading his former inmates to turn away from their world of unreality and to turn, as he had done, toward the contemplation of the true light he has seen for himself.

But the shock of the contrast between the light he inhabits and the gloom of the cave casts his eyes yet again into darkness as he descends. There, he debates with the prisoners and is ridiculed for his account of his own ascent, for they complain that his adventures have but ruined his eyesight. The prisoners resent his claims to a better vision of things and they will kill him if they can.

This image then...we must apply as a whole to all that has been said, likening the region revealed through sight to the habitation of the prison, and the light of the fire in it to the power of the sun. And if you assume that the ascent and the contemplation of the things above is the soul's ascension to the intelligible region, you will not miss my surmise, since that is what you desire to hear. But the Gods know whether it is true. But, at any rate, my dream as it appears to me is that in the region of the known the last thing to be seen and hardly seen is the idea of the good, and when seen it must needs point us to the conclusion that this is indeed the cause for all things of all that is right and beautiful, giving birth to the visible world of light, and the author of light and itself in the intelligible world being the authentic source of truth and reason...[14]

Plato, then, intended this fiction as an allegory of the philosopher's ascent to knowledge. Christians read it as an allegory of the ascent to God.

---

[10] Ibid., 516A–B. [11] Ibid., 516B. [12] Ibid., 516B–C.
[13] Ibid., 516E. [14] Ibid., 517B–D.

III

More diffuse, and by no means organized with the same intention
of allegory, are the narratives of two episodes in Exodus. In the
first (Exod. 19, 20) Moses ascends Mount Sinai at the summons of
Jahweh, there to meet with him and to be told of a visitation which
Jahweh will make to Moses 'in a dark cloud' (19, 9). The people of
Israel are told, on the other hand, that they are not to go up
Mount Sinai, or 'even touch the border of it' on pain of death (19,
12); they will, at the appropriate trumpet signal, be permitted to
approach the lower slopes.

'On the morning of the third day there were thunders and light-
nings, and a thick cloud upon the mountain...and Mount Sinai was
wrapped in smoke, because the Lord descended upon it in fire...'
(19, 16, 18). And the Lord said to Moses 'Go down and warn the
people, lest they break through to the Lord to gaze and many of
them perish' (19, 21).

Upon the mountain, Jahweh reveals the fundamental law which
will govern the people of Israel, the Decalogue (20, 1-17), but the
attendant paraphernalia of smoke, fire and lightning terrifies the
people of Israel. So they demand of Moses that he 'speak to us,
and we will hear; but let not God speak to us, lest we die' (20, 19).
And while the people stand afar off 'Moses withdrew to the thick
darkness where God was' (20, 21), there to hear Jahweh's further
warnings against idolatries and other such matters.

By no means are the warnings given prematurely, for the people
have already lost patience with Moses' long absence (32, 1) and
have fallen to the worship of idols. So Moses descends the mountain to confront them, and having violently restored order (32, 27-
28) returns to the mountain to plead with Jahweh on their behalf.
'Show me', he prays, 'your glory'.

And [Jahweh] said, 'I will make all my goodness pass before you, and will
proclaim before you my name "the Lord"; and I will be gracious to whom
I will be gracious, and will show mercy to whom I will show mercy. But',
he said, 'you cannot see my face; for man shall not see me and live'. And
the Lord said, 'Behold, there is a place by me where you shall stand upon
the rock; and while my glory passes by I will put you in a cleft of the rock,
and will cover you with my hand until I have passed by; then I will take
away my hand, and you shall see my back; but my face shall not be seen.'
(33, 19-23)

IV

A mind educated so thoroughly in the Platonic traditions as was Denys' could easily pick up the metaphorical resonances of the Exodus narrative; and on the other hand, it is not hard to see how some of the early theologians of the Christian Church came to the conclusion, as Justin Martyr did,[15] that the ancient Greeks must have plagiarized the Hebrew scriptures, so obvious did it seem to them that the best Greek thought depended upon the inspired writings of Israel. It is debatable which description is correct of Gregory of Nyssa's mind, whether he was a Greek Christian or a Christian Greek, but this is beside the point. In his mind, either, the Christian or the Greek, could evoke a response in the other and both the spontaneous harmonising of imagery and the perception of a common narrative structure are evident in that most Platonic of Christian Old Testament exegetes, as the following passage from his *Life of Moses* shows:

What does it mean that Moses entered the darkness and then saw God in it?...Scripture teaches...[that] as the mind progresses and, through an even greater and more perfect diligence, comes to apprehend reality, as it approaches more nearly to contemplation, it sees more clearly what of the divine nature is uncontemplated.

For leaving behind everything that is observed, not only what sense comprehends but also what the intelligence thinks it sees, it keeps on penetrating deeper until by the intelligence's yearning for understanding it gains access to the invisible and the incomprehensible, and there it sees God. This is the true knowledge of what is sought; this is the seeing which consists in not seeing, because that which is sought transcends all knowledge, being separated on all sides by incomprehensibility as by a kind of darkness...When, therefore, Moses grew in knowledge, he declared that he had seen God in the darkness, that is, when he had then come to know that what is divine is beyond all knowledge and comprehension, for the text says, *Moses approached the dark cloud where God was* (Exod., 20, 21).[16]

We could describe that common narrative structure as 'dialectical'. In both the Allegory and in Exodus, there is an ascent toward the brilliant light, a light so excessive as to cause pain, distress and darkness: a darkness of knowledge deeper than any which is the darkness of ignorance. The price of the pure contemplation of the

[15] *Apologia*, I, Migne: *Patrologia Graeca* (*PG*), 6, 396A – C.
[16] *The Life of Moses*, 2.162–164, trans. A. J. Malherbe and E. Ferguson, New York: Paulist Press, 1978, pp. 94–95.

light is therefore darkness, even, as in Exodus, death, but not the darkness of the absence of light, rather of its excess – therefore a 'luminous darkness'. In both, descent from the darkness of excessive light is return to an opposed darkness of ignorance, the half-light of the cave, where there is only incredulity and ridicule to be had from those who cannot credit the witness to anything more real. Light is darkness, knowing is unknowing, a cloud, and the pain of contemplating it, is the pain of contemplating more reality than can be borne: 'man may not see me and live'.

CHAPTER 2

Cataphatic and the apophatic in Denys the Areopagite

I

At the outset of our enquiry we need an explanation, if only of the most general sort, of two technical terms belonging to the vocabulary of late Platonist Christian theology, for without them the explanation of the purposes of this chapter is impossible. Those terms are 'apophaticism' and its complementary partner, 'cataphaticism'. They have a technical sense, and it is a principal purpose of this essay to clarify that sense, or those senses, which they acquire within the Latin traditions of Neoplatonic mysticism, but for the immediate purpose of getting that discussion going, they can be given an accessibly non-technical explanation. 'Apophaticism' is the name of that theology which is done against the background of human ignorance of the nature of God. It is the doing of theology in the light of the statement of Thomas Aquinas in the thirteenth century, that 'we do not know what kind of being God is'.[1] It is the conception of theology not as a naive *pre*-critical ignorance of God, but as a kind of acquired ignorance, a *docta ignorantia* as Nicholas of Cues called it in the fifteenth century. It is the conception of theology as a strategy and practice of unknowing, as the fourteenth-century English mystic called it, who, we might say, invented the transitive verb-form 'to unknow' in order to describe theological knowledge, in this its deconstructive mode.[2] Finally, 'apophaticism' is the same as what the Latin tradition of Christianity called the *via negativa*, 'the negative way'. These are among the things which are meant by the term 'apophaticism'.

---

[1] Even through the revelation of grace: 'and so we are united with [God] as to something unknown to us', *Summa Theologiae (ST)*, I, q.12, a.13, ad 1; cf also: '...in this life our understanding does not know him as he is', q.13, a.1 ad 2.
[2] *The Cloud of Unknowing*, see especially chapters 4 – 7.

It follows from the *unknowability* of God that there is very little that can be *said* about God: or rather, since most theistic religions actually have a great number of things to say about God, what follows from the unknowability of God is that we can have very little idea of what all these things said of God *mean*. And, strictly speaking, that is what 'apophaticism' asserts, as one can tell from its Greek etymology: *apophasis* is a Greek neologism for the breakdown of *speech*, which, in face of the unknowability of God, falls infinitely short of the mark.

On the other hand, if we attend to the Greek etymology of the word *theology*, then a curious state of linguistic affairs results from its combination with the word *apophatic*. For *theology* means 'discourse about God' or 'divine discourse', so the expression ᵢᵥ 'apophatic theology' ought to mean something like: 'that speech about God which is the failure of speech'. And, though more than a little paradoxical, as a sketch of what Christian theology is, or at any rate ought to be like, this definition rather precisely captures the Dionysian understanding of it, as we will see.

What, then, of the 'cataphatic'? The cataphatic is, we might say, the verbose element in theology, it is the Christian mind deploying all the resources of language in the effort to express something about God, and in that straining to speak, theology uses as many voices as it can. It is the cataphatic in theology which causes its metaphor-ridden character, causes it to borrow vocabularies by analogy from many another discourse, whether of science, literature, art, sex, politics, the law, the economy, family life, warfare, play, teaching, physiology, or whatever. It is its cataphatic tendencies which account for the sheer *heaviness* of theological language, its character of being linguistically *overburdened*; it is the cataphatic which accounts for that fine *nimietas* of image which we may observe in the best theologies, for example in Julian of Norwich or Bernard of Clairvaux. For in its cataphatic mode, theology is, we might say, a kind of verbal riot, an anarchy of discourse in which anything goes. And when we have said that much, narrowly, about the formal language of theology, we have only begun: for that is to say nothing about the extensive *non*-verbal vocabulary of theology, its liturgical and sacramental action, its music, its architecture, its dance and gesture, all of which are intrinsic to its character as an *expressive* discourse, a discourse of theological articulation.

So much, provisionally, for terminology. As for matters of substance, the first question to arise from these terminological remarks is also the main preoccupation of this chapter, namely, 'what is the relation between the apophatic and the cataphatic elements within Christian theology, between its wordiness and its astringency, between its desire to speak and its knowledge of when to stop?'. We turn first to the writings of Denys for an answer to this question, an answer which was to have, as I put it in the last chapter, ground-shifting consequences for the Latin traditions of mysticism.

II

Denys opens his *Mystical Theology* with a prayer:

> Trinity!! Higher than any being
>   any divinity, any goodness!
>   Guide of Christians
>   in the wisdom of heaven!
> Lead us up beyond knowing and light,
>   up to the farthest, highest peak
>   of mystic scripture
>   where the mysteries of God's Word
>   lie simple, absolute, unchangeable
>   in the brilliant darkness of a hidden silence.
> Amid the deepest shadow
>   they pour overwhelming light
>   on what is most manifest.
> Amid the wholly unsensed and unseen
>   they completely fill our sightless minds
>   with treasures beyond all beauty.[3]

Denys designs this prayer on the structural principle of what I shall call the 'self-subverting' utterance, the utterance which first says something and then, in the same image, unsays it. The divine light is a 'brilliant darkness'; the 'mysteries of God's word' are uttered in a 'hidden silence'. At the end of the same chapter, in a passage already quoted, Denys says that on the highest peaks of knowledge 'one is neither oneself nor someone else' and that one is 'supremely united' by 'an unknowing inactivity of all knowledge and knows beyond mind by knowing nothing'.[4] In chapter two of *Mystical Theology*, we are told of the necessity to deny all things of the 'primary' [God] 'so that we may unhiddenly know that unknowing which is itself hidden...so that we may see above being that darkness concealed from the light'.[5] But yet, in the last chapter

---

[3] *MT*, 997A–B.   [4] Ibid., 1001A.   [5] Ibid., 1025B.

of the same work, Denys says of God, the 'Cause of all': 'Darkness and light...*it is none of these*'.[6] So, it is both darkness and light; it is a luminous darkness and a dark brilliance; it is neither darkness nor light. What are we to make of this?

III

These opaque utterances are contrived, they are deliberately paradoxical, but they are not merely artful. They are, for Denys, the natural linguistic medium of his negative, apophatic theology: or, more strictly speaking, they are the natural medium of a theological language which is subjected to the *twin* pressures of affirmation and negation, of the cataphatic and the apophatic. We must both affirm and deny all things of God; and then we must negate the contradiction between the affirmed and the denied. That is why we must say affirmatively that God is 'light', and then say, denying this, that God is 'darkness'; and finally, we must 'negate the negation' between darkness and light, which we do by saying: 'God is a brilliant darkness'. For the negation of the negation is not a *third* utterance, additional to the affirmative and the negative, in good linguistic order; it is not some intelligible *synthesis* of affirmation and negation; it is rather the collapse of our affirmation and denials into disorder, which we can only express, *a fortiori*, in bits of collapsed, disordered language, like the babble of a Jeremiah. And that is what the 'self-subverting' utterance is, a bit of disordered language. Since that is also, for Denys, what theological language is when stretched to its fullest extent, that language naturally, spontaneously and rightly takes the form of paradox, and not merely for the sake of effect.

IV

What Denys has to say about theological language is but the transposition of the Platonic dialectics of the Cave Allegory into the domain of discourse. If the light of the sun is a mind-stunning darkness, so is the reality of the divine a language-defeating silence. We could say that the predicament for theology is rather like that of the verbose teacher, who in shame at having talked too much in

[6]   Ibid., 1048A.

the class, lapses into an embarrassed silence. Good theology, Denys thinks, has the same outcome, for it leads to that silence which is found only on the other side of a general linguistic embarrassment.

But that embarrassment has to be procured, and to reach that point – this is the essence of the cataphatic – it is necessary for theology to talk too much. Denys is insistent. Although we may properly attribute to God only those names which have the authority of Scripture, this is hardly for him a restrictive condition since scriptural writers 'praise [the Cause of all] by every name – and as the Nameless One';[7] and so as to reinforce the point, Denys lists fifty-two names[8] for which he can find a direct scriptural source and a further set of seventeen names descriptive of properties:[9] a list which in its variety and imaginativeness incidentally reveals the contemporary diet of theological metaphor to be very thin gruel indeed.

There is an ontological foundation for this profusion of trope: God is the cause of all things and so the names of God may be, indeed *must* be, derived 'from all the things caused'.[10] Anything that God has brought about provides a potential source of imagery for the description of God, so that only that which names a respect in which something is evil cannot serve as a name of God. For, as he argues in *Divine Names*, evil is not something we can say God has brought about, because there is no kind of thing which evil is.[11] Therefore we may say, without qualification, that any name which names a property of creatures can also be a name of God, for evil is not a property of anything at all.

The fact of their having been caused by God is what permits the names of all things to be used of God. But what makes it not just permissible, but a *requirement* of theological adequacy that we should use all names of God, is the fact that since God is the cause of the whole created order, God possesses in his own being and in an uncreated manner all the perfections which he causes:

And so it is that as Cause of all and as transcending all, he is rightly nameless and yet has the names of everything that is...[But] the unnamed goodness is not just the cause of cohesion or life or perfection,...but it actually contains everything beforehand within itself – and this in an

---

[7] *Divine Names* (*DN*), 596A, in *Pseudo-Dionysius*, trans, Colm Luibheid.
[8] Ibid., 596A. See also *Letter* 9, 1104C–1105C for a parallel list.
[9] Ibid., 597A–B.   [10] Ibid., 596B.
[11] Ibid., 716D: 'Evil is not a being; for if it were it would not be totally evil...'.

uncomplicated and boundless manner...Hence the songs of praise and the names for it are fittingly derived from the sum total of creation.[12]

Consequently, from the fact that we name God from his effects – and are justified in doing so *because* he is their cause – it does not follow that the names of God signify only that causality. We can *justify* describing God as 'a gentle breeze' because we know that God has caused all the gentle breezes we feel, but 'God is a gentle breeze' does not *mean* 'God causes gentle breezes'. For that is to say something rather about gentle breezes than about God. The metaphor, Denys says, tells us something, however inadequately, about what God eternally and in her nature *is*, it does not simply report on some act of the divine causality in time ('this or that providential gesture').[13] In the thirteenth century, Thomas Aquinas was to provide a general argument from logic for this conclusion, for he distinguished the grounds we may have for giving a name to a thing from the meaning which the name names.[14] The evidence we may have for saying that the swiftly moving shadow in the gloom was a cat may have been the miaow: but 'that was a cat' does not mean: 'that was a miaow causer', but rather: 'that was a feline quadruped'. So with the names of God. God's causality legitimizes our naming her by the names of her effects. But what we name is a being in whom is possessed in transcendent abundance all the perfections of the beings caused. Hence, to name God adequately, we not only may, but must, name God by all the names of creatures: only the 'sum total of creation' adequately reflects the superabundant variety of God.

Theological adequacy therefore requires the maximization of our discourses about God – and, whatever constraints an apophatic theology may impose, they cannot justify the restriction of theological language to just a few, favoured, respectful, 'pious', names. Denys is quite emphatic about this and he repeats the warning on several occasions, so fraught with dangers did he consider a limited theological vocabulary to be. In a pious vocabulary of unshocking, 'appropriate' names, lies the danger of the theologian's being all the more tempted to suppose that our language about God has succeeded in capturing the divine reality in some ultimately adequate way.[15] Tactically preferable is the multiplicity

---

[12] Ibid., 596C–597A.   [13] Ibid., 596C.   [14] *ST*, 1a, q.13, a.8, corp.

[15] *Celestial Hierarchy* (*CH*), 141A–B, in *Pseudo-Dionysius*, trans, Colm Luibheid. Here, admittedly, Denys is speaking of our language about angels, but the point here is an adaptation to that particular case of a more general point about theological language.

of vulgar images which, because they lack any plausibility as comprehensive or appropriate names, paradoxically have a more uplifting efficacy: 'Indeed the sheer crassness of the signs is a goad so that even the materially inclined cannot accept that it could be permitted or true that the celestial and divine sights could be conveyed by such shameful things'.[16]

There is good practical sense in this. A 'golden and gleaming'[17] God is too like what we might choose to praise; a God 'enraged', 'cursing' and 'drunk and hungover'[18] might have greater power to shock us into a sense of the divine transcendence by the magnitude of the metaphorical deficiency.

The inadequacy of theological language can therefore occur at two levels. For it is true that whatever we say about God, and that however vividly, and with however much variety of image we name God, all our language fails of God, infinitely and in principle. But it is also true that, should we arbitrarily restrict the names with which we name God, we will fall short of that point of verbal profusion at which we encounter the collapse of language as such.

Let us consider a contemporary example. Rightly, many Christians today regret as inadequate, misleading and as symptomatic of misogyny, that historical tradition whereby God is described exclusively in the language of the male gender. And there can be two quite different reasons why this is right, both of which flow from the logic of Denys' position. The first is that for every ground we have for describing God as male there is another for describing God as female. An exclusive use of male descriptions is therefore a misdescription of God by exclusion, since it rules out the ascription to God of the names distinctive of half her human creation. The second reason why the description of God as male is inappropriate has nothing to do with exclusivity, for it is perfectly obvious that God is not the sort of being who could have a gender at all.

Now we can know this in an a priori and 'higher' kind of way from our knowledge that God is not the sort of being who can have a body and so cannot be sexed. But, as Denys warns, the approach to the failure of gender language along this 'higher' route may well mislead us into supposing that since the reason God is not male is that God is 'spiritual' or 'disembodied', then that 'higher' kind of

---

[16] Ibid., 141B – C.   [17] Ibid., 141A.   [18] *MT*, 1033B.

talk is adequate to the description of God. Of course it is not, and it is less misleading to approach the inadequacy of male-gender language along the 'lower' route of its *self*-subversion in the simultaneous affirmation of contradictory gender descriptions: if we describe God both as male and as female, then we force upon our materialistic imaginations a concrete sense of the collapse of gender-language as such. For no person can be *both* male *and* female. Hence, if God has to be described in both ways, then he cannot possibly be either male or female; and if God is neither, then also she cannot possibly be a 'person' in any sense we know of, for every person we know of is one or the other. It is in the collapse of ordinary language, brought to our attention by the necessity of ascribing incompatible attributes, that the transcendence of God above all language is best approached. But an inadequate descriptive provision will not get us to that point where the inadequacy of all language in principle is met.

V

Within the profusion of discourse descriptive of God, Denys detects a hierarchy and a broad distinction: there are 'similar' and 'dissimilar' similarities,[19] a distinction which can be taken to coincide with another distinction he makes between the 'conceptual' and the 'symbolic'or 'perceptual' names of God.[20]

Nowhere does Denys give a sufficiently precise, formal account of how this distinction is to be made out, and his failure of precision, as we will see later on in this chapter, will cause some difficulty in the exact description of his negative theology. But an informal, pragmatic distinction is built into the division of the ascending scale of negated affirmations into two categories in chapters 4 and 5 of *Mystical Theology*. In chapter 4 Denys negates in turn all the attributes of God which are derived from 'perceptible' things, and in chapter 5 he denies the 'conceptual' names of God.

---

[19] See, for example, *CH*, 140C–145C for an extended discussion of the distinction itself and of the point of making it. Sometimes, as in this passage, Denys distinguishes between 'similarities' and 'incongruities' or 'incongruous dissimilarities'. But this is the same distinction.

[20] *MT*, 1033A. Denys discussed the 'conceptual' names of God in his *Divine Names*. He claims to have discussed the 'perceptual' names of God in a work which he calls his *Symbolic Theology*, which is either lost or, more likely, fictitious.

Thus, in the first instance it is denied that the Cause of all is material, has shape, form, quality, quantity, weight, is found in place, is seen, touched, perceived, suffers, feels, is deprived of light, changes, decays, is divided, is diminished, ebbs, flows, or that it is anything 'of which the senses may be aware'.[21] In chapter 5 we deny that the Cause of all is mind, has imagination, conviction, speech, understanding; it has no number, order, magnitude, equality, likeness or unlikeness; it is neither eternity nor time, life, wisdom, oneness, goodness, not even divinity. It neither exists nor does it not exist. Informally, then, we could say that the distinction of names denied is that between those which are derived from our perceptions of material things and those which are not so derived.[22] And it is fair to say that this distinction between 'perceptual' and 'conceptual' names corresponds with that between 'dissimilar' and 'similar' similarities. The more rooted our language about God is in the objects of our perceptual, bodily powers, the more 'dissimilar' is the similarity that language describes. The less our language is thus dependent, the more 'similar' are the similarities it describes.

Underlying this distinction within theological language is a metaphor of ontological distance and proximity: for, in Denys' doctrine of creation, existence itself is on a scale of more and less, or, as we may put it, things and properties are more or less 'real'. We, of course, have no way of thinking of such a conception comfortably, for the intellectual culture has long disappeared in which it was natural to think of a horse being 'more real' than a cabbage, a human 'more real' than a horse, an angel 'more real' than a human – still less are we able to think of a Cherub being 'more real' than a Principality. For us, existence cannot come in degrees, for the rules governing the logic of existence are those of the zero-sum: a thing either exists or it does not.

But within that lost culture – a distinctly Platonic one – the good sense it made to say that a horse is 'more real' than a cabbage consisted in the fact that a horse *realises* more than a cabbage does; and to say that with any hope of meaning something, requires a back-

---

[21] *MT*, 1040D.

[22] In advance of a discussion of the logic of 'negation' later in this chapter, this is the best we can do with this distinction. The difficulty of describing the 'conceptual' more positively than by contrast with the 'perceptual' names lies in the heterogeneity of the names given in chapter 5, for a comment on which see pp. 40–44 below.

ground in the Platonic doctrine of Ideas. For if, by contrast with another, Red Rum is a better horse, then this is because, Plato thought, Red Rum participates more fully in that complete reality which is equininity *as such*. That is to say, Red Rum *realises* more of what-it-is-to-be-a-horse than that other horse does. But what-it-is-to-be-a-horse includes being 'alive'. Hence, in the same way as Red Rum participates more fully in 'horseness', it will be possible to describe any horse as 'more real' than any cabbage because any horse *realises more* of what-it-is-to-be-alive than any cabbage does. For a cabbage lives only in its nutrition, growth and reproduction, whereas the life of a horse is a more flourishing realisation of life's possibilities, being in addition to what a cabbage is, self-moving, capable of perceiving its needs of nutrition, growth and reproduction and of desiring them too. In turn, a human realises all that a horse realises by way of life and more besides, and an angel realises all that humans do, and more. Each kind of thing on this scale makes 'real' – instantiates – more of what life is than those below it and less than those above. So a thing realises more or less of what *is*. It more or less exists.

Today we lack the conceptual schemas which enabled some ancient and mediaeval writers to think systematically in such terms, for we have abandoned that picture of an hierarchical 'chain of being' and its attendant scale on which the ancient and mediaeval thinker held every kind of being was placed; nor do we know of any account of the principles governing the relations of superiority and dependence between degrees on this scale. In Denys' conception of it, hierarchy was both an ontological structure and a rule of governance of the universe:[23] and we have no systematically hierarchical conception of either.

Because hierarchy not only regulates the good order of the universe, but also determines its degrees of 'reality', we can speak of this scale as determining degrees of 'distance' from the Cause of existence. The degree of a thing's 'reality' is directly related to its proximity to the Cause of all. Now if there are reasons, deriving from his Platonic inheritance, why Denys should favour this hierarchy of ontological 'distance' from source, there is a reason, deriving from his Christianity, why that ontological hierarchy should be a cause of difficulty. In fact, prima facie, the two seem scarcely consistent.

---

[23] 'In my opinion a hierarchy is a sacred order, a state of understanding and an activity approximating as closely as possible to the divine' *CH*, 164D.

Creation, for Denys, is, we might say, the divine *eros* in volcanic eruption.[24] It was in the fourteenth century that Meister Eckhart described the inner life of the Trinity as a 'seething and a boiling', a *bullitio*, a bubbling up of the infinite life and energy of the Godhead into the differentiation of Persons. Creation *ad extra*, however, is the overflow, the 'boiling over', the *ebullitio*, of that inner life and energy into all things,[25] an image which exactly captures one aspect of the Dionysian conception of creation. For Denys, creation is the erotic outpouring of the divine goodness into all things, it is the divine ecstasy, by which the One comes to stand outside itself in the multiple differentiations of the created world, while still retaining its apartness in its self-possessed Oneness. For

the very cause of the universe...is, as it were, beguiled by goodness, by love and by yearning and is enticed away from his transcendent dwelling place and comes to abide within all things, and he does so by virtue of his supernatural and ecstatic capacity to remain, nevertheless, within himself.[26]

And this is truly like a volcanic explosion in one respect. For as lava pours from the core, it descends from it, cooling and hardening as the distance from its source increases. The further the lava flows from the core the more it differs from it, the less it participates in the heat and flux of its origin, the more dissimilar it is to it.

Corresponding with this picture of the outflow of all beings in creation, in their multiplicity and differentiation, is Denys' picture of the tendency and flow of affirmative language about God. 'When we made assertions we began with the first things', he says, referring by 'the first things' to the few highest, simplest and most abstract 'conceptual' names of God, '[and] moved down through intermediate terms until we reached the last things',[27] referring to the most concrete, earthy 'perceptual' names, which are many. 'In my earlier books', he goes on,

my argument travelled downward from the most exalted to the humblest categories, taking in on this downward path an ever-increasing number of ideas which multiplied with every stage of the descent.[28]

---

[24] See my *Eros and Allegory: Mediaeval Interpretations of the Song of Songs*, Kalamazoo: Cistercian Publications, 1995, chapter 2, for a more extended discussion of the role of *eros* within the ontology and epistemology of Denys.

[25] Meister Eckhart, *Commentary on Exodus*, in *Meister Eckhart, Teacher and Preacher*, ed. B. McGinn, *Classics of Western Spirituality*, New York: Paulist Press, 1986, p. 46.

[26] *DN*, 712A–B.   [27] *MT*, 1025B.   [28] Ibid., 1033C.

And the reason for this is that 'when we assert what is beyond every assertion, we must then proceed from what is most akin to it, and as we do so we make the affirmation on which everything else depends'.[29] The dynamic of the cataphatic movement therefore depends on that of the movement of creation, the *proodos,* or progression, by which beings descending on the scale of being disperse into ever increasing multiplicity, variety and differentiation. Hence, the more distanced our language is from the simple, abstract, higher names of God, the more particularised and fragmented it becomes. Hence too, as names multiply and differentiate, each name taken singly becomes more limited in its expressive capacity, less adequate to the description of the Cause of all, less capable of being interchanged with other names, and more prone to literal inconsistency with the other names. It is from their characteristic of being more particular that is derived the necessity of multiplying the descriptions of the Godhead, of piling description upon description to supply for the increased inadequacy of each. And it is from their proneness to being inconsistent with one another that their conjunction results in the necessity of that paradox which will lead, ultimately, to the recognition of their collective deficiency.

Expressively apt as these images are of one dimension of Denys' understanding of creation, in another respect they very seriously misrepresent it. Exactly right is the expression such imagery gives to the underpinning ontology of degrees of reality, hence also to the relation of that scale to degrees of 'proximity' to the creating cause; equally, at the level of language, the imagery captures aptly the downward descent of affirmations. Exactly wrong is the failure of that imagery to give expression to that *immediacy* of the relation between Creator and created which is entailed by the doctrine of creation *ex nihilo.* For the imaging of creation as a laval flow is implicitly 'emanationist' and implies that the lower degrees on the hierarchical scale flow from those which precede them and are not in any immediate relation of ontological dependence on the One 'Cause of all'. So stated, this would not be a doctrine of creation *ex nihilo.* Rather it would imply that the One causes the existence of lower beings through the mediation of the higher; not therefore 'out of nothing' but out of a something which pre-exists.[30] In fact Denys

---

[29] Ibid.

[30] Which was, of course, the view of Proclus, one of Denys' major Greek sources.

does not hold with this: each being, at whatever point it is placed on the scale of beings, and in whatever relations of dependence it may stand to those ontologically higher than it, is in an absolutely *direct* and unmediated relation of existential dependence on God. Between each being and God there is nothing. Consequently, there could be little more mistaken than to conceive of the One as the being which tops off the ascending scale of beings, ontologically closer to those next to it than to those lesser beings lower down the scale. From this point of view 'existence' cannot be conceived of within the logic of an hierarchical sliding scale, its logic is that of the zero-sum. For each and every being the relation of its existence to its creating cause has the same immediacy. God has brought Cherubim and worms into existence in acts of creative causality which are, for want of a better expression, 'equidistant' from their effects.

So we are now presented with an *aporia*. The tendency of the hierarchical scale of ontological degrees, and the 'anti-hierarchical' tendency of the doctrine of creative immediacy, certainly appear to pull Denys' thought in opposed directions. Moreover, the tension between them may seem to be heightened by the fact that both seem to Denys to be necessary within an adequate theology. Christian orthodoxy imposes upon him the doctrine of creation *ex nihilo*, which demands that the dependence of creatures on God for their existence can allow of no degrees of distance between creatures and God. On the other hand, the manifest facts of our differentiated, hierarchically ordered theological language, constructed on a scale of degrees of descriptive adequacy, require him to find a basis for those facts in an *ontological* hierarchy.

For the distinction between 'dissimilar' and 'similar' similarities is founded upon this ontological basis. A horse is 'more real' than a cabbage and a human than a horse because each realises more of the perfection contained in the One cause than does its inferior. For this reason our equine imagery for God is a more similar similarity than our horticultural,[31] and a more dissimilar similarity than our human imagery. In chapters 4 and 5 of the *Mystical Theology* Denys represents this hierarchy as a sliding scale which admits of

---

[31] This is not a merely fanciful example: consider Gregory the Great's use of equine imagery in his *Commentary on the Song of Songs* in my *Eros and Allegory*, pp. 246–247 and the imagery of God as a garden in the Song of Songs itself, 5, 1.

many degrees, but more usually he simply divides the scale broadly into the two categories, the dissimilar and similar similarities, distinguished, as we have seen, on the lines of the 'perceptual' and 'conceptual'. And this broad hierarchical distinction within theological language is not just a convenient taxonomy which, under pressure from the contrary tendency of creation *ex nihilo*, could be abandoned as dispensable. As we will see in the next section, the distinction is required by weighty considerations of logic. Hence, for different reasons the two doctrines of language and of creation are equally required. And yet they seem difficult to reconcile.

But not, for Denys, impossible. In this, as in every other relation between God and creation, Denys sees that the relation of distance between God and creatures must be asymmetrical. Creatures may be more or less 'like' God. But there cannot be any respect at all in which God is 'like' any creature. Creatures may be nearer or further away from God ontologically; but there cannot be any degrees of proximity in which God stands to different creatures. God cannot even be, as we were tempted to say just now, *equidistant* from all creatures, for God is not and cannot be in any kind of relation of distance to any creature whatsoever. Now the only way we have of expressing the greater likeness some things have to God than others possess is by saying that the first are ontologically 'nearer' to God than the second. And the only way we have of expressing the ontological relation of God to creatures is by denying that it is mediated by distance. And the only way we have of giving expression to *both* is in the way Denys does it, in characteristic paradox, in the *Divine Names*: 'The Trinity is present to all things, though not all things are present to it'.[32]

So we encounter, once again, what we may describe as the basic law of cataphatic language. No partial, restricted vocabulary is adequate to express the inadequacy of theological language; only language under the requirement to say everything possible can do this. It is in the profusion of our affirmations that we encounter the limits of language, and then break through them into the the dark silence of the transcendent. And if this dialectic occurs within the 'first-order' theological language in which we strain to utter the names of God, then we have just seen that it also occurs in our 'second-order' discourse descriptive of the logic of that language.

[32] *DN*, 680B.

For just as the first-order language is revealed in its inadequacy by the necessity of our constructing simultaneously mutually can-celling images of God, so the second-order logic of that first-order language is imposed by the necessities which derive from our hav-ing to say mutually cancelling things about the foundations of the-ological language as such: both that all creation is hierarchically ranked in degrees of proximity to God and that God is in no con-ceivable degrees of proximity to creatures. If we can distinguish, as Denys does, between similar and dissimilar similarities *within* our speech about God, we can also distinguish, in a way Denys is rather less clear about, between that speech taken as a whole and the second-order language which is descriptive of its logical and epistemic foundations. And that second-order language is obedient to just the same constraints, productive of paradox, as we have seen the first-order speech to be.

VI

If in our affirmations about God we descend on a scale from greater abstractness and generality to the more particular and con-crete, in our negations the progression is reversed: we 'begin...from the lowest category when it involves a denial', and this is because 'we have to start by denying the qualities which differ most from the goal we hope to attain'.[33] This ascending scale of denials is the strategy of chapters 4 and 5 of the *Mystical Theology* which, as we have seen, constructs a ladder of negations from the denial that the 'Cause of all' is material[34] to the denial that it either exists or that it does not exist.[35]

In the last section I set out the case for saying that the apophatic in theology is simply the product of a properly understood cat-aphaticism and that we reach the point at which the apophatic begins by the means of the comprehensiveness of our affirmations, whose combined and mutually cancelling forces crack open the sur-face of language; and that it is through the fissures in our discourse that the darkness of the apophatic is glimpsed. In the last two chap-ters of *Mystical Theology*, however, the strategy appears to be differ-ent. The apophatic is represented as an hierarchical ascent, of serial negation, affirmation by affirmation, of the names that may be used

---

[33] *MT*, 1033C.   [34] Ibid., 1040D.   [35] Ibid., 1048A.

of God. First it denies the 'dissimilar' images, then the most similar, denying each affirmation in turn before denying the next.

There is no contradiction between these two ways of represent-ing the strategy of the apophatic, though they did tend to generate two quite different theological and mystical traditions in subse-quent Western Christianity. The device of embodying the transcen-dent primarily in negative theological language is characteristic, we may say, of that tradition to which Eckhart, the *Cloud* Author and John of the Cross belong. The device of embodying the transcen-dent primarily through the superfluity of affirmation is found most typically in the tradition to which Augustine, Bonaventure and Julian of Norwich belong. In view of this it would be all too easy to make the mistake of concluding that because the discourse of an Eckhart, *Cloud* Author or a John is characteristically negative, whereas the discourse of an Augustine, Bonaventure or a Julian is predominantly affirmative, it is helpful to distinguish between the first as 'apophatic mystics' and the second as 'cataphatic mystics' – though I fear the mistake is very commonly made. I shall not pur-sue the point here beyond saying that, on the contrary, leaving aside relatively marginal considerations of literary emphasis, theo-logically *The Cloud of Unknowing* and *The Shewings* of Julian are equally apophatic, but by the different routes which are anticipated in the distinct strategies of Denys' *Divine Names* and his *Mystical Theology*. When, for example, in a provocative paradox, Julian deliberately confuses the gender attributes of Jesus, her strategy is consciously apophatic: 'In our Mother, Christ, we grow and develop; in his mercy he reforms and restores us...So does our Mother work in mercy for all his children'.[36] And in a phrase preg-nant with Dionysian (and, as we will see, Augustinian) paradox, she says: 'Peace and love are always at work in us, but we are not always in peace and love.'[37]

It is of the greatest consequence to see that negative language about God is no more apophatic in itself than is affirmative lan-guage. The apophatic is the linguistic strategy of somehow showing by means of language that which lies beyond language. It is not done, and it cannot be done, by means of negative utterances alone which are no less bits of ordinarily intelligible human dis-

---

[36] *Shewings of Divine Love*, in *A Revelation of Love* (*Revelation*), ed. Marion Glasscoe, Exeter: University of Exeter Press, 1976, chapter 58.
[37] Ibid., chapter 39.

course than are affirmations. Our negations, therefore, fail of God as much as do our affirmations. Over and over again Denys repeats the refrain: '[The Cause of all] is beyond assertion *and denial*'; and again: 'We make assertions *and denials* of what is next to it, but never of it, for it is both beyond every assertion...[and] *also beyond every denial*';[38] and yet again: '[The One is] beyond...the assertion of all things and the denial of all things, [is] that which is beyond every assertion *and denial*'.[39]

Nor is the apophatic any better captured in negative images than in negative propositions. 'Silence'[40] we may say is the negative correlative of the affirmative image 'speech' or 'word',[41] 'the taciturn' of 'the eloquent',[42] 'darkness' of 'light',[43] 'sightless' of 'seeing'.[44] But a negative image is as much an image as the affirmative image it negates, the negativity of the image doing nothing to qualify its character as an image. A mysticism of negative imagery, therefore, even one, like Eckhart's, which is saturated with imagery of 'formlessness', of 'deserts' and 'silences', of 'spaces' and 'abysses', is not for all that any less cataphatic than is the robustly affirmative mysticism of Julian of Norwich.

For there is a very great difference between the strategy of *negative propositions* and the strategy of *negating the propositional*; between that of the *negative image* and that of the *negation of imagery*. The first of each of these pairs belongs to the cataphatic in theology, and only the second is the strategy of the apophatic. It is my view that Denys is clear about this in practice, but lacks the conceptual and logical tools in which to state the grounds on which the distinction is to be made. Like most Platonists, he lacks an adequate appreciation of the logic of metaphors.

It is possible for us, in the light of distinctions we make, to see that the 'perceptual' names of God, listed in chapter 4 of *Mystical Theology* as requiring to be denied, are all metaphors. And if Denys did lack our terminologies it is perfectly clear that he treats these affirmations and their corresponding denials in the way which is appropriate to metaphorical utterances. For he seems fully aware of the absurd, and quite unapophatic, results which would follow from treating the 'perceptual' names as being literally applied to, and then literally negated of, the Cause of all.

---

[38] *MT*, 1048B. [39] *DN*, 641A. [40] *MT*, 997B. [41] Ibid., 997A.
[42] Ibid., 1000C. [43] Ibid., 997B. [44] Ibid., 997B.

For, of course, if treated as literal, the attributions of the 'perceptual' names are all false, and no special strategy of denying them is required. We all know that God is not literally 'lifeless' or 'material' and that literally God does not have 'weight', 'quantity' or 'shape'. Since they are all literally false, the negation of these names, taken as literal, would simply yield the contraries of these names as literally true. And that is not at all what is involved in the apophatic strategy of denial.

For the logic of negation which applies to literal utterances is, we may say, straightforwardly 'Aristotelian'. In his *Peri Hermeneias* Aristotle remarks that 'to know an affirmation is to know its negation'.[45] Thomas Aquinas, following Aristotle, put the same point in similar terms: *eadem est scientia oppositorum*,[46] 'one and the same is the knowledge of contraries'. The point is not controversial: if we can know what it is to say that there is a cat on the mat then thereby we know what it is to say that the cat is not on the mat. The 'knowledge' is the same in either case, but in the one it is affirmed, in the other denied. If the knowledge were not 'the same' there would be no opposition between the two statements, for what the one affirmed would not be what the other denied. So they could not contradict each other.

Were we to suppose, therefore, that all the 'perceptual' names applied to God literally, then, on this Aristotelian rule of negation, it would follow that their contradictories are also literal truths. Thus the ascent begins with the denial that 'the Cause of all' is 'inexistent, lifeless, speechless, mindless'.[47] Now on an 'Aristotelian' negation the negation of 'inexistent' yields 'existent', of 'lifeless' 'alive', of 'speechless' 'speaking', of 'mindless' 'mind'. But this gives us an impossible result.

For if the predication 'is lifeless' is a literal falsehood, then, on the Aristotelian rule, the predication 'The One is life' is a literal truth. And if, in turn, we must deny that the One is 'life', then this 'not-life' of the 'higher' negation will, again on an 'Aristotelian' rule of negation, be synonymous with the 'lifelessness' which is negated at the lower level. The series of negations will cease to be an 'ascent' up a scale and will become a vicious circle, an endless series of contradictions returning upon themselves.

[45] *Peri Hermeneias*, 17a 31–33.
[46] *Quaestio Disputata de Veritate*, q. 2, a. 15, corp.   [47] *MT*, 1040D.

We get this result from falsely supposing that all the 'perceptual' names of God are literal utterances. But they are not. They are metaphors. Consequently the negations of a truly apophatic procedure of denial must be of the kind by which we negate metaphors, not of that kind by which literal utterances are opposed to one another, and in his own terms Denys at least implicitly acknowledges that *apophatic* denials involve something different from the literal negations of literal utterances, for he says:

we should not conclude that the negations are simply the opposites of affirmations, but rather that the cause of all is considerably prior to this, beyond privations, beyond every denial, beyond every assertion.[48]

Luibheid, however, in a thoroughly misleading footnote, comments that here Denys 'directly contradicts a passage from Aristotle, who uses identical terminology to argue that negations *are* the opposite of affirmations'.[49]

This is not a helpful comment, though it is not entirely false. To see why, let us note that it is in the nature of metaphors that they succeed in conveying the truths which they convey only on condition that they are recognized to be literal falsehoods, for it is part of their metaphorical meaning that they are literally false.[50] Thus, we might very well say, or imply, by means of the metaphor 'God is a rock' that God is 'lifeless'. And we will do this in order to convey, in a manner we otherwise could not, something about God's reliability, a reliability which is greater than any shifty living beings could be counted upon to possess. Hence, God's 'lifelessness' is part of the meaning of the metaphor, it is a metaphorical truth. Therefore it *cannot* be literally true. For this reason, you do not negate the metaphor by negating its literal falsehood. What negates a metaphor is only another metaphor. The utterance which negates the metaphor 'God is a rock' is the *metaphor* 'God is alive'. And what negates 'God is alive' is not the literal utterance 'God is lifeless', but the *metaphor* 'God is a rock'. The metaphors negate each other as metaphors, just as 'God is dark' is a negative metaphor in relation to 'God is light'. In fact we can say that they

---

48 Ibid., 1000B.
49 Luibheid, *Pseudo-Dionysius*, p. 136, note 6.
50 This may appear to be cast in doubt by such negative metaphors as Donne's 'No man is an island', which is, of course, a literal truth. But as we will see, a negative metaphor entails its *metaphorical* contrary, 'every man is part of the mainland', and *that* is a literal falsehood.

are one and the same metaphor, for *eadem est scientia oppositorum*, what the one affirms the other denies.

Therefore, what Luibheid says about Denys' abandonment of 'Aristotelian' negation is misleading *thus far*, for the relation between affirmative and negative metaphors is, and must be, straightforwardly 'Aristotelian': in that *in so far as* God can be said to be light he cannot be said to be dark; just as in so far as God can be said to be great she cannot be said to be small; just as in so far as he is said to be she, she cannot be said to be he. The metaphorical truths are mutually exclusive in the sense that the affirmation of the one excludes the affirmation of the other. Were this not the case, there could be no sense to Donne's negative metaphor, 'No man is an island'. For the point of the metaphor is precisely its entailment that every man is part of the mainland.

Negative metaphors are negations of affirmative metaphors and what holds of literal utterances and their contraries also holds of metaphorical utterances, affirmative and negative: *eadem est scientia oppositorum*, what the one affirms the other denies. But the logic of negation in respect of metaphors is beyond that different from that of literal utterances – and here Luibheid is right – in that opposed metaphors, unlike literal contradictions, can be simultaneously affirmed, in so far as to do so is to capture, by virtue of their conjunction, the failure of both to convey the reality of what is metaphorised. We can say metaphorically 'God is light' to convey something about God. We can say metaphorically 'God is dark' in order to convey something opposed to what the first metaphor conveys. And we can say metaphorically 'God is a brilliant darkness' in order to convey something of the failure of both metaphors to convey what God is. But this effect of conveying the transcendence of God beyond both metaphors can be produced only on the conditions *both* that they are (in an Aristotelian sense) opposed to one another *and* that, albeit opposed, they are simultaneously affirmed. So the Aristotelian negation is both presupposed to this effect and transcended by it. Apophatic denial is indeed not 'Aristotelian negation'. But it presupposes it. And by the juxtaposition of affirmative and negative images is achieved the negation, in the sense of the transcendence, of the imagery itself. It is as well, as I have said, not to confuse negative imagery with the negation of an image.

The negations of the 'perceptual' names of God do not, therefore, consist in the replacement of one set of literal affirmations with their 'Aristotelian' negations, nor do they consist in the substitution of negative images for affirmative. They consist in the negations of the negations between metaphors, so as to transcend the domain of metaphorical discourse itself, of both affirmative and negative, in the sense in which to negate is not to deny the truths which that discourse is capable of conveying, but is to denote their limitation.

Moreover, these negations can merely *exhibit* the failure of our language; they do not measure any particular extent to which the metaphors negated fall short of the mark. For whereas in non-theological cases, for example scientific, we are normally able to state in what respect a metaphor falls short of what it metaphorises, in the case of God the only language we have for describing the inadequacy itself falls short, as deficient in the description of the difference. We can only say that every utterance about God falls short of God 'infinitely'. But to say that *is* to say that we have no conception at all of the degree of shortfall, and therefore no language at all in which to describe it.

Therefore, we negate 'perceptual' names of God 'transcendently', not knowing how to describe their degree of inadequacy. For this reason, this kind of negation is an 'apophatic' negation, not a 'merely Aristotelian' opposing of an affirmative metaphor with its contrary. Since we have no language in which to describe the deficit between our metaphors and the reality they reach out to, we are in a position only negatively to express the deficiency. The position of the theologian is therefore like that of the person who, when lost for a word, can only say what it is not, with absolutely no prospect of ever finding the right one, the word which will do full justice to the thought. She may very well be able to judge some candidates to be more adequate than others, but this cannot be because she knows the *mot juste* as a standard of comparison. We can only know the inadequacy of our language from within it.

It is for this reason that the proper route to the apophatic is, as I have argued, through the dialectics of the cataphatic. We know the deficiency of our metaphors from the constraints we are under to employ the whole range of metaphorical language available and, precisely because our affirmative and negative metaphors *do* stand in relations of 'Aristotelian' contrariety to one another, we know their deficiencies from their mutual incompatibilities: God *cannot* be both darkness and light, both the Word and silence, both a rock and a breeze in any, even metaphorical, sense that we know of. Of no kind of thing at all can these metaphors be collectively expressive. But then that is *how* we know that God 'is not any kind of thing',[51] and that 'he does not possess this kind of existence and not that'.[52]

VII

All the 'perceptual' names of God denied in chapter 4 of *Mystical Theology* contain an intrinsic reference to something material, or to some property of material things. That is why when affirmed of God they have to be affirmed metaphorically and through their literal falsehood. Not so with the 'conceptual' names denied in the second stage of the ascent of negation, described in chapter 5. At any rate, this is not so of some of them, for on any account of the distinction between the 'perceptual' and the 'conceptual' some of the names listed in chapter 5 do not belong with the 'conceptual'. In fact, the 'conceptual' names of chapter 5 are a very heterogeneous bag, belonging to no single logical, or any other kind of common class.

For that list contains four quite different categories of predicate, and Denys' failure to distinguish them makes problematic any clear account of the logic of his apophaticism. For some are the names of 'perceptual' attributes, such as 'kingship', 'sonship', 'fatherhood', 'greatness' and 'smallness' and 'darkness' and 'light'. These are 'perceptual' in that they are, in their primary and literal senses, descriptive of perceptible, material things or of their properties or of their relations. Said of God, they are, therefore, metaphors. And their negations are the negations of their metaphorical meanings.

A second group includes names which, though not the names primarily of 'perceptual' properties of material things are certainly the names of intrinsically *created* things, such as 'speech', 'imagination', 'number' and 'order'. For even if the power of speech or imagination can be possessed only by a being with an immaterial soul, an immaterial soul is still a created thing, especially since only a soul united with a body could be capable of either. And any being which can be counted in a series or 'order' – even a being of which as a matter of fact there is only one instance – is a created

---

[51]   *DN*, 817D.   [52]   Ibid., 821D.

being. For if there is one being of any kind, there is nothing in the nature of that or any kind of being which can logically prevent there being more than one, and multiplicity is a possibility only for creatures.[53] But if these names contain an intrinsically creaturely reference, their predication of God is literally false. Hence, their predication of God must be metaphorical and their negations must be the negations of their metaphorical meanings.

Of the third category this cannot be said. If we say of God that she is 'good' this is not a literal falsehood, nor is it literally false to attribute existence, wisdom, oneness, knowledge or truth to God. For existence is not a predicate with any intrinsic reference to any *conditions* of existence whatever. Even if it is true – and it is true – that the human mind cannot conceive of what it is for an uncreated being to exist, if it is true, that is to say, that human minds can form conceptions only of created existence, there is nothing in the *logic* of existence, of goodness, of truth or of oneness, which limits these attributions to created things. In short, these predications are never literally false of anything whatsoever; for only nothing does not exist and there is nothing which is in no way good, true or one. And from this it follows that none of these names are ever predicated metaphorically of anything whatsoever, even of God.

The logic of these 'conceptual' names, which unlike those of the previous two categories are properly so called, therefore requires a different strategy of negation from that of the 'metaphorical' names. And this strategy of negation is best understood through an examination of the fourth group of names which are found in chapter 5 of *Mystical Theology*. But here we find a further puzzle – indeed, it has to be said, a characteristically Platonic confusion.

For Denys denies of the Cause of all that it is either 'equality' or 'inequality', 'similarity' or 'dissimilarity', and he does so as if these names, like the others in the list, denoted absolute and not, as we would be more likely to suppose, relational properties. For a thing is red or green because of a property it possesses absolutely and without relation to anything else. But a thing cannot be 'similar' or 'dissimilar' just in its own right, but only 'similar' to or 'dissimilar' from something else. Nor can a thing be just 'equal' or 'unequal', but only 'equal' or 'unequal' to another.

---

53 Of course if there is only one dodo then there is something *biologically* in the nature of dodos which prevents there being any more in fact, for one dodo cannot reproduce.

Plato got himself into all sorts of difficulties as a result of supposing these and other relational properties to be absolute in character. In the *Phaedo* he composed a notorious argument purporting to show how Socrates can 'change' as a result of being sometimes 'bigger' and sometimes 'smaller', since next to a small man he is the one and next to a tall man he is the other.[54] Manifestly, to treat such attributes absolutely can only generate absurdities: for if relational properties are treated as absolute then it will follow, on the argument of *Republic*, that a big mouse, being an animal, is a big animal; that a small elephant, being an animal, is a small animal; hence, that a big mouse is a bigger animal than a small elephant.

So what can Denys mean in denying of the One that it is either equal or unequal, similar or dissimilar? Though he misconstrues the logic of these relational attributes by treating them as if on a par logically with goodness, truth or existence, it is not difficult to make out his meaning if we think of the relational names not as names of God to be denied but as belonging within what I have earlier called the 'second-order' description of the logic of negation itself.

In negating metaphors of God we have to be content with what we saw to be a kind of pure negativity, for we possess only a deficient language, and the degree of the deficiency of our theological language cannot be known to us, nor do we have the language in which to describe it. For the reality of God transcends our language not to any describable degree, but 'infinitely'. And 'infinitely' is not itself the name of some measurement of the degree of difference between what we can say of God and what God is. It says, simply, that no such language of measurement is possible.

This follows from the logic of 'difference' itself. 'Difference' is, after all, a relational property. One thing can differ only *from* another and for one thing to differ from another it must do so in some common respect. I may differ from my friend in height or in strength or in sex or in intelligence. I differ from a sheep as animals differ, from a plant as living things differ, from a stone as material objects differ. Nothing can differ from another in no respect nor, either, in every respect. Not the first, for that is not to differ. Not the second, because there has to be something in common between things which differ, as being *the respect in which* they differ – whether they differ as animals, as living beings, or as material objects.

[54] *Phaedo*, 102 B–C.

Now if we ask 'In what way do God and any creature differ?' we are in a quandary for an answer. For if an answer could be given this would have to be in terms of something which both God and creation possess in common, such that they differ in respect of it. But there is nothing at all which God and creatures possess in common, nor is there any language in which to describe God which does not fall infinitely short of the divine reality, even if the affirmations we are capable of making are true, so far as they go. But if there is no ground which God and creatures occupy in common, then there is no respect in which God and creatures are 'similar'; and from that it follows that there is no respect in which we can describe how God and creatures 'differ'. From this it does not follow that they do not differ. It simply follows that 'difference' and 'similarity' are terms which are themselves infinitely deficient in describing features of our language about God. We cannot say what God is because we cannot express what that degree of difference is which falls between what we can say of God and what God is. We know that our language about God fails. But we have no language about our language about God which can adequately describe the extent of the failure of our descriptions.

When, therefore, Denys says that we deny of God 'similarity' and 'difference' he writes, unintelligibly, as if these were somehow properties of God as goodness and existence are. But what he says is perfectly intelligible if these properties are thought of not as referring to properties of God but as referring to properties of language. For it makes sense to say of our language about God that it gets to the point of 'stretch' at which its categories of similarity and difference fail, so that, when stretched out to God, our language encounters its own failure to name the difference it stretches out across.

For in ascending the scale of negations we successfully deny respects in which God and creatures can be said to be 'similar'. We deny that God shares the properties of material beings, from which it might appear that God differs from them in the way in which minds differ from matter. So next, we deny that God is 'mind' in any sense in which we possess them, from which it might seem to follow that God differs from the human mind as an angelic mind differs from the human. Hence, we must deny that difference too. What are successively denied, therefore, are any respects of difference between God and every member in turn of the hierarchy of beings.

But this same operation of denying the similarity and difference must be performed on the most general 'conceptual' names as well. Any affirmation of the goodness of God has to differ in what it affirms from any we make of the goodness of creatures, or even of their existence. In affirming 'God exists', what we say of God differs infinitely more from what we affirm when we say 'Peter exists', than does 'Peter exists' from 'Peter does not exist'. For the difference between Peter's existing and Peter's not existing is a created difference, and so finite. Whereas the difference between God's existing and Peter's existing is uncreated, and so infinite. Hence, any understanding we have of the distinction between existence and non-existence fails of God, which is why Denys can say 'It falls neither within the predicate of nonbeing nor of being'.[55] But if even this distinction fails – and after all, it is the most radical distinction of which we can conceive – then what is demonstrated by this apophaticism is the failure of distinction itself. Our language of 'similarity' and 'dissimilarity' fails of God, and that means that our language fails and is known to fail to an unutterable degree.

This, then, is what Denys means when he says that the Cause of all is 'beyond assertion and denial'.

VIII

Let us summarize. The progress of the mind towards God ascends from complexity of image to simplicity, from many names in potential conflict to abstract and increasingly interchangeable names, from 'dissimilar' to 'similar' similarities, from prolixity to terseness and, ultimately, to silence. As the mind ascends through the hierarchy of language, it moves therefore, from that which is most distinct from God to that which is progressively less obviously so, from the more 'unlike' to the more 'like'. For God is more obviously not a rock than he is not a spirit, more obviously not a shape than he is not a mind, more obviously not a mind than he is not a being, more obviously not a being than he is not divinity, ascending the scale until everything that God can be compared with, however 'like', is negated. But the progression by which we eliminate what God can be compared with must also be the progressive elimination of everything with which God can be contrasted, for

55 *MT*, 1048A.

eadem est scientia oppositorum. Therefore, as comparisons fall away, so must contrasts, for as we find more and more ways in which God is 'unlike' anything at all, our hold on the logic of 'like' and 'unlike' begins to weaken. Hence, as we move from complexity to simplicity, from the multiplicity of creatures to the oneness of their cause, from differentiation to lack of differentiation, we must encounter, and then transcend the last differentiation of all: *the difference itself between similarity and difference.* We cannot describe the difference of God from all creation in terms which do not also attest to her similarity to all creation. But there is nothing in creation which God is like. Therefore, the only way in which we can attest to the absolute transcendence of God is by transcending the language of similarity and difference itself.

From this it follows that we cannot know God's distinction from, and transcendence of, creation through any analogy with how anything at all differs from anything else, any more than we can know the intimacy of God's relation with the world in terms of how any things at all are similar to one another. For God transcends the difference between similarity and difference.

Nor can we say that Denys' apophaticism consists in the recognition that before the transcendence of God our affirmations fall away into the silence of negations. We shall have to say that what falls away are both our affirmations and our negations, whose inadequacy is demonstrated in the necessity of affirming both, in what I have called the characteristically apophatic 'self-subverting utterance', the 'negation of the negation'. It is on the other side of both our affirmations and our denials that the silence of the transcendent is glimpsed, seen through the fissures opened up in our language by the dialectical strategy of self-subversion.

The divine transcendence is therefore the transcendence even of difference between God and creation. Since there is no knowable 'distance' between God and creation, there is no language in which it is possible to state one. For all our terms of contrast state differentiations between creatures. There is none in which to state the difference between God and creatures. God is not, therefore, opposed to creatures, cannot displace them and this consequence of the dialectics of apophaticism entails another which is of some importance for judging Denys' influence upon subsequent Western mysticism.

For that influence, and the influence of Neoplatonism generally, has sometimes been thought to have had the damaging effect of distracting the Western mystical tradition down paths of an exaggerated and one-sided 'absorptionist' account of mystical union. Heavy with the imagery of the erotic 'oneness' of the lover and beloved in dark and secret places, the Platonic mysticism has, some think, created the fantasy of a mystical 'onening' of the soul with God which, by transcending all 'differentiation', absorbs the created, finite soul in the infinite abyss of the Godhead; and in its apophaticism has dissolved the identity of the lover in the Beloved. Thus, for example, Kerr[56] and from within a quite different set of theological presuppositions, Nygren.[57]

In due course we will have the opportunity to explore some of the language and doctrines of later mystics, but let it be said here simply that such an unbalanced emphasis on union at the expense of the distinct identity of the soul can claim no support whatever in the dialectics of Denys' apophaticism. On the contrary, what those dialectics specifically show is that in the description of the soul's oneness with God we have no language, because that union transcends it, in which it would be possible to contrast the union of the lovers with their distinctness of identity. For the achievement of that union is possible only at the point where the mind has surpassed all discourse in which to state the contrast. Hence, if our language of distinction fails, so too has our language of union. Denys himself says precisely that, for in that union, all that the mind may conceive 'being renounced', Moses does indeed 'belong completely to him who is beyond everything'. But here, not only Moses, but any person who climbs the same mountain of negation, is *'neither oneself nor someone else'*.[58]

IX

I have construed Denys' 'apophatic' mysticism as if it could be explained as the systematic exploitation of the convergence between a Greek and a Hebrew allegory, the one of knowledge as such, the other of the knowledge of God. The distinctive manner in which Denys articulated the elements of Hebrew and Greek allegory within his theology had considerable influence, as I have

[56] Fergus Kerr, 'Charity as Friendship', in ed. Brian Davies O. P., *Language, Meaning and God*, London: Geoffrey Chapman, 1987, pp. 1–23.
[57] Anders Nygren, *Agape and Eros, A Study of the Christian Idea of Love*, trans. A. G. Herbert, London: SPCK, 1932.   [58] *MT*, 1001A.

suggested, upon the subsequent development of Western Christian mysticism and not merely upon its vocabulary and imagery. For his legacy consisted as much in an agenda of substantive theological and conceptual issues, an agenda which did not always determine the solutions to the questions it raised, but did very decisively determine many of the questions. We may conclude by noting the chief items on that agenda, all of which will much preoccupy us in the ensuing discussions.

One of the most powerful effects of the Platonic allegory on the mysticism of Denys is to be found in its resolute 'intellectualism'. Even were more emphasis to have been given than I have allowed for the presence in Denys' theology of a richly erotic imagery – and I have given it elsewhere[59] – the conclusion would be the same: it is the ascent of the *mind* up the scale of negations which draws it into the cloud of unknowing, where, led by its own *eros* of knowing, it passes through to the darkness of union with the light. It is therefore the *eros* of knowing, the passion and yearning for the vision of the One, which projects the mind up the scale; it is the dialectics of 'knowing and unknowing' which govern that progress, and it is not in the traditional metaphors of affectivity, touch, taste and smell, but in the visual metaphors of light and dark, seeing and unseeing, that that progress is described.

Nor, as we will have occasion to observe in some later mediaeval 'Dionysians' – in a Thomas Gallus or a *Cloud* Author – is Denys' 'cloud of unknowing' a vehicle for an anti-intellectualism, for a displacement of the role of intellect, at least ultimately, in favour of that of love in the making of the ecstatic union of the soul with God. Rather, in Denys, it is the immanent dialectic of knowing and unknowing *within* intellect which governs the pattern and steps of its own self-transcendence to a union, principally, of *vision*. Denys' is a mysticism which, as the psalmist puts it, 'seeks the face of God' (Ps. 24, 6), but under the condition imposed by Exodus: 'no one may see me and live' (Exod., 33, 20). That 'death' which is the condition of 'seeing' is Denys' 'cloud of unknowing': a death in an apophatic darkness which will rise in the knowing-unknowing vision of God.

Secondly, there is the problematic question of the role of hierarchy, and so of the metaphor of 'ascent', within the theoretical and

---

[59] See my *Eros and Allegory*, especially chapter 2.

metaphorical articulation of Denys' theology. It is because, we saw, the world *is* hierarchical in its ontological structure that the *metaphor* of ascent is constitutive within the dialectical epistemology. Because 'ascent' is constitutive within the epistemology it is indispensable within the description of the mind's spiritual journey towards the One. Hierarchical ontology and 'ascent'; dialectical epistemology and 'light-darkness'; these subtle combinations and interweavings of image and concept articulate the language of the spiritual journey towards a uniting vision of the One in which all negations are negated, all oppositions transformed and transcended. In Denys, at least, it is impossible to unpick this complex tissue of imagery and concept, to detach the epistemology from the ontology, the metaphors from their foundations in both or the description of spiritual experience from any of them.

And yet the 'hierarchical' elements of mediation in this complex threaten to run into headlong confrontation with a doctrine as fundamental to Denys' theology as any other: the doctrine of the ontological immediacy of the relation of created dependence. There are tensions here which Denys is able to resolve dialectically, but the stress of these tensions will leave their mark upon the imagery which he left as his legacy to Western theologians. Eight centuries later, the representation of the soul's journey to God as an 'ascent' is as powerful an image in Bonaventure as it is in Denys, but Bonaventure can no more detach the metaphor from an hierarchical ontology than can Denys. Consequently, as we will see in chapter 5, Bonaventure has to face for himself Denys' problem of how to reconcile the language of 'ascent', and so of hierarchy, with that of 'immediacy' and he faces it as a difficulty compounded by factors which appeared to have been far less pressing for Denys: Bonaventure's profoundly *Christological* vision.

By no means, however, is Denys' language of hierarchy the unique determinant of subsequent imagery of spiritual ascent. At least as important is Augustine's where it has equally significant Platonic sources, traceable ultimately back to Plato's Allegory of the Cave. Moreover, we find in Augustine a similarly complex and subtle interweaving of this metaphor with another, which has no place in Denys, that of 'interiority'. From at least the twelfth century apophatic spirituality in the Christian West is distinguished in its vocabulary and imagery by the attempt to harmonise Dionysian emphases on the dialectics of light and darkness with Augustinian emphases on interiority and ascent; and within these attempts the underlying foundations in a Dionysian hierarchical ontology are placed under increasing pressure. This, at any rate, is part of the story which we will have to follow out, though there are sub-plots and diversionary episodes in which other issues will sometimes assume greater importance. In short, it is not Denys' agenda alone which determines the main lines of narrative, but the relation between Denys' and Augustine's. Hence, it is to Augustine's contribution to the formation of the spiritual language of Western Christianity that we must now turn.

CHAPTER 3

The God within: Augustine's Confessions

For, wondering how I recognized the beauty of bodies, whether heavenly or earthly, and by what criterion I might rightly judge concerning mutable things and say: 'This ought to be so, that ought not to be so', wondering therefore what was the source of my judgement when I did thus judge, I had discovered the unchangeable and true eternity of truth above my changing mind. And so, by degrees passing from bodies to the soul which uses the body for its perceiving and from this to the soul's interior power, to which the bodily senses present exterior things, as indeed the beasts are able to do, and from there I passed to the reasoning power to which whatever is received from the bodily senses is referred for judgement. This also finding itself mutable in me awakened itself to its own understanding and withdrawing my thought from its usual ways, removing it from the confused crowd of phantasms so that it might discover what light suffused it, without any doubt cried aloud that the unchangeable was to be preferred to the changeable and that it had come to know the changeable itself; for if it had not arrived at some knowledge of the unchangeable, it could in no way have preferred it with certainty to the changeable. And then in the flash of a trembling glance my mind arrived at that which is. Now indeed I saw your 'invisible things, understood through those things which are made'. (Rom. 1, 20)[1]

This passage from Augustine's *Confessions* raises many questions for the contemporary reader, but the question which will concern us in this chapter is provoked by what may seem to us to be a curious, even possibly an illegitimate, confusion of literary genres, the narrative, autobiographical and experiential on the one hand and the

[1] *Confessions*, 7.17.23. For the most part I quote the English translation of R. S. Pine-Coffin, Harmondsworth: Penguin Books, 1961 and the Latin text from the edition of L. Verheijen, CCSL, 50, Turnhout: Brepols, 1981. I have used the paragraph divisions and enumerations from this Latin text.

dialectical and epistemological on the other. This conjunction of genres is, moreover, typical of the *Confessions* as whole. For it is not just that Augustine's masterpiece contains many instances of both kinds of writing; more than that, it is a structure put together on two apparently rather different, and not obviously complementary, organizing principles, those which organize it as autobiography and those which organize it as argument.

In this connection it is perhaps worthwhile to remind ourselves of the most visibly puzzling feature of the external structure of *Confessions*, divided as that work is into two groups of Books: the first, comprising Books 1–9, being fairly unambiguously autobiographical in character, the second, comprising Books 10–13, being of no auto-biographical significance at all, at any rate in the simple sense that it contains no narrative of Augustine's life and is rather a set of exegetical and theological reflections on memory, creation and time. It has taxed the ingenuity of most commentators to explain how, otherwise than in terms of rather indirect connections between them, these two parts of Augustine's work form a coherent unity. And it is hard to avoid the impression that, for all their ingenuity, these commentators in practice rather doubt that they do. It has to be said that in terms of modern conceptions of autobiography the two parts of Augustine's work simply fall apart. *We*, at least, have difficulty in seeing the inner coherence between them. Yet Augustine appeared not to have our difficulty, or at any rate he apparently saw no need to justify putting together what are for us heterogeneous genres. Looked at from his point of view, however, the fact that Augustine saw no need for justification, together with the fact that we do, might cause us to raise questions about the relevance of our taxonomy of genres in the understanding of Augustine's *Confessions*. In what sense is *Confessions* autobiography?

It is fair to say that there is a level at which the work is an intellectual and spiritual biography in a recognizably contemporary sense. The contemporary reader is likely to be impressed by *Confessions* primarily in that character. It seems true to say that *Confessions* is distinctive as autobiography, if it is not quite unique, until the sixteenth-century *Vida* of Teresa of Avila.[2] Since we think

---

[2] Clark's evidence of precedent and subsequent works of intellectual and spiritual self-analysis serves mainly to reinforce our sense of the distinctiveness of *Confessions*, at least until Teresa's work. See Clark, *Augustine, The Confessions*, Cambridge University Press, 1993, pp. 45–53.

of an autobiography primarily as a narrative, what is likely to disturb us is the intrusiveness of the technical philosophical dialectics within the recognizably narrative outline. Naturally, in an *intellectual* autobiography we ought not be surprised to find accounts of how Augustine's intellectual life developed, accounts of the problems which he had learned to solve first in one way and then in another, of the arguments which came to persuade him and of those whose power to convince diminished; and in an intellectual autobiography we would expect to find some account of how his own experience interacted with his intellectual development so as to produce the outcomes, both intellectual and personal, which they did. So it ought not to surprise us to find these things in Augustine's *Confessions*. In fact it is not the presence as such of elements of both which disturb us, or even their occurrence within the same passage, but the *manner* in which they relate. This can strike us as curious, and nowhere more clearly than in the passage quoted above.

It is possible to imagine the historian of ideas, or even the philosopher, seizing upon the character of this text purely as an argument in the theory of knowledge purporting to demonstrate the dependence of human powers of knowledge upon the divine Light of Truth. It is, indeed, that, a distinctively Augustinian argument, to be found in many places elsewhere in Augustine's corpus,[3] and its nature as argument is reflected in the presence within it of the language of inference. Augustine wonders 'By what criterion' he recognized the beauty of bodies, or was able to judge mutable things; he concludes that had he not somehow grasped the nature of the unchangeable it *would not have been possible* for him to know the changeable as changeable or to discriminate degrees of more or less between mutable things; and so *there must be* some inner, unchangeable light to which he, Augustine, had some access, by virtue of which he was able to make such judgements. Nothing in the nature of this account, *qua* argument, relies on Augustine's having had any particular experiences, whether of himself or of the world outside him. It is, as arguments go, in the general form of

---

[3] For example, in that most rigorously academic set-piece, *De Trinitate* (*De Trin.*), as we will see in the next chapter. For the English translation of *De Trin.* I have generally used A. W. Hadden's version in *The Works of Aurelius Augustine*, ed. Marcus Dods, VII, Edinburgh: T & T Clark, 1873; and for the Latin text, the edition of W. J. Mountain for CCSL, 50 and 51, Turnhout: Brepols, 1968. I have followed the enumeration of paragraphs in the Latin edition.

what a later, Kantian, philosophy called a 'transcendental deduc-
tion' from which first person pronouns are eliminable: *since* anyone
can make judgements of comparison between changeable things,
and *since* it is possible to do so only if the mind is illuminated by
the unchangeable light of truth, *it follows that* in some way the mind
does have access to that eternal light of truth.

Historians of ideas and philosophers, therefore, will attend to the
logical force of these connectives and are likely to neglect as logically irrelevant the first-person, experiential language which also
characterizes this passage and is interwoven with the language of
inference. And in this they will, from their point of view, be right.
For *qua* argument Augustine's reflections offer hostages only to *logical* fortune and their further character as autobiographical can do
nothing to protect Augustine from the logician's scrutiny of that
argument's validity. Nonetheless it is also the description of a personal *itinerarium mentis*. Grammatically the double character of the
passage is reflected in the manner in which it is built up out of the
alternation of logical connectives (the 'if', the 'therefore' and the
'since') with first-person pronouns ('*I* passed...', 'withdrawing *my*
thought...', '*my* mind arrived...', '*I* saw...'). In this second character
– of being the description of Augustine's experience – it reads as
the narrative of a mental process, perhaps even of introspection,
which parallels in microcosm, as it were in a single experiential act,
the story of his life as a whole: for that too is the story of a progression from a life lived 'in exteriority' among changeable things
towards a gradual awakening of the depths of his own interiority;
from that condition in which he lived, as he puts it, 'outside himself', to that in which he is able to find both God and himself
'within'. This is Augustine's personal *itinerarium mentis*, which is
above all an *itinerarium intus*; it is a journey most aptly paraphrased
in Augustine's own paradox: *et ecce intus eras et ego foris et ibi te quaere-
bam* – 'but see, you were within (me) and I was outside (myself); it
was there that I sought you'.[4]

Considered as his own life-story in small, therefore, this passage
is primarily experiential reporting; its language from one point of
view serves the purpose of describing epistemological conditions of
true judgement, and from another point of view gets its autobiographical force from the experiences which it reports. This is above

---

4   *Confessions*, 10.27.38.

all true of the structuring metaphors of 'interiority' and 'exteriority' which more than any others serve this dual purpose. 'Without' and 'within': at one level these function as concepts which give shape and form to Augustine's experience, indeed to his life as a whole; but they are also metaphors for what he experienced, and in that character they give psychological content to the bare categories of an epistemology. The true excitement to be gained from Augustine's story of his life lies in following through the subtle interplay of the conceptual and the experiential language in which he tells it.

We, however, can all too easily miss the subtlety, indeed, can be forced to deny its existence if on the strength of an a priori classification of methods we judge Augustine to have confused argument for a proposition with the reporting of experience, epistemology with psychology and the converse. Today we have denied ourselves that flexibility of mind with which Augustine is able to weave a single strand of thought out of what we may regard as heterogeneous strands of 'experience' and of 'dialectic'. The contemporary philosopher can feel unsatisfied at the appearence of an inference being broken into by intrusions of felt experience; and the psychologist may be equally disconcerted by Augustine's strange tendency to see himself in the light of purely intellectual considerations.

But perhaps our ambivalence is more revealing of a rupture in our culture than of any in Augustine's. No doubt it would be unwise to take for granted as some timeless necessity of thought a disjunction between reason and emotion, between inference and autobiography, between logic and psychology. It is this rupture which concedes the legitimacy either of a *philosophical* account of what 'the self' is, or of an *autobiographical* account of who 'I' am, but disallows the breeding of what inevitably seem to us to be hybrid genres. Whereas, as we shall see, for Augustine, the discovery of who *he* is depended in good measure on his discovery of what *the self* is. The two standpoints cross-fertilise. He knows that in his youth he misunderstood himself because he had very false ideas of what a self was – for example materialist and Manichaean; and he knows that he did not know what a self was because his life had been that of a person fleeing from self through sin, through the intellectual and moral blindness which goes with a life lived through exteriority. Both sorts of ignorance kept him from God, because they reinforced each other as tendencies to disperse himself, morally, emotionally and intellectually within the multiplicity of the changeable, 'external' world. He neither knew, as we might put it, 'propositionally', *that* the self lies in interiority; nor did he know, as we might put it 'experientially', the personal depth within himself in which, alone, God is to be found.

II

In the structure of *Confessions* as autobiography, therefore, the interplay of the conceptual with the experiential is crucial. In terms of its content, in those terms which will most generally describe what it is the story *of,* it is the story of a search, the search for God. But it is the story not only of *a* search for God, but of *Augustine's* search for God, written by Augustine. And as such, that is to say, as autobiography, it is also descriptive of Augustine's search for himself. Augustine came to see that these two pursuits, the search for God and the search for himself, were in fact the same search; that to find God was possible only in and through the discovery of the self and that the self, his self, was discoverable only there where God was to be found. And that place, where both he, Augustine, and God were to be found was in the depths of his own interiority: *tu autem eras interior intimo meo,* 'But you were more inward than my own inwardness'.[5] For Augustine, God, self and interiority all point to one and the same place.

But if *Confessions* is therefore the story *of* Augustine's search for self and God within interiority, it must also be said that in a certain way Augustine's writing of *Confessions* was part of the search which it describes. We know that what provoked Augustine to write *Confessions* may well have been an apologetic purpose. Christians in North Africa had needed to be convinced of the genuineness of Augustine's conversion and perhaps Augustine for his own part felt the need to justify himself to them. But this purpose by no means excludes other, self-motivated reasons, and from this point of view, we might say that Augustine wrote *Confessions* in order to know himself, as part of, indeed, perhaps as the culmination of the exploration and searching which it describes. For it is in the very nature of the sort of autobiography which Augustine writes that it is in its own right an act of self exploration and not merely the report of

5   Ibid., 3.6.11.

such acts. In fact, the interrelations between Augustine's life reported in *Confessions* and the act of reporting it which is *Confessions* are more complex even than that. Augustine tells how his life has been a search for God and for himself. And we can say that *Confessions* is also the demonstration, from a standpoint ten years or so after his conversion, that his life is indeed story, that it is a narrative of something, of a self, of the workings of divine grace in and through a self, of a search whose meaning as the search for God was at first not grasped at all, was then dimly grasped but within concepts which betrayed its true nature and then, finally, was revealed fully as the search which it was; all this – that is to say, the possibility of its being written as that story – is something demonstrated precisely by the act of writing *Confessions*. *Confessions* itself, the fact that Augustine could write it at all, both demonstrates that Augustine has become a self and contributes to the making of the self it is the story of.

There are some difficult concepts here which we will discuss more fully later in this chapter. Here let us say in a preliminary way that any autobiography which offers more than a mere sequence of isolated events at once *tells* of a self and *constructs* the self it tells of. Unless I am a self, there is no story to be told. Unless there is some thread of meaning, in terms of selfhood, to the events of my life, there is no coherence to the story. We might say, 'no self, no autobiography'. What Augustine could certainly have said is that until his conversion he was not in that sense a self at all in which it would be possible to tell the story of it. His conversion was the discovery of the love by which he was loved by the Christian God and that this discovery was what he had all along been searching for. Because it was then that he discovered himself, it was then and only then that the coherence of the narrative of his life could be grasped. And so his autobiography, from that moment, became the possibility which, until then, it was not.

But if in this sense we might say, 'no self, no autobiography', we might also say, and for the same reason, 'no autobiography, no self'. For Augustine's writing of *Confessions* is his act of appropriating his own selfhood by means of appropriating the narrative which gives it its coherence and meaning. Augustine writes of his exploration; but his writing is itself an exploration of the significance of his life's exploring. He *can* write of the significance of his seeking only because he now knows what he was seeking for; but equally, he writes in order

not merely to communicate that significance to others, but also so as
to know it for himself: to *make* the self he *reveals*.

III

There is, moreover, another layer of complexity within the structure of *Confessions*. Not only does Augustine wish to describe his
search for self and God; nor only is his writing *Confessions* the culminating act of the exploration which he describes in it; typically,
he has a philosophical problem about the nature of 'searching' as
such. And once again, he cannot keep this conceptual problem
from intruding into the text of his narrative. In the very first chapter of *Confessions* Augustine at once subjects God (and his reader) to
a barrage of questions, not all of which strike the contemporary ear
as pressingly *ad rem*, and among them is the question 'whether a
man is first to pray for help...and whether he must know you
before he can call you to his aid'. But then, 'If he does not know
you, how can he pray to you'.[6] Readers who know *Confessions* will
recognize this as but the first occurrence in a particular form of a
more general, conceptual question which will preoccupy Augustine
throughout the work, but especially in Book 10: how can we be
said to be searching for something if we do not know what we are
searching for; and how, by contrast, if we do know what we are
searching for, can we be said to be *searching* for it at all. And
indeed, in the highly abstract form in which the problem is discussed in Book 10 it may be hard to see equally how the problem is
of any interest and how it could possibly be solved.

Yet the issue is a real one and if within the narrative of the first
nine books it is kept in a relatively subordinate place, in Book 10,
when the narrative proper has been completed, Augustine embarks
upon a full-scale, systematic exploration of the meaning of 'searching'. It is not hard, after all, to see why, nor why the question of
how a person can be said to 'know' what he is looking for should so
preoccupy him. He has represented his own life as a searching for
God, and, at the same time, as a searching for himself. In so far as
his life can be so represented its progression has been from various
kinds of not-knowing to the corresponding forms of knowing –
from not knowing God to knowing God; from not knowing himself

<hr />

[6]   Ibid., I.I.I.

to knowing himself; and from the failure to recognize that to know God and to know the self are one and the same knowledge, to knowing this. And yet it cannot, he sees, have been a progress from unqualified ignorance to wholly new knowledge, for once again the question presses of how a person can be said to be searching for something if he does not know what he is searching *for*? How can it be that when, at the end of a successful search, a person recognizes that he has found what he was looking for, and can characteristically exclaim: 'there it is, I have found it!', unless, in *some* sense at least, he *did* know that which he sought? If in this way an act of *re*-cognition is at the heart of finding, how can this be if there was no *pre*-cognition there to be revived in the moment of discovery?

Now we know that in post-conversion writings which pre-date *Confessions*, Augustine had toyed with Neoplatonic ideas of *anamnesis*: the theory according to which all knowledge is a form of remembering of that which once, before birth, we fully knew, but in the cataclysm of birth, had been caused to forget. Augustine had toyed with this idea, for example in the earlier *Soliloquies*.[7] He was probably never fully convinced by this explanation but by the time he wrote *Confessions* he had decisively abandoned it: more precisely, he had rejected the argument, found in Plato's *Phaedo*, that the character of learning as *anamnesis* demonstrated the pre-natal existence of the soul.[8] Yet in an important way Augustine never abandoned the notion of knowledge as *anamnesis*: throughout his writings, from *Confessions* to *De Trinitate* and beyond, Augustine held fast to the centrality of memory in the process of knowledge-acquisition, to the idea, on which the Platonic doctrine was based, that all knowing is a form of *recognition*. It was this idea which mattered to Augustine and when, in his *Retractationes*, he records his disapproval of the *Soliloquies* passage, it is the explanation in terms of the pre-existence/oblivion model that he retracts, not the character of learning as a recognition which that model was meant to explain, for in the *Retractationes* he offers his alternative account in terms of eternal truth.[9]

Nowhere is this residual, revisionary Platonism more evident than in *Confessions*. The discovery of God is the *re*discovery of God, the return to a truth already somehow known, to a knowledge

---

[7] *Soliloquies*, 2.20, 34–35, PL, 32, 902–3.
[8] *Phaedo*, 72e–76a.
[9] *Retractationes*, 1.4.4, Migne: Patrologia Latina (PL), 32, 590. See also *De Trin.*, 12.15.24.

already somehow present within the searching itself. But again, how can it be said that we already know a thing if, truly, we are still searching for it? On the other hand, how can we be said to be searching for it if we do not know what we are searching for?

This question matters to Augustine in a peculiarly fundamental way, for theological reasons of his own and not merely for those arising out of specifically Neoplatonic preoccupations or out of a personal taste for dialectics. If we have emphasized, very properly, the element of Augustine's own activity of seeking God in his story, this emphasis ought not to allow us to neglect the fact that the primary agent in Augustine's seeking is not Augustine but God. It is because – indeed, emphatically, it is *only* because – God has been and is seeking out Augustine that Augustine seeks God; if, for Augustine, his seeking is always *for* God, his seeking is before that *from* God. This is the foundational truth which, as we will see, underlies all Augustine's paradoxes about seeking and finding: God is not to be sought outside the self, for God is already there 'within', eternally more intimate to me than I am to myself. It is I who am 'outside' myself and it is the God within who initiates, motivates and guides the seeking whereby and in which God is to be found. Not only is God within my interiority; it is from the God within that the power comes which draws me back into myself, and so to God.

This being so, Augustine's seeking God originates both in and from a power which is already active within him. For which reason, Augustine's apparently abstract, dialectical question about how he can seek God if he does not already know God becomes the more urgently practical question of how far, even at the beginning of his search, he was aware of that inner power which is both the source and object of his searching. If God was *in* his searching and not just the object of it, must not Augustine have in some way known this as and while he searched?

His answer is complex. Certainly he could not have been fully aware of the God he was seeking – not, at any rate, in the way he has become aware of God now that he has found him. For, of course, in principle he could not have been genuinely *seeking* God if, in the articulate manner of hindsight, he was from the outset in full possession of the knowledge he was seeking. Nor is this possible in fact, for Augustine wants to represent himself as in some way seeking God even when, as he wants us to think of him as having been, he was lost in the thickets of passion and pride in his young manhood in Carthage. But then, of course, he was very far from consciously seeking God. He was, as he says, not consciously seeking anything at all, except, perhaps, the satisfactions of lust and ambition.

And yet he wishes, *post factum*, to describe even the uncontrolled hedonism of his youth as having been driven in some way by, and to be in some way a manifestation of, his search for God. Augustine is unwilling to be forced off this ground by the consideration of the philosophical difficulty in describing a life lived without a thought for God as being somehow, perhaps 'really', a search for God. Nor does he propose merely to ignore the philosophical issue, which is why he engages in the very full treatment of it in Book 10. In the end, however, what will win out in this struggle between primitive theological belief and the philosophical difficulty it gives rise to is the theological belief, which consists, as I have said, in three propositions: that Augustine was, all the time, seeking God; that this can be said because all the while God was in his seeking, with whatever twists and turns of vicissitude it progressed; and that this is shown by the fact that his eventual discovery of God had all the character of a recognition, a 'home to his Father's house, private returned'.[10]

We should not, however, set these beliefs in sharper opposition with the philosophical difficulty than Augustine's own discussion warrants. Augustine thinks he can resolve the antinomy and sets about doing so in Book 10 where it beomes quickly clear that the solution lies within an adequate understanding of memory.

Prima facie, it is not difficult to see why this should be so. To seek something one does not yet possess is, at the cognitive level, at least rather *like* trying to remember something one has forgotten: and, as we have seen, for Augustine the discovery of God is at least to this degree like an act of memory in that it comes to us as a kind of recognition. Augustine clearly felt that at the dawning of his discovery of the true Christian God he was able, as it were, to say : 'Ah, yes. Now I see that that is what *all the time* I was seeking'. The past tense of the emphasized phrase is essential in the description of the discovery of God. To recognize God is to grasp the continuity of one's life in God. And, for all that his life appeared to be the pursuit of anything but God, indeed, it appeared to be the pursuit

---

[10]   Milton, *Paradise Regained*, last line.

of fantasies and illusions, it was, nonetheless, in some deeper way now grasped, also the seeking of God. To say this now is not an arbitrary act of *post factum* rationalisation. It is to recognize a truth then obscured, now revealed. To appropriate this truth is to appropriate one's past for what it truly was; it is therefore to set one's past in a true, ordered, coherent relationship with reality, it is to appropriate a continuity and so a new selfhood, a new identity. Consequently it is to put within one's grasp the power of autobiography, the power to describe what I am in terms of what my past has been leading to and of what my past has been in terms of what I now am. And the mechanism of this retrieval of my selfhood is memory, the power, as we might put it, of selective, meaningful personal continuity. It is in memory that I am what I am, for it is there that this continuous 'I' who writes the autobiography is also constructed by the autobiography it writes.

But if the claim to have been always seeking God is to be distinguished from arbitrary rationalisation after the event, this can only be because there is evidence that in some sense I *did* know that what I was looking for was God. And this requirement sharpens the philosophical problem: with what kind of knowledge did Augustine, in Carthage say, know the God he would later recognize he had been seeking, if, *ex hypothesi*, he had not yet found him?

In three chapters of Book 10 Augustine attempts to meet the philosophical difficulty head on. In chapter 18 Augustine considers the case of the woman who has lost a coin (Lk., 15), who, he says, 'would never have found it unless she had remembered it'. Otherwise, when it was found, 'how could she have known whether it was the one she was looking for?' The case is, indeed, conceptually unproblematic, for it is unarguable in such a case that a person who has lost a coin can recognize it when she finds it only if, *before* she finds it, she can give a sufficiently rigid identifying description of what it is that she had lost.[11] In fact, when what is forgotten is not *what* one has lost but *where* it is, the knowledge of what we are looking for is, or at least may be, every bit as full as the knowledge we have of it when it is in our possession. As

---

[11] It does not, of course, have to be a wholly accurate and full description. I can think that what I am looking for is a ten pence coin. But when I find it I am reminded that it was a fifty pence coin. So I was wrong in what I had thought I had lost, I was seeking the wrong thing, but still legitimately 'recognize' what I had lost when I find it, so long as it is the coin I remember losing which I find and not, by serendipity, some other coin.

Augustine says: 'If a thing vanishes from sight but not from memory...its image is retained within us and we look for it until it comes to light again'.[12]

But just for the reason that in such cases the knowledge of what we are looking for is explicit and unproblematic, the analogy does little to help us to understand how I can be said to 'know' what I am looking for when I seek God. For I cannot be said to know the God I am looking for in the way I now know the God I have found. And so, in *Confessions*, 10.19, Augustine considers a case whose epistemic complexity comes at least closer to that of his own search for God: that of the person who is trying to find the right word for a thought or, rather like it, the case of a person who cannot remember someone's name. When, in the act of writing I am looking for the right word for a thought it cannot be said, by analogy with the lost coin case, that I have the thought, but cannot find the right word for it. We might say, more precisely, that I am looking for the *articulation* which the right word, when I find it, will give to my thought. So in the sense that I have not yet found the right word I do not yet know what I am looking for. In what sense do I know what I want to say? In this sense at least that in spite of my not having yet found the word which will articulate the thought, I am perfectly able, as Augustine points out, to reject any number of inappropriate words. 'No, not this, not that', I can say. Moreover, when I stumble over the word, even by trial and error, I may instantly be able to say 'Ah, that's it!', recognizing, as we would legitimately say, 'just the word I *was* looking for'. The kind of knowledge we have of what we are looking for is in this case like that which we have in solving crossword puzzles: we possess a clue and the *shape* of the answer, and possibly even some part of the answer itself; we possess, therefore, some parameters of fittingness which determine what could and what could not count as an answer. This, I suspect, is something like what Augustine means when he says that we may 'partly' remember the word we are looking for, partly forget, the part we remember 'giving a clue to the remainder'. Though it is better put by saying that what we know when we are seeking is the shape which the answer must fill; and that what we recognize when we find the answer is that it fills the

---

[12] *Confessions*, 10.18.27.

required shape.[13] To use a term of ours, not Augustine's, our knowledge of what we are looking for is, in such cases, 'heuristic'.

Finally, in 10.20, Augustine asks: 'How then do I look for you, O Lord?' and his answer, as we might expect, is to explain the nature of his seeking God by partial analogy with the 10.19 case. He begins by suggesting that the search for God has both the general epistemological character of the search for happiness and is the only genuine form of it. Hence he can equally say: '...when I look for you, who are my God, I am looking for a life of blessed happiness',[14] and: 'Happiness is to rejoice in you and for you and because of you'.[15] Everyone desires happiness, 'so much so that there can be none who does not want it'.[16] But if they seek it this can only be because they do not possess it. If they seek it, then, the question arises: is it that they seek it in memory, as if they had forgotten it, but remembered at least this much about it that once they knew it and had somehow forgotten it? Or is it that they have so far forgotten it that they do not even remember having once known it and that they have since forgotten it?

This last, Augustine says, is not a real possibility, for, once again, how could they be seeking it if they possess it in no way at all, not even as something that they can remember once having known? For even those with very low expectations of happiness long for it and they 'must possess happiness in a certain sense, otherwise they could not long for it as they do; and there can be no doubt they do long for it'.[17] No seeking for happiness would be possible, Augustine concludes, if happiness were not to be found somewhere in everyone's memory.

We are, therefore, back with the same question all over again: how do we know the happiness which we seek, or as Augustine puts it, *where in memory* is this knowledge of happiness to be found? What follows, in 10.23, is a tortuous and at least apparently specious argument. No one, Augustine says, could be satisfied with happiness on a basis known to be false. Yet true happiness consists in God. So the search for happiness is one and the same with the search for God.

[13] Compare *De Trin.*, 10.4: 'And so [the mind] seeks that which is wanting, as we are wont to seek to recall to the mind something that has slipped from the mind, but has not altogether gone away from it, since we can recognise it, when it has come back, to be the same thing that we were seeking.'
[14] *Confessions*, 10.20.29.   [15] Ibid., 10.22.32.   [16] Ibid., 10.20.29.   [17] Ibid.

Naturally, Augustine concedes, many people do think, falsely, that happiness is to be found in activities or states other than the possession of God. Augustine knows this because at one time *he* did. Yet they would not search for happiness in what are false claimants to the name if they knew the falsehood of those claimants' credentials. So everyone desires true happiness, however degraded may be their desires and however self-deceived may be their search for it in false objects of desire. Everyone, even a mind 'in this wretched state...would still rather find joy in truth than in falsehood'.[18] But since only the possession of God is true happiness, 'one day (such a mind) will be happy, if it learns to ignore all that distracts it and to rejoice in truth, the sole Truth by which all else is true'.[19]

At first sight this argument appears to commit an obvious and well-known fallacy, of the general form: Everyone desires **x**; though it is possible to be wrong about what **x** consists in, no one desires to be deceived about what **x** is; true **x** consists in **y**; therefore everyone desires **y**. Everyone wants happiness and no one wants to be deceived about what happiness is. But happiness consists in God. Therefore everyone desires God. So formulated, the argument is manifestly invalid: for what people desire when they desire happiness is what they *think* happiness consists in, whether or not happiness truly consists in that thing. For desires are characterized by their *intentional* objects, by the descriptions under which those objects are desired, even if those descriptions are false. Hence, if I think happiness consists in sexual satisfaction then that, sexual satisfaction, is the description under which I desire happiness and is the intentional object of my desire. I do not desire God, even if God is what happiness truly is.

So clearly fallacious is this argument that one prefers to acquit Augustine of guilt. Nor is he in fact guilty of it. He knows perfectly well that he, and many another, has sought and does seek happiness in things that cannot truly yield it. But if I so misdescribe what happiness is as to think that it consists in sexual satisfaction, can I truly be said to desire happiness? Augustine, like Aristotle before him,[20] thinks of the desire for happiness as absolutely irreducible: you can never cease to desire it. Yet, also like Aristotle, Augustine knows that there is scarcely any limit to the perversity and deprav-

---

[18] Ibid., 10.23.33.   [19] Ibid.   [20] *Nicomachean Ethics*, I.8.

ity of human desire. Hence the desire for happiness can be present in desires for utterly self-destructive and self-defeating objects. It is still the desire for happiness, however misconceived and under whatsoever misdescription, so long as in any relevant respect what one desires has some capacity to reflect what true happiness consists in. And nothing human beings desire can wholly lack that capacity. For nothing can wholly fail to represent the beauty and goodness of God. No one, therefore, can desire anything so as in every respect to miss the mark of true happiness. Hence, no matter how mistaken may be my pursuit of happiness it is always in some way a desire for God.

In every human desire, therefore, there is some echo, however faint, of God, who in every human desire is in some way desired, not necessarily or always *as* God, but always as happiness; and true happiness is always in some way desired, even happiness sought in false pursuits, and this may be said even if the only evidence for the desire for true happiness will, in such cases, be negative, consisting in the trail of restless frustration which such false satisfactions leave behind them. Hence, too, the *awareness* of God as the true object of desire is always present, if only, often, in the form of the dissatisfaction which flows from the pursuit of anything else.

Dissatisfied longing, I suggest, is the key to Augustine's conception of 'remembering God', and so, as he sees it, to the shape and form of his life – hence, too, to the shape and form of his *Confessions*: after all, this is the meaning of perhaps the best known of Augustine's *dicta*, among the opening words of the book: 'our hearts are restless until they rest in you'.[21] All his life Augustine sought God. But this was no straightforward search as for something once clearly known, but now lost. It was a search along false trails, up blind alleys and into *culs-de-sac*. Sometimes that searching was more or less unconscious, like that of a person who finds herself absently rummaging through a drawer, having forgotten what she was looking for. But as his search met with more and more frustration, and the gap of longing, intellectual and emotional, widened, the longing itself acquired shape and definition and direction, became focused, at least negatively. For as this or that solution to the problem had to be abandoned, the blurred outlines of *what* he was searching for sharpened, and as the form of what he sought hardened into shape,

---

[21] *Confessions*, I.I.I.

so the dissatisfaction itself intensified. Augustine knew what he was looking for in the increasingly defined shape and intensity of his unhappiness, in the same way that the crossword solver becomes more, not less, frustrated as the solution moves nearer and nearer to the tip of her tongue, but eludes her yet.

IV

Let us draw some threads together. Augustine's seeking God was *of* God. From the beginning of his life, even when Augustine was far from consciously seeking God, God was in his seeking; and so it is appropriate that, at the very beginning of his *Confessions*, Augustine should so emphatically 'confess' the absolute priority of the divine initiative. For this is what Augustine, the author of *Confessions*, now knows about Augustine the subject of *Confessions*. This is what Augustine, upon his conversion, so emotionally 'recognizes' – that the God he had always been seeking was familiar to him as having always been in his seeking.

But *where* was this God who had been in his seeking? In Augustine's interiority. There Augustine had been unable to recognize God because he had been living *foris*, 'outside himself'. The God within had been beckoning him on, drawing Augustine within himself on an *itinerarium intus* – but inwards towards what? Towards 'memory', to that most intimate part of himself, to that depth within himself in which it would be possible to recognize the God whom he could not possibly wholly 'forget'.

But in what sense of 'remember' does Augustine 'remember' God, however minimally, within the erratic and apparently random course of his journey within? Augustine remembers God in the form of a restless dissatisfaction with all else that he seeks, a dissatisfaction which sharpens and intensifies as he draws ever nearer the goal of his seeking. That dissatisfaction is a 'remembering' because it is at once a longing for what he lacks and a recognition of the failure to reach it, which implies at least negative knowledge of the true nature of the goal. That remembering is at once a knowing and a not-knowing of God, a knowing, we might say, in the form of a not-knowing.

But now we must ask: *what* was it that left Augustine so dissatisfied with all that he sought besides God? Whence his unhappiness? There is no doubt about the answer to this question: it was the character of all created things as 'mutable'. Augustine could not contemplate the changeableness of creation without a shudder of dismay, even of apprehension, and if Augustine could be said to be a 'Neoplatonist' in any one respect alone, it would principally be in this, so characteristically 'Platonic', emotion of distress at the mutability and instability of all things. And yet it is not only under the influence of the *Platonici* that Augustine learned to feel this distress. It was the emotional key to his life before he encountered Platonism – at any rate, he came to see that this was so, and the significance of the encounter with Platonism lay in the ability it gave him to formulate the epistemology of what had become for him an emotional rising tide of dissatisfaction with all that he had been seeking until then. Platonism, therefore, made such a powerful impression on him because it met his personal needs at a point in his development where there was no way forward for him *emotionally* unless he could be released *intellectually* from the prison of his materialist philosophy. Platonism, therefore, explained to him the dissatisfaction he had already recognized in himself. Platonism explained the restlessness of his search as lying in the fact that the things of creation teeter, as it were, on the edge of a precipice: they are what they are, but only just, for so easily could they be otherwise; they exist, but in a condition so precariously close to nothingness as to be separated from it by nothing at all in themselves. It taught him, moreover, that there is nothing in ourselves, who know these things, other than acts of knowing which are themselves mutable – or rather, there is nothing in us which is *of* us to distinguish our condition of mutability from that of the things which we know. We are perishable beings among the perishable, and were it not for the presence within us of that which is not of us, the immutable light of Truth itself, we could not even know the perishable for the perishable thing which it is.

For that, indeed, is what it is to live and know in our 'exteriority': it is to be wholly immersed within the mutable, unable to see it *as* mutable. That is how Augustine had lived until his reading of the *Platonici* rescued him from his blindness. Not to know the mutable for what it is is simply not to know it at all. But we cannot know the mutable for what it is except in the light of the immutable. Hence, if we do experience the unhappiness of mutability this is, in itself, a minimal grasp of the immutable Truth in whose light we are aware of that unhappiness as the unhappiness which it is. But this 'pre-explicit'[22] hold on the immutable is not so minimal that memory cannot retrieve it in an act of *re*cognition when, at last, the Truth is encountered explicitly in 'a moment of awe'.

V

Let us, then, return to the passage with which we began. The logic of the progress from 'without' to 'within' paraphrases both the life of Augustine itself and the logic of any individual act of cognition. What *Confessions* recounts biographically the epistemology recounts inferentially, and the double nature of the passage is reflected in the duality of the central organizing image of interiority: 'interiority' denotes both an ascetical practice of turning away from the changeable 'without', 'inwards' to the light of truth, and an epistemological structure, both something to be achieved by a life and the foundation of knowledge, both *an* experience and the presupposition of *all* experience.

My 'interiority' is memory: that is what is most 'within' me. And yet, though Augustine will certainly allow the proposition that God is 'within' me, he prefers to say that I am 'in' God.[23] Indeed, God is only within my memory at all in the sense that, having penetrated most deeply within myself into memory, God is discovered on the *other side of* memory and 'above' it:

Where, then, did I find you so that I could learn of you? For you were not in my memory before I learned of you. Where else, then, did I find you, to learn of you, unless it was in yourself, above me? Whether we approach you or depart from you, you are not confined in any place. You are Truth, and you are everywhere present.[24]

There is observable here a concern lest the metaphor of inwardness should become interpreted in too 'physical' a way, as the *Cloud* Author was later to put it, and there is the suggestion in this passage of the *Cloud* Author's paradox that the journey 'inward' toward memory leads to the recognition of the God there encountered as beyond all boundaries, less in us than an 'everywhere' we are in. For the God encountered 'within' memory is personalised Truth as such, present within us in our capacity to judge of the

---

[22] See chapter 4, pp. 83–84, for an explanation of this theme of 'pre-explicit' as distinct from 'explicit' self-knowledge.
[23] *Confessions*, 1.2.2.   [24] Ibid., 10.26.37.

changeable, but altogether beyond the confines of our limited and themselves changeable minds. The paradox, then, is that there, where God is most intimately and 'subjectively' interior to us, our inwardness turns out beyond itself towards the eternal and boundless objectivity of Truth. The language of 'interiority' is, as it were, self-subverting: the more 'interior' we are the more our interiority opens out to that which is inaccessibly 'above' and beyond it.

This is the paradox which Augustine presents to himself at the very outset of *Confessions* in the form of a question: is he to say that God is within him or that he is in God? Though *Confessions* itself is, as we have said, the story of Augustine's searching for and finding the God 'within', that, for Augustine, is not the primary, foundational metaphor for his search: the 'true answer to my question' is 'rather that I should not exist, unless I existed in you'.[25] Memory is, epistemologically, the point of juncture between the 'within' and the 'above', the point at which my deepest interiority intersects with the eternal objectivity of Truth, so that my knowing any truth becomes at least an implicit acknowledgement of Truth itself, a recognition of the Truth particular truths 'remind' us of. Memory, then, is the epistemological key. It is also the key to Augustine's autobiography because memory is the experiential root of his identity: hence, to the story of his personal search for the God within. These two elements, the epistemological and the autobiographical, subtly interact within Augustine's narrative so as to produce that unfamiliar and apparently hybrid mix of the inferential with the experiential which is so pervasive a feature of *Confessions*. And, as I have pointed out, the two genres are never so startlingly combined than in the passage with which this chapter begins. He both *infers that* and, as it were, *mystically encounters* the reality of 'that which is' 'in the flash of a trembling glance', which is at once the recognition of a philosophical truth and a personal encounter with Truth itself. I see absolutely no reason why we, contemporary readers, should even ask, as if the answers excluded one another, which of these it is, never mind devote either time or scholarship in a pointless quest for the answer, for it is manifestly both, the key to the understanding of his life and the key to the understanding of understanding itself.

Thus was God always 'within', but not always known through that 'inwardness'. Knowing God as he had through various modes

---

[25] Ibid., 1.2.2.

of exteriority, in his early life Augustine had been unable to recognize the God he had always been seeking, so that, although in some way it truly *was* God whom he sought, it was a God misrecognized whom he repeatedly believed he had found; and he could not come to recognize the true God until he had discovered his own inwardness. Indeed, the truth Augustine discovered was that to discover his own inwardness was the same thing as to discover God and that to discover God was to discover his own inwardness – either discovery was the discovery of his true selfhood. That is why Augustine's discovery of God was also the discovery of the power of autobiography. For to possess the power of autobiography is to possess the power to represent oneself to oneself in a coherent narrative, that is, *as a self,* which one can own. As I put it earlier, 'no self, no autobiography'.

One dimension of this narrative, therefore, is its character as a journey of self-discovery. There is a sense, which I have tried to clarify, in which, for Augustine, the existence of his true self was always a pre-existing fact, albeit, until his encounter with the *Platonici,* one hidden from him. That deeper 'self' was there in spite of his incapacity to make it his own within his conscious, experiencing selfhood. It was there within an inwardness which betrayed its presence, obscurely indeed, within his very capacity to judge the beautiful, mutable things of this world and in his constant, questing desire for beauty itself. But that inwardness had eluded his grasp in so far as he had persistently misconstrued his own selfhood through an exteriorised, theoretical and practical materialism of vision. *Et ecce intus eras et ego foris*: all the work of Augustine's seeking was therefore *for* God, but equally it was all *of* God. All was the work of pre-emptive grace, for the God whom Augustine sought was the immanent cause also of Augustine's seeking, a cause he had come to recognize to be more inward than his own most intimate being.

In this recognition we find Augustine's spirituality of *memoria,* the spirituality of a journey which retraces the steps back towards a self lost sight of, but still present and active within the very acts of return. Hence that journey is essentially a journey of memory back to that primitive relationship, never wholly lost to it but lingering, as it were, on the tip of memory's tongue, there to be recovered as a conscious recognition of the infrangible union which the soul had always enjoyed with God. This is the spirituality of memory as 'storehouse', of memory as the passive repertoire of experience and knowledge in which is contained the depths of selfhood and knowledge awaiting rediscovery.

But if the imagery of *Confessions* is that of the discovery of a selfhood already possessed immanently within him, that imagery also bears the meaning of a more active, dynamic, dramatic spirituality of *self-making*. If, from one point of view, the progress of Augustine's life towards conversion is the act of *memoria* retrieving the residual, 'dormant' true self of interiority from the depths of the soul's amnesia, from another point of view that progress is the creative activity of making a self which, before his conversion, was *not* already there. If, in his pre-conversion life, Augustine had lived on the surface of his own true selfhood in exteriority, it is not so much that he had neglected a depth of selfhood which already existed as that, on the model of self-discovery, he *was* only a surface, that he *lacked* the depths of interiority in which alone God could be found. From this standpoint the story of his conversion is less the story of grace illuminating a pre-existent but misrecognized space than the story of grace making the space which it occupies: it is the story of the making of a soul, not of its rediscovery.

It is therefore the story of the making of memory in a man who had lacked it, or in whom memory was but a feeble power of perception of the mutable world, not the power of knowledge proper which both possesses and knows itself to possess the inner source of immutable light in which to judge that mutable world. That power which, from one point of view he already possessed dormantly, needing only to be activated, from this other point of view is a new creation of grace, which opens up spaces in the soul previously lacking to it.

These two 'spiritualities' – of self-discovery and of self-making – possess, as it were, different moods. In the one predominates the mood and the language of passivity, of calm certainty, an untroubled sense of everything having been in place all the time; it is a spirituality whose metaphors of spiritual progress are those of restoration of lines of continuity which in fact were never wholly severed, so that what is restored is the sense of how things truly are and always have been – indeed, in at least an implicit and inchoate sense, were always recognized to have been. It is a spirituality in which sin and failure are represented as the rupture of the conscious, actively desiring and knowing self from its true relationship with its true centre, in which sin is the condition in which the conscious self is focused upon a point 'outside' that centre within, like an image in double focus. It is therefore a characteristic of this spirituality of self-discovery that the goal of the spiritual life is reintegration, the readjustment of the image into single focus, the re-establishment of a unity, which sin has fractured, between conscious empirical selfhood and the pre-existing depths of one's being from which God can never be expelled.

The mood of the spirituality of self-making is, we might say, more 'existential'. If the emphasis of self-discovery is on continuity, the emphasis of self-making is on breaks, crises and novelty; less on the Plotinian theme of the soul's return to its source, more on the soul's reaching out to that which is not yet; less on the domestic emotions of return to what is already, however dimly, known, more on the erotic passions of a yearning for the inaccessible. And the narrative of the soul's progress in the spirituality of self-making is punctuated by crises of loss of the familiar and of startling encounters with the unexpected, for it is the spirituality less of memory as recollection than of memory as reconstruction, of memory constantly challenged to re-make the past in new terms and, as of the past, so of personal identity. For the spirituality of self-discovery, I am what I was in my origins; for the spirituality of self-making, I am what I may hope for.

The presence of these two spiritual tendencies within Augustine's narrative may have some role in explaining the presence of that other duality within *Confessions*, between the dimensions of the conceptual–theological and the experiential. The raw autobiographical materials of *Confessions* are its key moments of experienced crisis, of discontinuity followed by renewed perception of continuity, each a break with a phase of the past but each inaugurating a new language in which to recapture the continuity of present self with past self broken with. Each crisis therefore inaugurates a new perception of his personal identity. This is the language of the spirituality of self-making, in the narrative of which Augustine is at his psychologically most acute: he can describe in detail what each crisis felt like in its own terms and at its own time.

But this narrative is set within an overarching frame of theological and conceptual interpretation which Augustine was able to discover only after the events he recounts and from the standpoint of his conversion and so is the retrospective hermeneutic of *Confessions*. That frame is the spirituality of self-discovery, the *post-factum* recognition that, for all the experience of discontinuity and crisis, those ruptures had had the effect of but leading him back to a self and a God who had been continuously with him. In part, at least, that retrospective hermeneutic was an intellectual discovery, both sustaining and depending upon his personal conversion in the garden in Milan. Augustine discovered 'interiority' as such and *his* own interiority in one and the same act, was startled at once by the novelty and by the continuity of what his conversion gave him, wrote *Confessions* at once to *rediscover* and at the same time to *re-create* his own identity and met with all these things in a single 'moment of awe' which fused the conceptual and the experiential in a single experience, the experiential and the conceptual in a single concept.

All of these dimensions of Augustine's *Confessions* are fused in its one, dominating preoccupation, with Augustine's seeking God and with his seeking of the meaning of seeking. And the dialectics of the 'inner' and the 'outer', the sense of a self restored and of a self renewed, of the discovery of the truth of his life and the Truth itself, of memory as recall and of memory as reconstruction – this multiple complexity of dimension is all embodied in that second most famous passage of his *Confessions*:

Late have I loved you, o Beauty ever old, ever new, late have I loved you. You were within me, and I was outside myself and it was there that I sought you and, myself disfigured, I rushed upon the beautiful things you have made. You were with me but I was not with you. They held me far from you, those things which would not exist if they did not exist in you. You called, you cried out and you broke through my deafness, you shone out, cast your radiance and put my blindness to flight, you shed your fragrance and I drew breath and pine for you, I tasted you and so I hunger and thirst for you, you touched me and I burn with love of your peace.[26]

[26]   Ibid., 10.27.38.

CHAPTER 4

Interiority and ascent: Augustine's De Trinitate

I

The language of interiority is a metaphorical discourse which at once structures Augustine's thought about selfhood, and organizes his personal sense of himself. It has, that is to say, both a conceptually and an experientially structuring power. As a metaphor it has no merely decorative purpose, nor in any other way could Augustine's understanding of self or of God survive its removal; nor are there any other terms to which that metaphor could be reduced.

This much I have tried to show in the last chapter. In this chapter we must raise some more detailed questions about how the metaphor articulates Augustine's thought, in particular about how the 'inner' as a category of thought and experience is to be distinguished from the 'outer' – for manifestly they are correlative, mutually defining, terms. Above all we must try to determine where the line of demarcation is meant to fall between the 'inner' and the 'outer': *at what point* do I cease to think or experience in an 'outward' way and begin to think or experience 'inwardly'? And then we must ask how this discourse of inwardness relates with that other, complementary, discourse of ascent. We might say that if the last chapter was concerned with the dynamics of these metaphors, in this we will be concerned with their epistemological structure, their statics.

It would be a mistake to expect from Augustine any single, consistent and formal statement of how this distinction is to be made out even in any one work, let alone throughout his vast *œuvre*. Augustine's intellectual development is too exploratory, his temperament too tentative, for such expectations ever to be reasonable. That having been said, Augustine inherits with the metaphor of 'interiority' some broad indications of its structure. This is only to be expected. 'Interiority' and 'exteriority' are, as I have said, correlatives. One could not simply say, in the relativistic spirit of

74

some 'structuralist' thinkers, that the meaning of 'interiority' *consists* in its modes of contrast with 'exteriority' and vice versa, but there is no work of illumination which the metaphor can do except in the light of the contrasts in which those terms stand to one another: and *what* work it does depends on how those contrasts are made out. Hence, with the metaphor of interiority Augustine inevitably inherits some sense of how the 'inner' and the 'outer' are to be distinguished, and there seems little doubt that his chief source in this connection is the *Platonici* who figured so importantly in his intellectual conversion, especially Plotinus.

Undoubtedly one can say, whether on Augustine's own authority or on the strength of an assessment of the traces of Neoplatonic influence throughout his writings, that Augustine's encounter with the *Platonici* was decisive in his intellectual and moral formation. Our assessment of that debt inevitably brings us back in the first instance to *Confessions* where the history of that indebtedness is recounted. There we find three *loci* in which the metaphor of 'interiority' is expanded with some rigour, 7.17, 9.10 and 10.6. Of these the first holds a particular interest for the assessment of Augustine's debt to Platonism. For in that passage, quoted in full at the beginning of the last chapter, Augustine paraphrases the essence of what he felt able to retain of his own pre-Christian Platonism within his later Christian perspectives.[1]

That he felt able later to retain within his Christian faith the distilled Plotinianism of his pre-conversion period is perhaps best evidenced by the fact that although in 7.17 Augustine describes little that Plotinus could not have described – indeed, as we will see, somewhat less[2] – the significant steps in the ascent to 'interiority' which he there describes are all to be found in the other two passages (9.10 and 10.6), both of which refer to his post-conversion period. Hence these latter passages are equally 'Platonic' but

---

[1] Again, it would be risky to assume that the passage paraphrases objectively the commitment of Augustine to Platonism at the time reported; here, as elsewhere, we must assume that Augustine is giving an *assessment* of what he thought at the time and one ought always to suppose that the assessment has at least to some degree found its way into the thing assessed.

[2] It is often noted that no parallel to Plotinus' heady rhetoric of mystical 'union' can be found in Augustine's *Confessions*, or, for that matter, anywhere else in Augustine. This kind of 'mysticism' was evidently uncongenial to Augustine, and McGinn is quite right to insist that Augustine found place for the ideal of 'union in love' principally within his understanding of the Christian community, the Church. See Bernard McGinn, *The Presence of God*, 1 *The Foundations of Mysticism*, New York: Crossroads, 1992, pp. 248–251.

describe Christian experiences. Whether Augustine was ever *more* a Platonist than he describes himself in *Confessions*, 7 as having been is another matter, to be judged on a more detailed analysis of the early post-conversion writings which precede *Confessions*.

Be these things as they may, nothing is easier – and perhaps in inverse degree interesting – than to cull the *Enneads* of Plotinus for sources of vocabulary and imagery picked up in our three passages from *Confessions*. What concerns us in this chapter is the structure of the metaphors of 'inwardness' and 'ascent' and while there seems to be very little doubt that Augustine found the chief lineaments of that structure in Plotinus, at least as revealing as the similarities are the differences.

In *Confessions*, 7.17, that structure is reduced to the bare essentials of the Plotinian three-stage progression, away from the things of sense, inwards to the soul and upwards to Truth and Beauty. The progression begins for Augustine, therefore, where it begins for Plotinus, with the 'beauty of bodies', but immediately with a question about that beauty: *how* was Augustine able to recognize it? To put bodily beauty in question was also the first move of Plotinus: bodily beauty 'ravishes', but 'the beauties of the realm of sense' are 'images and shadow pictures, fugitives…'.[3] What accounts for the seductive beauty of bodies? What accounts for the *beauty* of bodies is Beauty itself. What accounts for the *seduction* is the fact that the human soul, in its deepest being, has its own source in Beauty, and in turning in upon itself the soul discovers there imprinted the image of that Beauty from which it proceeds. The soul therefore longs for Beauty, as an exile longs for home. 'Let us flee', Plotinus says, 'to the beloved Fatherland…The Fatherland to us is There whence we have come, and there is the Father.'[4]

But a turning 'within' is, in the first instance, a turning away from what is 'without' and for both Plotinus and Augustine the 'without' is the 'changeable'. For Plotinus this mutability is due to the contagion of matter, the force of dispersal and disunity which drags the soul towards 'the outer, the lower, the dark'.[5] Augustine's distaste for the material is less emphatic, but the identification of 'the outer, the lower, the dark' with the 'changeable' (and conversely, of 'inner', 'higher' and 'light' with the immutable and the

---

[3] *Enneads* (*Enn.*), 1.6.3. Throughout I have used Stephen McKenna's translation as abridged by John Dillon, Harmondsworth: Penguin Books, 1991.

[4] Ibid., 1.6.8.   [5] Ibid., 1.6.5.

eternal) is no less marked than in Plotinus. For, once removed 'from the confusing crowd of phantasms...[the mind] discover[s] what light suffused it...[and] cried aloud that the unchangeable was to be preferred to the changeable...'.[6]

In the second step, then, the mind, having turned away from the changeable, turns inward upon itself to find there the source of its own power to judge the changeable beauty of bodies. Not in *Confessions*, but only later in *De Trinitate*, will Augustine develop the Plotinian theme of the image of eternal Truth and Beauty in the restored soul. For Plotinus, the soul purified by detachment from the seductions of changeable beauties is a reflection of Beauty itself. But, he asks, 'How are you to see into a virtuous soul and know its loveliness? *Withdraw into yourself and look.*'[7]

Augustine's 'turning inward' to the mind's own nature is at once more detailed and in one important respect, quite different. It is more detailed in that Augustine distinguishes between three levels of interior power in the soul: that at which the 'soul uses the body for its perceiving'; that at which the soul has the 'interior power to which the bodily senses present exterior things'; and finally, that of the 'reasoning power' (*ratiocinans vis*) to which 'whatever is received from the bodily senses is referred for judgment'. In the 10.6 passage, and later in *De Trinitate*, these steps are further divided, but at any rate the second level referred to in 7.17 is what in those later places Augustine calls 'imagination', the source of 'the confused crowd of phantasms'. This, and the later more detailed distinctions of human powers not only goes further than Plotinus, but differs from him in a way whose importance will be best seen from the vantage point of his own, developed, theology of image in *De Trinitate*.[8]

Augustine never followed Plotinus in finding the soul's image of God in its own self-achieved degree of *moral* perfection. For Augustine that image was to be found in the interior structures of the mind's cognitive and affective powers, but above all in those powers by which the mind can reflect upon itself as a knowing agent – as he will later say, memory, understanding and will. The source of the mind's ability to image that which transcends it is therefore its own nature *as a mind*, not any moral beauty it may possess. Here, in *Confessions*, that later account of image is not found, but the principal stages of the argument which leads to it in

---

[6] *Confessions*, 7.17.23.   [7] *Enn.*, 1.6.9.   [8] See pp. 94–100 below.

De Trinitate are present in the hierarchical ascent by which the mind progressively reflects upon its own self, seeking out within its own changeable powers those in which evidence of the unchangeable truth can be found. Thus, even when the journey within leads him to the power of judgement, it finds that too to be 'a changeable thing', so that the mind is forced to transcend even itself in quest of that which is both itself unchangeable and the means by which the reasoning power is able to judge the changeable for what it is. There, then, where the mind exceeds its own powers (*in excessu mentis*), it strikes upon *id quod est, in ictu trepidantis aspectus.*

Therefore, whereas the emphasis in Augustine's journey 'within' is on an epistemic progression of self-reflection upon the mind's natural powers, the emphasis in Plotinus is on the soul's awareness of its own moral beauty, on its having become – made itself – a 'perfect work'.[9] For one reason above all Augustine could not have followed Plotinus here. For Augustine, no soul could claim to be a 'perfect work', least of all by virtue of its own efforts. The power of the soul to image unchangeable Beauty could not depend on its having met any *moral* conditions. When, therefore, Augustine hears, as Plotinus did, the summons 'withdraw into yourself', he responds: 'And I entered into my inward being, with you as my guide, and I was able to do this because you made yourself my helper.'[10] Where Plotinus' soul reaches out, solitary and unaccompanied, toward the ultimate, uniting vision – 'strike forward yet a step – you need a guide no longer – strain and see'[11] – Augustine is passively 'opened out' and it is God who does it. Both the steps on the ladder and the means of ascent differ.

The second passage, the 'vision' with Monica at Ostia (9.10) is constructed upon the same threefold schema of turning away, turning within and opening up to that which is above. There is, however, a wealth of Plotinian trope not found in the other two *Confessions* passages which is easily identified from a comparison with *Enneads* 5.1.2[12], though it will not particularly serve our pur-

---

9 *Enn.*, 1.6.9.　　10 *Confessions*, 7.10.16.　　11 *Enn.*, 1.6.9.

12 For example: 'The great soul must stand...holding itself in quietude. Let not merely the enveloping body be at peace, body's turmoil stilled, but all that lies around, earth at peace, and sea at peace, and air and the very heavens. Into that heaven, all at rest, let the great soul be conceived to roll inward at every point, penetrating, permeating, from all sides pouring in its light'. Compare *Confessions*, 9.10.25: 'Suppose...that the tumult of man's flesh were to cease and all that his thoughts can conceive, of earth and of water and of air, should no longer speak to him; suppose that the heavens and even his own soul were silent, no longer thinking of itself, but passing beyond...'.

poses to explore the similarities here. Suffice it to say that the Ostia 'vision' is notably more 'experiential' in tone than are the descriptions of the other two, though by no means does Augustine suppose some incommunicably 'individual' experience; on the contrary, what Augustine tells of is an experience shared with Monica, a *dialogue*, itself literally punctuated by the rhythms of their words and silences in the way that what they experience is metaphorically punctuated by them. As the description of a 'mystical' experience, the Ostia passage is altogether out of character with the Plotinian 'flight of the alone to the alone'.[13] But then, nearer to the 'inferential' spirit of the 7.17 passage is the third of our three *loci*, Augustine's interrogation of creation about God in *Confessions*, 10.6.

In a series of overlapping questions and answers Augustine interrogates successively the creatures of the external world, asking 'What is my God?', and he hears in response successively, 'I am not God, but he made me', and, 'Not I', and, 'Look above us...'. So again, in the familiar pattern, Augustine turns his attention away from the things which surround the externality of his flesh and directs his attention upon himself, asking 'Who are you?' The answer is, 'A man', a being composed of body and soul, *unum exterius et alterum interius*. But since it was with his body that he sought God in creatures, it must be within his soul, his 'inner and better self', that he must question further. For it was by means of his soul, the *homo interior*, that he came to know that the creatures of the external world were not God.

Once again, therefore, the progression 'within' is achieved by successive moments of self-reflection by the mind on its own powers of knowing. And that progression spirals ever further within and above, the steps being considerably multiplied in number and detail beyond those described in the Ostia and pre-conversion visions. We will have the opportunity to examine those steps more closely when, in *De Trinitate*, Augustine gives a more formalised and analytical description of the powers of the mind, but it is fair to say that all the steps are already in place in *Confessions*. In the meantime, let us take note of a puzzle which has a direct bearing on the principal concern of this chapter, which is with the point of demarcation at which 'inner' and 'outer' are distinguished.

The puzzle arises because at the point where Augustine's ques-

---

[13]   *Enn.*, 6.9.11.

tionings turn away from the 'exterior' to the 'interior', Augustine places the body firmly on the side of the 'exterior' and the soul on the side of his 'interior' and 'better' part – *unum exterius et alterum interius*. Moreover, at least as Pine-Coffin translates, Augustine even identifies *himself* with his soul: 'I, the inner man...I, the soul'.[14] On the other hand, as the questioning proceeds up the hierarchy within the soul, new distinctions of 'interior' and 'exterior' are made: imagination is more interior than the senses of the body, reason more interior than imagination, memory the most interior of my rational powers. How is this?

A full discussion of this difficulty must await consideration of *De Trinitate* later in this chapter. Provisionally we may say that what this passage in *Confessions* shows is that the distinction between 'inner' and 'outer' is not an *absolute* distinction which occurs just at one point. Levels of interiority are in degrees of more and less, for that which is interior in one relation is exterior in another. In short, degrees of interiority are also degrees of hierarchy and 'the' distinction between 'inner' and 'outer' is not a two-term polarity, in which all that does not fall on the one side of a fixed point of distinction falls on the other. Thus, for Augustine the language of interiority fuses with the language of ascent. The two metaphors interact, interdefine and complement each other at every stage, and not merely at the end of the chain of questioning where, as I have put it, the 'within' opens up to the 'above'. There, certainly, the question becomes: *quis est iste supra caput animae meae?*, but if reason is a more 'interior' power than imagination it is also, as we say informally, a 'higher' power. And just as one power can be higher than another, but lower than a third, so can a power stand between that which is more exterior than it and that which is more interior.

That having been said, one part of our problem remains unresolved. In *Confessions*, 10.6, Augustine does, after all, appear to 'absolutise' the 'interior/exterior' distinction into a body/soul polarity, assigning the 'I' to the side of the soul with apparent firmness. If this is so, if I am to be identified with my interiority and my interiority with my soul, then does not Augustine's metaphor of 'interiority' in the last resort commit him to, or perhaps presuppose, some kind of body/soul dualism? The answer to this question

---

[14] Pine-Coffin, p. 212.

will be found within the more extended discussion of *De Trinitate*, to which we must now turn.

II

In his *De Trinitate*, 10, though written much later,[15] Augustine returns to ground familiar to us from our discussion of *Confessions* in the last chapter. His problem, as *De Trinitate*, 10 opens, is with self-knowledge. We seek to know ourselves. For our minds love themselves, and everything which loves, loves to know what it loves. But since *a fortiori* we can only love what we know, and since that which we seek to know we do not actually know, how can we desire to know (and so love) something of which we are ignorant?

For sure, the problem must not be excessively complicated by the failure to make an obvious distinction: 'It must be understood that it is not the same thing to say that [a person] loves to know things unknown, as to say he loves things unknown.'[16] That being clear, however, the problem of *Confessions* remains, that of how a person can want to know something, whatever it is, without already possessing the knowledge he seeks, and the problem is especially acute in the case of *self*-knowledge. This may seem strange, since, on the contrary, one might have expected self-knowledge to be the least problematic case, less problematic, certainly, than our knowledge of *other* minds. For standing between us and the minds of other people is the opaque wall of their embodiment: yet we do know the minds of others, that opacity notwithstanding, whereas to our own, surely, we have immediate access: 'Why, then, when it knows other minds, does [the mind] not know itself, *since nothing can possibly be more present to it than itself*?'[17]

Complicated as his statement of the problem is by some unnecessarily tortuous dialectics, there is no difficulty in seeing what Augustine's problem is here, nor, for the modern mind especially, that it is a very real one. It is the problem of how anything at all can be 'in' the mind and yet not be known to it. For 'self-presence', as Augustine says, is a distinctive characteristic of mind, it is what sets mind apart from all else: 'nothing is more immediately present to the mind than it is to itself'.[18] The non-mental may or may not

---

[15] The dating of individual books of *De Trinitate* is uncertain. But if *Confessions* was written between 397 and 401 AD, the later books of *De Trinitate* were written perhaps nearer to 420.
[16] *De Trin.*, 10.1.3.   [17] Ibid., 10.1.3.   [18] Ibid., 14.5.7.

be present to that which has a mind, but it can never be present to itself. Minds may or may not be present to other minds, but, it would seem, no mind can ever fail to be present to itself. It is not at all clear, therefore, *how* a mind can fail to know itself; nor, therefore, can it be clear how a mind can be said to be seeking to know itself, since that too supposes that there is something 'in' the mind but opaque to it, in the way that what is in another's mind can be opaque to mine. And yet it is a fact that we do not know ourselves and that we do seek self-knowledge. *How*, then, is this possible? For to deny that minds are self-transparent reduces them to the status of the non-mental and material; to affirm the self-transparency of mind seems to make self-ignorance impossible to describe. Augustine is faced, therefore, with a genuine *aporia*: both propositions must be true, yet they are mutually inconsistent, since either excludes the truth of the other.

The general problem, discussed in *Confessions*, of how we can be said to be seeking that which we have not already found, is therefore reinforced in its difficulty in the case of the desire to know oneself. And Augustine approaches the solution in a series of stages, the first of which requires the making of a distinction between two kinds of presence by which the mind is present to itself.

The first is the presence of the mind's own activities to itself. The mind knows what it does. In so far as its activities are conscious they are *self*-conscious. Now, clearly, there are senses in which it is possible for agents 'not to know what they are doing'. I may *think* I am helping to reconcile enemies, while all the time I am, without knowing it, making things worse. But even if I may be ignorant of what my intentions bring about, if I intend to reconcile, then I cannot fail to know that that is what I intend. My intending is self-transparent. And this is so even if, in a psychoanalytic spirit, an observer may wish to doubt that my motives in intending to reconcile are quite as selfless as I suppose them to be. For even if it is true that I do not always know what underlies what I intend, or what the causes of my intentions are, I cannot fail to know what I *think* I intend. Such knowledge is primitive and incorrigible, it cannot be revised away in the light of any *theory*, purporting to explain why I intend what I do in terms of causes unknown to me.

It is along these lines that Augustine distinguishes between that respect in which I cannot fail to know myself from that in which I can:

In what way, then, does that which does not know itself, know itself as knowing anything? For it does not know that some other mind knows but that it itself does so. Therefore it knows itself. Further, when it seeks to know itself, it knows itself now as seeking. Therefore again it knows itself. And hence it cannot altogether not know itself when certainly it does so far know itself as that it knows itself as not knowing itself. But if it does not know itself not to know itself, then it does not seek to know itself. And therefore, in that very fact that it seeks itself, it is clearly convicted of being more known to itself than unknown. For it knows itself as seeking and not knowing itself, in that it seeks to know itself.[19]

Clearly, then, there are two possibilities of self-knowledge being distinguished, the first of which, the primitive, incorrigible sort which can never fail, is perfectly compatible with the absence of the second. If I *seek* self-knowledge, then manifestly I lack it; but seeking is an intentional activity, so I cannot engage in seeking self-knowledge without knowing that I am seeking and to that degree I do 'know myself'. But the self-knowledge which I lack when I am seeking it is of a quite different order from that which I necessarily possess in my activity of seeking. There is no paradox here once the distinction is made.

The distinction is that between pre-reflexive and reflexive forms of knowledge. What in Augustine we have described as the incorrigible 'self-knowledge' always present in the course of any conscious activity is, it seems, of an entirely 'pre-reflexive' kind, for the 'I' of this self-consciousness is entirely implicit within the conscious activity itself: it is not the object of any distinct conscious act. This self-awareness is pre-reflexive in that it always accompanies conscious activity in the way enjoyment may sometimes accompany the playing of golf: for in such cases the enjoyment *is* the form consciousness of playing takes; it is the golf not the enjoyment we are conscious of. It is this sort of self-knowledge which is what enables me to remember, after the event, what I did, a knowledge which differs from that which I have when I recall what another did, for it is what *I* did that I remember; and it differs from remembering *myself*, because it is what I *did* which I recall. Neither *un*conscious of myself, nor yet *reflexively* conscious of myself, my conscious activity was, we may therefore say, *pre*-reflexive.

In this pre-reflexive sense I cannot fail to know myself, even when I seek to know myself – a seeking which implies that, in

[19]   Ibid., 10.1.3.

another sense, I do not know myself. What is this second sense of self-knowledge and self-ignorance? When, Augustine says, the mind turns back upon itself and sees that it does not know itself, it wants to know itself. Here, that pre-reflexive self-knowledge becomes the object of my attention and scrutiny: I can, in a second act of self-reflection, scrutinize the self who is consciously acting and so thematise the agent rather than the action. And when I do enquire into myself I discover that I am not a self-transparent presence to myself. Augustine knows that he can be wrong about himself, that he can be mistaken as to his true nature, for he knows that he can think of himself as being that which he is not. And he knows this because he remembers that once he was so mistaken. But what do I not know when, in this second, reflexive, sense, I do not know myself?

III

The typical case of self-ignorance – the only case Augustine considers – is that of the person who believes herself to be entirely, or 'as a whole', that which she is only in part. This is Augustine's own mistake as he recounted it in *Confessions*: for in the years before his encounter with the *Platonici*, he, who is indeed partly a material, embodied being, believed himself to be *nothing but* a material body.

Let us remind ourselves that here Augustine is talking about *reflexive* self-ignorance which, unlike the pre-reflexive self-awareness, is corrigible. In this case, therefore, the mind makes itself its own object, but it should now be clear that what is in question is a conceptual knowledge or ignorance about the mind's own nature. In *De Trinitate* at least, Augustine shows no interest in the quality of the mind's *psychologically* introspective awareness, in that kind of 'self-knowledge' which consists in being able accurately, say, to diagnose one's own motives for action. Of course, it is just as possible for a person to be mistaken, even wilfully mistaken, about herself in this sense. But Augustine's problem in *De Trinitate* is not with self-knowledge of this kind.

The mind can be mistaken about its own nature, then, by supposing itself to be in whole that which it is in part. But, Augustine adds, in an unconscionably rebarbative (and virtually untranslatable) passage: 'It is absurd to say that [the mind] does not as a whole know what it knows. I do not say that it knows wholly; but what it knows it as a whole knows.'[20]

This somewhat opaque utterance is best understood in the light of a later passage in Book 12 where Augustine explains that although I may mistakenly believe myself to be wholly that which I am only in part – to be wholly material, say, fire or air – nonetheless, my understanding, albeit mistaken, itself reveals that I am more than what I believe myself to be. For if I understand myself to be nothing but fire or air, then certainly I am neither of these things, precisely because I *understand* myself to be such. Neither fire nor air can understand themselves to be anything at all, even mistakenly. Therefore, more generally, a materialistic account of self-understanding is *ab initio* self-defeating. For in understanding myself to be nothing but matter I show myself to be something more than matter. And *what* differentiates me from matter is precisely that mistaken act by which I understand myself to be nothing but matter. For that act cannot itself be material. Hence, when I understand myself in part, it is by means of the whole of myself (including my understanding) that I do so. So, once again, though I can misunderstand myself – and in that way be ignorant of my own nature – my true nature is nonetheless revealed in the very act of being mistaken.

Moreover, not every kind of self-ignorance consists in being mistaken about what I am. I may, more innocently, simply not know what I am, or rather, I may *think* that I do not know what I am. In that case, I will seek to know what I am, but the act of seeking, since that too is the act of the whole of what I am, reveals the true nature of what I am:

[the mind] seeks that which is wanting [i.e., knowledge of itself], as we are wont to seek to recall to the mind something that has slipped from the mind, but has not altogether gone away from it; since we can recognise it, when it has come back, to be the same thing that we were seeking.[21]

In what way is the discovery of my true nature a kind of 'recognition'? In this way, that my true self, that which I seek, is already present and revealed to me in the very act of the seeking: for it is

---

[20] *Non dico, Totum scit, sed quod scit, tota scit. Cum itaque aliquid de se scit, quod nisi tota non potest, totam se scit. De Trin.*, 10.3.

[21] *De Trin.*, 10.3.

the 'mind as a whole' which does the seeking, and this cannot fail to be at least implicitly, pre-reflexively present to us in the seeking, and always has been, in every act of the mind. Therefore, just as the person who mistakenly understands himself to be but a part of what he is, is revealed in that act of mistaken understanding to be the whole he denies, so the person who does not know what he is and seeks to know himself already knows himself in the very act of seeking and, as it were, 'remembers' himself, for in a pre-reflexive way he has always known himself. Mistaken self-understanding is self-defeating; seeking to know oneself is self-fulfilling.

All of which is very well and good, but since the manner in which my true nature is revealed to me in either mistaken understanding or in seeking to understand myself, is of the pre-reflexive sort, given in any human act whatsoever, this level of self-knowledge does not get us very far. For, being inexplicit, and just because it is present even in acts of mistaken self-perception, its existence does nothing, by itself, to overcome the *reflexive* self-ignorance in which it is revealed. Moreover, the practical problem remains that people persist in their *reflexive* self-ignorance and fail to attend to the significance of their pre-reflexive awareness, implicitly revealing as it is of their true natures.

For a practical materialism of the mind is fixed within images of corporeality; the mind persistently misreads itself

through vicious desire, as though in forgetfulness of self. For it sees some things as intrinsically excellent, in that more excellent nature which is God; and whereas it ought to remain stedfast that it may enjoy them, it is turned away from him by wishing to appropriate those things to itself, and not to be like him by his gift, but to be what he is by its own and it begins to move and slip gradually down into less and less, which it thinks to be more and more...and so through want and distress it becomes too intent upon its own actions and upon the unquiet delights which it obtains through them.[22]

Augustine speaks graphically of a *glutino amoris*[23] by which the mind becomes wedded fast to that which it most loves. If the mind is inordinately fixed upon *exteriora* then it becomes incapable of prising itself away from images of itself in terms of those *exteriora* which, as it were, it 'adds' to itself. Consequently it will construe itself as something other than, or as he puts it, 'withdrawn from', itself:

<hr/>

[22] Ibid., 10.3.   [23] Ibid., 10.8.

When, therefore, it is bidden to become acquainted with itself, let it not seek itself as though it were withdrawn from itself; but let it withdraw that which it has added to itself. For itself lies more deeply within (*interior est enim ipsa [mens]*), not only than those sensible things, which are clearly without, but also than the images of them...As therefore the mind is within, it goes forth in some sort from itself, when it exerts the affection of love towards these, as it were, footprints of many acts of attention. And these footprints are, as it were, imprinted on the memory...[so] that even when those corporeal things are absent, yet the images of them are at hand to those who think of them. Therefore let the mind become acquainted with itself, and not seek itself as if it were absent, but fix upon itself the act of attention of the will, by which it was wandering among other things, and let it think of itself. So it will see that at no time did it ever not love itself, at no time did it ever not know itself; but by loving another thing together with itself it has confounded itself with it and in some sense grown one with it.[24]

Two things seem clear in this passage: the first is that there is contained in it an implied strategy for the acquisition of self-knowledge. The semi-materialism of self-knowledge which consists in 'imagining' ourselves, causes us to see ourselves as quasi-material objects. This, in turn, will lead us to suppose that we can know ourselves only in the way in which we know material objects: after all, if we think of ourselves as being fire or air, then we will suppose that we know ourselves as we know fire and air.[25] But this is to think of ourselves not just as being the wrong *kind* of thing (fire or air), but in the wrong *kind of way*: as we know *exteriora* – 'external' objects. But we do not know ourselves as objects:

'Know thyself' is not so said to the mind as is...said 'know the will of that man'...Nor again as is said 'Behold thy own face'; which he can only do in a looking glass...But when it is said to the mind, 'Know thyself', then it knows itself by that very stroke by which it understands the word 'thyself'; and this for no other reason than that it is present to itself.[26]

The way for the mind to seek self-knowledge, therefore, is by turning away from itself 'as absent' (as if it were an object of that attention by which we attend to a physical object); and, positively, by eliciting from its own conscious activity the mind's implicit, but luminous, self-presence. Adequate reflection upon the very act of seeing oneself corporeally will yield an explicit knowledge of ourselves as the kind of beings who are capable of judging and mis-

---

[24] Ibid., 10.8.   [25] Ibid., 10.10.   [26] Ibid.

judging themselves, as the kind of beings who can love themselves for what they are or for what they are not, as the kind of beings who remember or misremember themselves.

This is the act which Augustine describes in those three accounts in *Confessions* which we have just considered. It is the act of seeking ourselves 'within', of which we can say so far this much: it consists principally in an act of explicitating self-reflection, when we attend to what it is in ourselves which makes us the believing, doubting, fallible, creatures that we are.

Yet who ever doubts that he himself lives, and remembers, and under-stands, and wills, and thinks, and knows, and judges? Seeing that even if he doubts, he lives; if he doubts, he remembers why he doubts; if he doubts, he understands that he doubts; if he doubts, he wishes to be cer-tain; if he doubts, he thinks; if he doubts, he knows that he does not know; if he doubts, he judges that he ought not to assent rashly. Who ever there-fore doubts about anything else, ought not to doubt of all these things; which if they were not, he would not be able to doubt of anything.[27]

The second point which emerges clearly is that this act of self-knowledge is primarily an act of epistemological inference, not an act of psychological introspection. Indeed, there is implied in Augustine's account of this act a potential critique of 'introspec-tionism'; for it is precisely the placing of the mind's mental con-tents before the eye for the purposes of self-scrutiny which leads to the error of thinking of oneself in terms of semi-material images. It would, moreover, be the ultimate irony if that metaphor of interi-ority which shapes Augustine's critique of a materialist psychology of 'selfhood' should after all be pressed back into the service of just that same semi-materialism: which is what would be done by those who would read the metaphor as commending a 'quasi-physical' psychological act of 'turning of the mind inward' towards its own mental contents.[28]

IV

'Self-knowledge', therefore, is, for Augustine, of two kinds. The first, the pre-reflexive kind, is simply the kind of self-awareness which is given in any conscious activity whatever. It is not an

---

[27] Ibid., 10.10.
[28] As we will see, p. 204 below, this is precisely what the *Cloud* Author fears from an uncriti-cal, 'naturalistic', 'physical' understanding of the metaphor.

explicit, conceptualizing kind of knowledge and is, we might say, 'experiential' in the sense that it is an intrinsic constituent of all conscious human experiencing.

The second kind of self-knowledge is reflexive and conceptual. It is achieved by the redirecting of the mind upon its own activities so as to explicitate that inexplicit self-awareness which is present in them. It is a knowledge of *what* we are, and we are as capable of being wrong about what we are as we are capable of being wrong about what anything is. These are the kinds of self-knowledge to which Augustine admits, as being relevant to the discussion of the nature of our 'interiority'.

This being so, it follows that there is no such thing in Augustine as the experience, explicitly, of ourselves; or, to put it in another way, there is no such experience as that for which the *direct object* is 'the self'. If 'the self' is the direct object of anything, it is the direct object of studied, conceptual reflection, which is, as Thomas Aquinas was later to explain, 'a diligent and subtle investigation'.[29] If, on the other hand, the 'self' is in any way experienced, it is so inexplicitly and indirectly, within our experience of things other than the self.

Nonetheless, if this distinction must be made, it is not as if these two forms of self-knowledge are unrelated. For reflexive self-knowledge is gained by a 'diligent and subtle investigation' into the nature of the first. In other words, it is only within our inexplicit self-experience that our explicit acts of self-investigation can take place.

V

This having been said by way of summary of our discussion so far in this chapter, we must now turn to the question which is its chief purpose, of how Augustine distinguishes between the 'inner' and the 'outer' and, in particular, at what point the line of demarcation between them falls. And we can begin with the following, highly intriguing, passage from *De Trinitate*:

Whatever we have in the mind common with the beasts, this much is rightly said to belong to the outer man. For the outer man is not to be considered to be the body only, but with the addition also of a certain

[29] *ST*, I, q.87 a.1 corp.

peculiar life of the body, whence the structure of the body derives its vigour, and all the senses with which he is equipped for the perception of outward things; and when the images of these outward things already perceived, that have been fixed in the memory, are seen again by recollection, it is still a matter pertaining to the outer man.[30]

This passage is intriguing because the intention of Augustine's remarks is to establish that the boundary between the inner and the outer falls not between the mind and the body, but between the part of the mind which is intrinsically dependent on the body for the exercise of its powers (the 'outer') and the part of the mind which is not so dependent (the 'inner'). But in the course of explaining this boundary-line Augustine implies a different line of demarcation between 'inner' and 'outer' apparently presupposed in the defining of the first. For when Augustine says that the 'outer' is not the body alone, but all those powers of the soul which are directed toward the 'outer' (*exteriora*), he appears to be presupposing that we know what counts as the *exteriora* (as distinct from *interiora*) in virtue of which the 'outer' powers of the mind are said to be 'outer'. Therefore, we apparently need to know how to distinguish between 'outer' and 'inner' *objects* of the mind as the basis for distinguishing between 'outer' and 'inner' *powers* of the mind. It might seem, therefore, that Augustine is guilty of a *petitio principii* in that he uses an implicit distinction between 'inner' and 'outer' in the course of trying to define it explicitly.

In fact, of course, this is not so. It will help to explain why if we distinguish between a quite basic and highly general mode of contrast between inner and outer and a more specialized distinction which Augustine is trying to establish for his theological purposes. The first, the 'basic' distinction, is so primitive as perhaps to be rooted in a physical fact of the greatest generality about the human body. This is the fact that the organs of the human body are distributed spatially around and within its frame and that those organs which have the most fundamental role to play in human life – the brain, heart, nervous system and so on – lie below the surface of an opaque covering, namely the skin. They are, literally, 'inside' the body. On the other hand, the most immediate intentional objects of the acts attributed to those organs lie on the other side of that opaque covering, and so are, also literally, 'outside' it. These

[30] *De Trin.*, 12.1.

facts are, therefore, simple spatial facts and the distinction between 'inner' and 'outer' in this connection has no metaphorical character of any kind.

Nonetheless, human self-awareness appears to be structured by these facts so that inevitably our ways of perceiving ourselves are governed by *some* contrast between 'inner' and 'outer' and by the inevitable allocation of that which is most to do with ourselves as conscious, intending beings, to the 'inner'. Thus do the spatial relations of the body to the 'world' become a metaphor for consciousness in its relation to its objects. And this metaphor is so thoroughly embedded in our language descriptive of mental acts that we could only imagine ourselves not perceiving ourselves in this way if we were to suppose, in some merely fantastical thought experiment, that our vital organs of perception and thought were exposed in transparent bubbles on the surface of our skins, and so 'outside'. Then, perhaps, we would metaphorise our 'selfhood' as 'outer'. Short of such an anatomical revision, however, it seems inconceivable that human beings could perceive of themselves otherwise than in terms of the priority of the 'inner' over the 'outer'. And short of our becoming wholly disembodied beings, it seems an equally safe presumption that human beings must experience themselves in terms of *some* contrast between them.

I emphasize the 'some' because, being rooted in facts of so utterly fundamental a kind, the distinction between 'inner' and 'outer' is of a correspondingly general and innocent kind. That is to say, the language of interiority is, at this level of generality, neutral as between any particular epistemology whatever – it is as near to being a 'pre-cultural' and 'natural' fact of human cognitivity as any is. Even an out-and-out materialist can happily use it, or at least need not be unhappy to, for in the language of 'inner' and 'outer' itself, at least at this primitive level, there is no obstacle to his materialism. It is only on a further theory that the 'inner' becomes contentiously identified as the region of an immaterial soul; on another theory it could equally be identified with higher functions of the body; or on other theories, other identifications of the 'inner' are possible. But for each theoretical construction of the basic metaphor the boundary between the inner and outer will be *specified*. And in that specification of the boundary between inner and outer, the 'basic', physiological, distinction will be presupposed to the functioning of the metaphor.

We may, therefore, distinguish in general between a specialized, theory-laden, and, no doubt, culturally specific manner of construing the root metaphor of 'inner' and 'outer', and the root metaphor itself which is at once presupposed to and often revised by, that construction. In the light of this distinction we can therefore see that in the *De Trinitate*, 12.1 passage, Augustine is proposing a specialization of the basic distinction; and according to that specialized distinction the 'interior' is not to be contrasted with the 'exterior' as mind is to body, but is a distinction which occurs *within* the mind itself: the lower part of the mind (that part which the human being shares with brute animals) belongs to exteriority, whereas the higher part belongs to our interiority. But the only way in which Augustine can get at this specialized distinction is by employing the language of the generalized, physiological, metaphor. For those powers belong to the 'outer' part of the mind whose proper objects are *exteriora*: that is to say, they are objects which fall on the other side of that divide which is the surface of my body. This basic distinction is presupposed to, but differs from, Augustine's own, specialized, distinction, for the line of demarcation falls in different places in the one and in the other.

VII

Within the 'specialized' distinction which Augustine is feeling his way towards in this passage, the line of demarcation between the 'inner' and the 'outer' powers of the mind is said to fall in that same place where it is said to fall in *Confessions*: at the point of demarcation between 'imagination' and 'reason'. For, both the 'external' senses and our powers of sensory imagination and memory collectively comprise the 'outer' man; and this is because all have as their natural objects the things of the 'external' world. Those powers are 'inner' to the human mind in which consist its power of conscious reflective activity: and they, taken collectively, are 'reason'. The fundamental disjunction, therefore, which distinguishes the 'inner' from the 'outer', occurs at the point of disjunction between reason and any higher power on the one hand and imagination and any lower power on the other. This, then, is Augustine's 'specialized' distinction between 'inner' and 'outer'.

Moreover, once equipped with the distinction between the 'primitive' and the 'specialized' forms of the 'inner/outer' disjunction, we are in a position to clear up the ambiguity we noted to exist in the *Confessions*, 10.6 passage. There, it will be remembered, Augustine appeared at one and the same time to situate the point of distinction in two quite different places: on the one hand between body and soul – *unum exterius alterum interius* – and on the other, as in *De Trinitate*, between imagination and reason. It is now possible to see how this is not a simple confusion; indeed, it is possible to see not only how Augustine can, but also how he *must* make both distinctions, in both cases as between the 'inner' and the 'outer', and do so consistently.

For when Augustine says that relative to the body the soul is 'within' he is calling upon the root metaphor which places the distinctively human powers 'within' relatively to the body's spatial 'exteriority'. And he needs this distinction if he is to explain in what way imagination is, within his 'specialized' distinction, an 'outer' power. For what makes the imagination an 'outer' power of the soul is the fact that the objects and contents of its cognitions are *exteriora* in the primitive sense – objects which lie beyond the body's perimeter, such as fire, air, or whatever. On the 'primitive' distinction, therefore, it is the body's point of juncture with the soul which determines the boundary between 'outer' and 'inner'.

The specialized distinction, however, is partly made out in terms of the primitive and partly *contra*distinguishes it. As the *De Trinitate*, 12.1 passage indicates, *anima* is to be further distinguished into its 'inner' and 'outer' powers and this is done in terms which are anticipated in the Latin text of *Confessions* 10.6. Sadly, however, this further distinction is thoroughly misconstrued in Pine-Coffin's English rendering. Pine-Coffin translates:

The inner part of man knows these things [*exteriora*] through the agency of the outer part. I, the inner man, know these things; *I, the soul*,[31] know them through the senses of my body.

The Latin text, however, gives:

Homo interior cognouit haec per exterioris ministerium; ego interior cognoui haec, ego, *ego animus*,[32] per sensum corporis mei.

There seems little doubt that Pine-Coffin's translation of *ego animus* as 'I, the soul' wrecks the sense of the argument of *Confessions*, 10.6. *De Trinitate*, 12.1 helps us to see why.

[31] My emphasis.   [32] My emphasis.

Let us remind ourselves of how the *De Trinitate* argument goes: 'the outer man', Augustine says, 'is not to be considered to be the body only, but with the addition also of a certain peculiar life of the body, whence the structure of the body receives its vigour...'.

This conjunction of the body and its life [*corpus et anima*] collectively comprise the 'outer' man, for the soul is the principle which 'animates' the body: that is its reality. Correspondingly, a body which lacks a soul is not truly a body, for the body of a living being is only its body when it is alive. Hence, body and soul constitute one reality, an animated body and an embodied *anima*, one and the same thing, neither being what it is without the other.

But an animated body, though indeed possessed by a human being, is not all that a human being is, for that much, Augustine says, is the common possession of humans and brute animals. Human beings do indeed possess an animal soul: it is that which accounts for the whole structure of the animal life of humans, their growth, their nutrition, their capacities for feeling and responding to pleasure and pain in desire and aversion. And these capacities are greatly intensified by imagination and memory. All these powers, then, belong to embodied soul, the soul as animal. With respect to the body, of course, the soul is 'interior', for it is the *life* of the body. But with respect to Augustine's specialized distinction, it is still part of the outer man, because it is *of the body* that it is the life. For this reason, Augustine could never have said what Pine-Coffin translates him as saying: *ego, anima*, nor does he say it. What Augustine says is: *ego animus*.

For by *animus* Augustine means those truly interior powers – those of the rational mind – which enable humans to reflect consciously upon their own activities and thereby distinguish humans from animals. And they distinguish humans from animals because it is by means of them that humans can both know that they are animals 'in part' and, in knowing that, know that they are more than animals. In this power lies our interiority. It is with this power of self-reflection that 'I' can be identified, *ego interior...ego animus*.

VIII

But what is *animus*? What do I know, when *in animo* I know myself as *animus*? The answer to that question is what the entire argument of *De Trinitate* is constructed to provide. And the answer is: I know myself to be an image of God, specifically an image, or at least, *in* the image, of the Trinity.[33] For that, in the fullest, deepest, most interior and highest sense, is what I *am*.

It is quite beyond the scope of this study to consider in any detail Augustine's complex and rich discussions of the image of the Trinity in the human *animus*.[34] Necessarily paraphrasing, therefore, we can attend only to those particular emphases which relate to the main purposes of our discussion. And these, principally, are two.

In the first instance, there is the theme of interplay between what I shall call the 'mimetic' and 'participatory' aspects of image. The powers of the human soul which are known in my self-knowledge are three: memory, intellect and will. These constitute the self which is *animus*. Adopting the terminology of a later period, these are my 'spiritual' powers; and if that term were to have any sense for Augustine, it would be because in their presence in the soul, in their mutual interactions and indwellings, they are an image of the Trinity of persons. And the image they form of the Trinity may be said to be 'mimetic' because it is only by means of the formal character of their mutual relations, by means of a kind of proportionate analogy, that they exhibit a similarity with the mutual, 'internal', relations of Father, Son and Holy Spirit.

Memory, the source, generates understanding: for just as our implicit, pre-reflexive self-knowledge, continuous with all our conscious activity in memory, is articulated and expressed in the reflexive self-knowledge which memory 'generates', so the Son, the Word, articulates and expresses the self-knowledge of the Father, who generates that Word. And just as our reflexive self-knowledge – intellect – seeks out and 'loves' the self in the memory which generates it; and just as, in complete mutuality, memory seeks out and 'loves' the self-knowledge which intellect expresses – a mutual seek-

---

33 Strictly speaking, I know myself to be not *the* image of God, for only the Son, the Second Person, is that. I am, strictly speaking not *the*, or even *an*, image of God, but, following the text of Genesis 1, 26 in the Old Latin version (as also in the Vulgate) I am made, Augustine says, '*in* the image of God' (*ad imaginem Dei*).

34 But see David N. Bell's excellent account in *The Image and Likeness, The Augustinian Spirituality of William of St Thierry*, Cistercian Studies Series, 78, Kalamazoo: Cistercian Publications, 1984, chapters 1 and 2; see also, Bernard McGinn, *The Presence of God, A History of Western Christian Mysticism*, I, *The Foundations of Mysticism*, New York: Crossroad, 1991, pp. 243–48; and John Edward Sullivan, *The Image of God: The Doctrine of St Augustine and its Influence*, Dubuque: Priory Press, 1963.

ing and loving which is 'will'; in the same way does the Father love the Son and the Son the Father. And this mutual love is the Holy Spirit.

And just as the image of the Trinity is not found in those powers of the soul – sense and imagination – which may be distinguished only by virtue of their diverse relations with *exteriora*, but may be found alone in those powers of *animus* which are distinguished by their *internal* differentiations; so are the Persons of the Trinity which those powers image differentiated only by their relations with one another, and not by any 'external' relations with created beings.

And just as the image of the Trinity is found not in those functions, powers or activities of the soul which are inherently time-bound and historical – not even, as Augustine says in Book 8, in that 'temporal' faith which will eventually pass away,[35] – but only in that of its nature which is immortal,[36] so is the Trinity itself eternal in its generation and procession of Persons, eternal in its mutuality and differentiation, eternal in the interplay of its self-knowledge and self-love.

The 'mimetic' aspect of the image of the Trinity in the human soul therefore consists in the fact that there are formal similarities, or proportionalities, between the structural interactions of those human powers and the internal, structural differentiations and relations of the Persons of the Trinity. But the character of *mimesis* does not necessarily bring with it any element of participation.[37] In some later writers, for example Hugh of St Victor and Bonaventure, who are without doubt influenced by Augustine's discussion in *De Trinitate*, the distinction becomes formalised and hardened into that between the merely mimetic 'image' (*imago*) and the mimetic and participatory 'likeness' (*similitudo*).[38] In Augustine one hesitates to make too much of the distinction, for though it may legitimately be made as between dimensions of image, Augustine never suggests that there may be images of the Trinity which are purely mimetic and not participatory, as these later authors do. Indeed, as we will see, Augustine expressly denies this.

---

[35] *De Trin.*, 8.5.8.   [36] Ibid.

[37] In my *Eros and Allegory* I give a more extended account of how the mimetic and participatory dimensions of the Augustinian and later mediaeval doctrine of image are related. See pp. 139–149.

[38] On the basis of the same text from Genesis 1, 26: *ad imaginem et similitudinem faciamus.* Many mediaeval theologians took it that the author of Genesis must have intended a distinction between *imago* and *similitudo*.

Nevertheless, the distinction is capable of clarifying even within Augustine's doctrine of image. The human *animus* is mimetic in so far as in its mutual relations of memory, intellect and will, it 'maps' onto the internal relations of the Persons of the Trinity. Now a map is a formal replica of the ground it maps, in just the same way as the internal relations of the soul's higher powers in some way replicate the internal relations of the Trinitarian Persons. For, as symbol **a** is to symbol **b** on the map, so proportionally are the features on the ground which **a** and **b** stand for related by direction and distance.

But a map, though *formally* similar to the ground it maps, has no *material* continuity with it. A map of Durham is a design in paper and ink. It does not in any way share materially in the brick, stone and mortar of the city. The distances on the one are *proportionately* 'the same' on the other. But a map would be useless if its distances were *actually* the same. Moreover, not all the formal properties of maps are properties of what they map. Some of us like maps for their own sakes. But you do not, in your liking for the map, *thereby* engage enjoyably with Durham. In any case, no doubt true map-lovers enjoy reading maps of Slough as much as maps of Durham. But no one can enjoy Slough.

A map, then, is formally or mimetically an image of what it maps, but otherwise than by purely formal analogy it does not share in the real world of the territory mapped. By contrast, a child's doll is not only mimetically 'like' the baby it is a model of, but can also be used within a behaviour which *participates* in what it models. For a child can learn about the adult behaviour of caring for an infant − can play 'parent' − by playing with the doll. In some way, therefore, the child's imitation of playing with a baby participates in the real world of baby-care. Hence, we may say, a doll is more than the purely mimetic image which a map is, for it is an image whose use engages the user in some way in the reality it images: it makes real that which it is an image of.

Augustine's account of the relations between the mimetic and participatory dimensions of image is complex. He insists that in none of its powers, even in its most interior, could the soul be truly in the image of the Trinity merely by virtue of the formal analogy in which it stands to its analogate. As he says:

this trinity of mind is not on that account the image of God because the mind remembers itself, understands itself, and loves itself, but because it can also remember, understand and love him by whom it was made. And when it does so it becomes wise; but if it does not, even though it remembers itself, knows itself and loves itself, it is foolish.[39]

On the other hand, were we not formed in our creation, and so in our immortal natures, in the mimetic image of the Trinity, were we not constituted in our *animus* as memory, intellect and will, we would lack the capacity to be raised into a participatory relationship with the Trinity our souls mimetically image. And without that participation, even that natural mimesis of the soul would fail as image. Mimesis is the necessary but insufficient condition of the image of the Trinity in the soul. Except through the theological virtues of hope, faith and love, except, that is to say, through grace which engages memory, intellect and will in the actual life of the Trinity itself, those powers would have no capacity to image God. But otherwise than in those human powers grace cannot operate.

Moreover, the natural image in the soul, though immortal and indelible in itself, is obscured by sin. For sin is shown in our failure to remember, know and love ourselves, in our ignorance and misconstructions of what we are, in our love of ourselves for what we are not, in our seeking our identity in the claims of a false memory. All these distortions of the image in the soul have their common root in our fallen life, a life which has so fallen into exteriority that we construe even ourselves in the images of that exteriority. This is how we are able to be 'outside ourselves', as Augustine so often put it in *Confessions*, 'outside' ourselves while yet God was 'within': so that I, where I see myself, am not there where in my true being I may be found; so that God is where I truly am and I am where truly I am not – I am 'absent' from myself, alienated, self-exiled. The 'I', then, which is the outcome of this misrelating of self-image and God, is a composite mismatch of true selfhood lived through a false image; an image blurred, because it is the product of two unsynchronized focuses.

And yet just because I am not an image destroyed, but a complex of both image and its distortions, within the obscurity of false self-image and love there are glimmers of the true light which we may approach along the track of self-knowledge and interiority. Here we take up the second of the two points of emphasis within Augustine's doctrine of image, one which brings us back to those themes central to *Confessions* discussed in the last chapter.

[39]   *De Trin.*, 14.12.15.

My true selfhood is my interiority. And, as we saw, that place where the self and interiority intersect opens out to the God, the eternal light of Truth, who is *above*. The *itinerarium intus* is also an *ascensio superius*. The two metaphors of inwardness and ascent themselves intersect at the point where God and the self intersect, so that that which is most interior to me is also that which is above and beyond me; so that the God who is within me is also the God I am in.

There is nothing accidental about this fusion of metaphors, with their divergent directional tendencies. Both are needed for different purposes specific to each, namely to embody different aspects of Augustine's theological epistemology; but both are needed also so that each may limit and correct the tendencies of the other and to complete the epistemological picture.

For, as we have seen, the 'interiority/exteriority' polarity both embodies and is governed by the epistemological principle which distinguishes the powers of the soul inherently incapable of self-reflection from those which are inescapably engaged in it. Reflecting ever more deeply upon itself, retreating, as it were, ever more deeply into the abyss of memory, the mind strikes upon the light itself which informs all its powers of perception, imagination and judgement.

But if that is so, if through successive phases of self-reflection, the memory tracks horizontally along the paths of my identity in time, that memory, so to speak, stumbles across the eternal light of Truth which shines upon it from above. At that point, then, where greatest inwardness has been achieved, the memory is also projected 'above' itself on a contrary, vertical axis. Here, where time intersects with eternity, the mind's most intimate interiority is also its 'highest' point, a point which Augustine calls the *acies mentis*,[40] the 'cutting edge' of the mind, the place 'in' it which overlaps with the eternal Light it is in. It is the point at which the mind can most truly contemplate the Trinity and in which the Trinity dwells by participating image.

---

[40] For this phrase, see for example, *Enarrationes in Psalmis*, 134.6; (PL), 37: 1742. As we will see, this Augustinian idea that the highest kinds of contemplation occur in that point at which the soul, at its utmost point, overlaps with the Light which is the source of all its knowledge and love, is immensely influential in the Middle Ages. This *acies mentis* is variously described in other terms as the *scintilla rationis* (Augustine, *de Civitate Dei*, 22, 24. 2; PL 41: 789), *apex intellectus* or *mentis* (Thomas Aquinas), the *apex amoris* or *affectus* (Thomas Gallus, Bonaventure), the *acies intellectus* (Bonaventure), 'the divine spark in the soul' (Eckhart) or, as in the *Cloud* Author, the 'nakyd entente' for God.

But this second, complementing, image of hierarchical ascent embodies an equally central element of Augustine's epistemology, for that hierarchy is determined in its stages, as we saw in the last chapter, by the scale of degrees of unchangeableness. The 'higher' a thing is the more it approximates to the eternity, necessity and immutability of Truth itself; the 'lower', the more it lapses into temporality, contingency and so into changeableness.

And as these metaphors embody the distinctness of their associated epistemological theses, so they embody their complementarity. That which is most inward in the soul is also its intrinsically immortal part. And that is why only the soul in the deepest intimacy of its immortal being can image the eternity of the Godhead it reaches up to. 'Within' *is* 'above'. The immortal self *is* a participative image of the Trinity: it is not something else, *plus* image, for its reality consists in its being 'like' God.

Moreover, these metaphors embody not only the complementarity of distinct elements in Augustine's epistemology, they embody also the unity and coherence of his theory of knowledge with his 'spirituality'. For the metaphors of inwardness and ascent both explain something and make personal demands; they call upon the Christian to embark on a journey whose course they illuminate; they tell what the human is and challenge the hearer to become it; they tell us what and how we can know and elicit the desire to know it. Augustine could not have envisaged a case of doing the one which was not to be doing the other, any more than a flame can shed light without heat or heat without light. And the metaphors of interiority and ascent perfectly embody this conviction of the unity of theory and practice.

IX

I conclude with some unfinished business which I do not propose yet to embark upon. There is an apparent paradox at the heart of Augustine's spatial imagery, whether of inwardness or of ascent. The language of interiority both describes and demands an *ascesis* of mind and spirit away from its captivity by the imagination, towards those recesses of interiority where it encounters the bare, imageless light of eternal truth which is above. There is in the description of this *ascesis* an implied apophaticism, powerfully developed in some later writers, such as the *Cloud* Author and

Ruusbroec, who are, like Augustine, profoundly suspicious of the imagination. And yet Augustine's discourse of interiority and ascent is itself riddled with imagery indeed, it is an inherently metaphorical language, a language of imagination which both describes and is borrowed from 'exteriority'. Is this not a contradiction, however inevitable?

CHAPTER 5

Hierarchy interiorised: Bonaventure's Itinerarium Mentis in Deum

I

It is appropriate, though in an important way misleading, to open a discussion of Bonaventure's *Itinerarium Mentis in Deum*[1] with an acknowledgement of his intellectual debts. 'Bonaventure's work is regarded with good reason as the supreme example of mediaeval Augustinianism', writes Grover Zinn,[2] and in no work of Bonaventure's is this debt more manifest than in his *Itinerarium*. But if, as we will see, Bonaventure's Augustinianism is often filtered through the prism of an equally enthusiastic Augustinian of the twelfth century, Hugh of St Victor, the effect of Hugh's influence was to bring that Augustinianism into play with the other main stream of Christian Neoplatonism, the Dionysian. Zinn therefore adds: 'This confluence of Augustinian and Dionysian materials in Hugh of St Victor's thought is most important for the development of theology, and especially in relation to Bonaventure.'[3]

Having begun our discussion with extended reflections on these two great streams of Christian Neoplatonism, their convergence in Bonaventure gives him a pivotal importance for our discussion. But though it is appropriate to begin this chapter with a mention of Bonaventure's major sources, it is potentially misleading. For a reader of the *Itinerarium*, uninstructed in these and other, lesser

---

[1] I have used the parallel Latin and English edition of Philotheus Boehner, II of *The Works of St Bonaventure*, ed. Philotheus Boehner OFM and M. Frances Laughlin SMIC, New York: The Franciscan Institute, 1956. The title of this work is usually translated as 'The Soul's Journey into God', but since the Latin *itinerarium* suggests as much the map of a journey as the journey itself, 'The Route of the Soul's Journey into God' is a more literal, if more cumbersome, translation.

[2] 'Book and Word. The Victorine Background of Bonaventure's use of Symbols', in *S. Bonaventura, 1274–1974*, II, Grottoferrata: Colegio S. Bonaventura, 1973, p. 144.

[3] Ibid., p. 146.

sources,[4] the most vivid impression will be of both the unity and coherence of thought, style and imagery and of the personal distinctiveness of Bonaventure's theology. Consequently, an analysis which did no more than to fragment this integrity into the multiplicity of its 'influences' – an effect of source-critical method which is always to be resisted – would miss the point, more particularly in this work than in many another, less integrated, text. Yet a compromise must be struck. For if the modern reader may not know Bonaventure's sources, Bonaventure most certainly did and he expected his reader to know them.[5] And in any case one of the features of Bonaventure's distinctiveness consists precisely in the delicacy with which Augustinian and Dionysian emphases are poised in equilibrium, the points of contact between the elements of structure being placed with the exactness and accuracy of an engineer who knows his structural dynamics and of an architect who is confident of his own aesthetic. Indeed, one might fairly say that in Bonaventure's *Itinerarium*, as in a mediaeval cathedral, the engineering of the structure does much of the work of the aesthetic.

II

When all the differences between Dionysian and Augustinian forms of Neoplatonism have been duly noted, as very properly they should be; when, running risks of obfuscating generalization, the Dionysian emphasis is said to be placed upon objective, cosmic hierarchy, that of the Augustinian upon subjective interiority, then it is time to make as much of the commonality of mind which informs every mediaeval Platonist, whichever of these two forms of it he favours. We can, in truth, identify one aspect of the distinctiveness of Bonaventure's theology as consisting in the manner in which he fuses the Dionysian hierarchy with Augustinian interiority – this is what causes the formula of an 'interiorised hierarchy' to spring to mind as a description. But having said that we would have to add that the organizing perspective of that synthesis lies in a view of the created world common to nearly all forms of mediae-

---

4 We will have occasion to mention in addition Richard of St Victor and Thomas Gallus, both 'Victorines'.

5 Occasionally, Bonaventure does little more than paraphrase the most obvious source with a compression which presupposes that the reader knows the source in question, for example at *Itinerarium (Itin.)* III, 5, which summarizes Augustine's *De Trin.*, 14 in a single paragraph.

val Platonism: creation is, above all, to be understood as 'symbol', 'representation', 'image'.

The root of Bonaventure's thought is thrust firmly into this Platonic soil. And from wherever specifically he got the idea, his language is indebted to Hugh of St Victor. For Hugh, all theology – 'theology' being understood in its widest sense to include natural as well as revealed – is constrained by a quite general epistemological condition: 'It is impossible', he says, 'to represent things invisible except by means of things visible. Necessarily all theology must, therefore, make use of visible representations in the showing forth of the invisible'.[6] Nor is this way of seeing the world as representation a necessity merely for *theology*, as if there were other points of view from which one might see the world differently. The constraint is quite general epistemologically: *nothing* invisible is capable of being described or known otherwise than in and through the representations of the visible, not even the soul. And the constraint is quite general ontologically: it is because of the way the world is that theological method is constrained to work by means of the symbolic; it is not because of some imperative of theological method that we need to see the world in that way. The world's character of being created means that it *is* symbol, representation, image. That is its reality and its truth.

We encounter here one of those characteristic features of the mediaeval world-view which modernity consciously and deliberately swept away as antique. 'Modernity', at least as a seventeenth-century modern such as Thomas Hobbes saw it, supplanted this view of the world as a web of symbolic representations with the view of the world as a mechanical system of interacting efficient causes.[7] It may be said that in this respect at least 'post-modernity' has returned to an older idea in conceiving of the world as a text to be read by means of an adequate hermeneutic rather than as a system of causes to be explained by means of hypothesis and verification. It is therefore possible to be struck by the contemporary, as distinct from 'modern', feel of Hugh's description of nature as a 'book'[8] in which are inscribed the simulacra of its author, who otherwise than by means of these simulacra is unknown to us. Hence,

---

[6] *In Hierarchiam Coelestem S. Dionysii Areopagitae (In Hier.)*, I, I, PL 175, 926D.
[7] *Leviathan*, prologue.
[8] *De arca Noe Morali*, II, 12, PL 176, 643B–644C.

we may read the author only from the book, we cannot read the book from the author.

In the book of nature, therefore, are written the simulacra of its invisible author. From the scrutiny of these simulacra is generated what Hugh calls the *theologia mundana*, a 'worldly' theology and a deficient, which can attain only to that description of the God which natural symbols are capable of revealing, God the Creator: for nature, Hugh says, is the *opus conditionis*. But the best the *simulacra naturae* can give us are 'signs' of their Creator, simulacra which can tell us about, or signify God,[9] but they cannot provide us with the key to understanding their proper meanings; they gesture towards God, but God is not in any way made present by them; they signify from a distance and only in a partial way,[10] and so they are, as we would say, 'signs', not 'symbols', because, like street signs, they point the way, but themselves possess none of the character of what they point to.

Moreover, this objective limitation of the *simulacra naturae* is further compounded by the obscuring effects of sin on the ability of the reader to interpret them. In their original constitution humans possessed three 'eyes' with which to see the simulacra of the divine; the 'eye of the flesh' through which they could see the external world (*ex se*); the 'eye of reason' through which they could perceive the soul within (*in se*); and the 'eye of contemplation' through which they were able to see God and things divine (*intra se et supra se*). But through sin humans have become blinded in the eye of contemplation and myopic in the eye of reason, with the result that they can see neither the soul nor God except through the eye of the flesh.[11] To pursue the book analogy, post-lapsarian humans possess the book of nature and can be aware of the simulacra it contains, but they lack the interpretative apparatus which would enable them to read it with any degree of understanding. They are like students with no palaeographical skills in possession of a beautiful manuscript. The beauty itself says something to them, but they cannot decipher the words.

By contrast *theologia divina* reads the simulacra of grace. But grace offers not only what are more powerfully revealing signs in them-

---

9   *Demonstrare, significare, In Hier.*, I, I, 926C.
10 *De longe...pro parte, De sacramentis*, I, iii, 21, PL 176, 225B.
11 *In Hier.*, III, 976A.

selves, they also restore the power to read all simulacra, whether of nature or grace, with an eye unblurred by sin. For the *simulacrum gratiae* is, Hugh says, the human nature of the Word of God itself. And in that human nature of Christ there is both a recapitulation of the representational power of all creation and the source of that light, lacking to the unregenerated eye, in which it is possible to read with understanding the symbolic text of the world. For, switching metaphors, Christ's humanity is the medicine which restores light to the eye, as Jesus did to the blind man, and he pro- vides the teaching which instructs the blind man, once cured, in what he sees:

He made a paste out of spittle and he smeared the eyes of the blind man, washed them and then he saw (Jn, 10). And what then? He said to him, who could see but could not as yet understand: It is I, and he who speaks to you is the Son of God. First, then, he gave light to his eyes and then he showed him. Nature can show things but it can give no light. And through its beauty of form it can speak of its creator, but it cannot impart any understanding of the truth into men's hearts.[12]

Thus, through Christ's curing which enlightens, and his teaching which explains, is the *opus restaurationis* achieved: the regenerate soul can read the whole world. Through that work of restoration, the sign which gestures from a distance at that of which it cannot convey the meaning, becomes the symbol in which humans can both read what is signified and appropriate what is made present. Consequently, the *simulacra gratiae* are no longer but natural signs of the Creator, they are *sacraments* which contain what they signify, they are at once text and hermeneutic, word and the reality spoken of.

Truly, for Hugh, the sacramentality of things is universal. For these sacraments are not only those instituted in the New Law, the sacraments of the Church. The whole universe is in some way a signifier of its Creator, not only nature, but even more visibly and clearly, the whole continuum of salvation history, from Adam until the end of time. Thus the rituals and observances of the people of Israel had a double significance. They had their own sacramental significance and efficacy, but they also had a typological signifi- cance as prophetic signs of the future Christian dispensation and in some way made present then the future which they anticipated.

---

[12] Ibid., I, 1, 926C–D.

Wider than that still, all the events of Jewish history, before and after the giving of the Law, were at least quasi-sacramental, for again not only did they have their own significance as history, through that significance they were and are now revelatory of the providential purposes of the Holy Spirit within the economy of salvation which they embody. Hence too, as nature is a book of signs, so too is human history, and so therefore are the Scriptures, the book in which that history is recorded. The Scriptures are therefore another 'Book' of signs which are sacraments, having both a literal and a spiritual significance, the former signifying the latter: for 'the literally recorded facts [*res*] which in this way [in Scripture] represent spiritual realities, are called "sacraments".[13]

Therefore, all nature, all history and all Scripture are, within the dispensation of grace, a complex of symbolic representations of the divine, a universe whose reality is sacramental. In essence, all the visible world is sacrament of the invisible. And that sacramentality of the Book of nature and of the Book of Scripture is resumed in the human nature of Christ, the Book of Life, who is at the same time the hermeneutical key by means of which the Books of nature and of Scripture may be understood.

III

In the most mechanical sense of the word structure – denoting the formal plan of its argument – the structure of the *Itinerarium* is instantly recognizable from Augustine as mediated by Hugh of St Victor. Three organizing principles overlap with one another to govern a plan which is at once extraordinarily complex and lucid.

Bonaventure begins where Hugh began. His book, Bonaventure says, will describe the steps of the soul's ascent to God[14] and 'we are so created that the material universe itself is a ladder by which' we may make that ascent.[15] And in what must have been a conscious paraphrase of Hugh, Bonaventure explains:

For creatures of this visible world signify the invisible things of God: partly because God is the origin, exemplar and end of every creature and the effect is the sign of the cause...partly by their own proper representation; partly because of their prophetic prefiguration; partly by reason of angelic operation, partly by reason of superadded institution. For every

---

[13] *De Scripturis et de Scriptoribus Sacris*, I, 3, PL, 176. 12C.
[14] *Itin.*, I, 2.   [15] Ibid., I, 2.

creature is by its very nature some kind of image and likeness of the eternal Wisdom, but especially one who, according to the Book of Scriptures, has been raised by the Spirit of Prophecy to prefigure spiritual things; and more especially those creatures in whose likeness it pleased God to appear through the ministry of the angels; and finally, most especially, that one which he willed to institute for signifying, and which not only has the character of sign in the ordinary sense of the term, but also the character of sacrament as well.[16]

And in the *Breviloquium* Bonaventure combines the Hugonian metaphor of the world as book with the scalar image which predominates in the *Itinerarium*:

the creation of the world is a kind of book in which the Trinity, the world's maker, shines forth, is represented and read in three modes of expression, namely in the modes of vestige, image and likeness: thus the meaning of vestige is found in all creatures, of image in intellectual or rational spirits only, of likeness in those alone who are godlike; and from these human understanding is destined to ascend step by step to the highest Principle, God, as if up a kind of ladder.[17]

'Vestige', 'image', 'likeness'. In the books of creation and restoration are contained, as it were, three kinds of trope, three forms of simulacra. As such this terminology is not to be found in Hugh, and Bonaventure's greater precision enables him to outline a broad threefold division of steps on the ladder of ascent to God, and so of his *Itinerarium*. The visible 'external' creation contains vestiges of the divine, the interior world of the human soul contains images of the divine and, through the work of grace, the images of the divine become likenesses of it which raise the soul 'above' itself. But the distinction is implicit in Hugh, for it corresponds well enough with his threefold distinction of 'eyes' in the Commentary on Denys' *Celestial Hierarchy* which, like Bonaventure's distinction, is based upon the Augustinian triad of 'without', 'within' and 'above'. Vestiges are what are seen with Hugh's 'eye of the flesh', for they are found in what is *extra nos*; images are what are seen with the 'rational eye', for they are found *intra nos*; likenesses raise the mind so as to see with the 'eye of contemplation' those things which are *supra nos*. Vestige and exteriority, image and interiority, likeness and ascent: these three pairings determine the basic division of the text of the *Itinerarium* into three pairs of chapters:

[16] Ibid., I, 12.   [17] *Breviloquium*, II, 12, I.

In order to arrive at the consideration of the First Principle, which is wholly spiritual and eternal and above us, we must pass through vestiges which are corporeal and temporal and outside us. Thus we are guided in the way of God. Next we must enter into our mind, which is the image of God – an image which is everlasting, spiritual and within us. And this is to enter the truth of God. Finally, looking at the First Principle, we must go beyond to what is eternal, absolutely spiritual and above us. This is to rejoice in the knowledge of God and in the reverent fear of his majesty.

The secondary principle which governs the subdivision of each of these three steps into a further two, yielding a total of six, is less easy to understand. Contemplation of God by means of vestiges and images can each be of two kinds: contemplation *per vestigia* or *per imaginem* and contemplation *in vestigiis* or *in imagine*. What is this distinction between *per* and *in*? The text of the *Itinerarium* does not help us with any explicit definition, nor is it made much clearer what this distinction entails from the discussions in the corresponding chapters. But Bonaventure makes the distinction elsewhere and presumably he expects us to recognize it. Thus in his *Commentary on the Sentences* of Peter Lombard it is evident that what Bonaventure has in mind is a distinction which might loosely be related to Hugh's distinction between those simulacra which reveal God merely (*per vestigia, per imaginem*) and those which not only reveal God but make God present in some way in what they reveal (*in vestigiis, in imagine*).[18]

It is one thing to know God in a creature, another [to know God] through creatures. To know God in a creature is to know his presence flowing into the creature. But to know God through a creature is to be raised up by the knowledge of the creature to the knowledge of God, as by means of a ladder between them.[19]

---

[18] This distinction in Bonaventure between *per* and *in* is not, however, *as such* that between Hugh's simulacra of nature and the simulacra of grace. For though the nature/grace distinction serves to distinguish between the *per imaginem* of step three and the *in imagine* of step four, as we will see below, the distinction between *per vestigia* and *in vestigiis* of steps one and two is not between that of *vestigia* of nature and *vestigia* of grace, but more generally between *vestigia* which only reflect something of what God is like and the *vestigia* in which the divine power itself is capable of being experienced. So there is, perhaps, a Hugonian connection in Bonaventure's distinctions between *per* and *in*, but these distinctions are not the same as Hugh's.

[19] *1 Sent.* d.3, p.1, a.1, q.3. In *Commentarius in IV Libris Sententiarum*, in *Doctoris Seraphici S. Bonaventurae Opera Omnia*, I–IV, Quaracchi: Collegium S. Bonaventurae, 1882-1902. It is by no means a safe assumption that what Bonaventure distinguishes in one place applies in the same sense in another. But the degree of dependence of the *Itinerarium* on Hugh and the similarity of Bonaventure's terminology in the *Commentary on the Sentences* to Hugh's, suggests that in both places he has Hugh's distinction in mind.

From this twofold distinction within vestige and image we get, therefore, the first four chapters of the *Itinerarium*: in order, the contemplation of God is described *through* the vestiges of God in the external
world (chapter 1); *in* those same vestiges (chapter 2); *through* the image
of God within the soul (chapter 3) and *in* that image (chapter 4).

More problematic, perhaps, is the principle which yields the distinction between the chapters 5 and 6 of *Itinerarium* and between them
both and the previous four chapters. Here, as far as concerns the distinction between the fifth and sixth steps, the distinction between *per*
and *in* is dropped in favour of chapter titles which denote the two
highest kinds of contemplation of God through affirmative attributes:
the contemplation of the divine unity through its primary name of
being (chapter 5), and the contemplation of the Trinity through its
primary name of goodness (chapter 6). And as far as concerns the distinction between the last two steps and the preceding four, it is tempting to take up the clue provided by the *Breviloquium* distinction,
quoted above, which told us that the representations of God are of
three kinds, vestiges, images and likenesses, and so to distinguish
between the contemplations of the third and fourth steps and those of
the fifth and sixth in the way that images are distinct from likenesses.
And this is especially tempting since Bonaventure himself offers it as
one of the many principles of the structure of the *Itinerarium*. This
tempting proposition, however, runs up against a difficulty.

The difficulty is that, once again, Bonaventure gives no formal
account of the distinction between 'image' and 'likeness' in the
Itinerarium. And where he does, as again in his *Commentary on the
Sentences*, the distinction is worse than useless in helping to explain
the distinction between the last two steps and the preceding four.
For the distinction made between 'image' and 'likeness' in the
Commentary on the Sentences is that between the soul's natural power
to reflect God as image and that of the power to reflect God as
likeness which is found only in the soul restored by grace:

an image occurs in the order of nature and likeness in the order of grace;
...for...an image...is exemplified in the case of the natural powers of the
soul, namely memory, intellect and will; so it is that an image is something in the natural order. But because a likeness is an actual sharing, and
is the common possession of a quality; and because the quality by which
the soul is made like to God is grace; for this reason a likeness is said to
be something in the order of grace.[20]

[20]   II *Sent.*, d.16, a.2, q.3, resp.

What seems to be at stake here is a distinction not unrelated to that which it was possible to make within Augustine's concept of 'image', between its mimetic, purely formal character of correspondence with what it images and its participatory character of sharing, through grace, in the reality which it represents. Now what in Augustine is a distinction within the one concept of image, becomes in Bonaventure the distinction between 'image' and 'likeness',[21] the one mimetic but not participatory, the other both mimetic and participatory. But then, this distinction appears to be one and the same with the distinction between the *per imaginem* and the *in imagine* of chapters 3 and 4. For in chapter 3 Bonaventure paraphrases Augustine's account of the formal analogies which obtain between the internal relations of the natural powers of the human soul – intellect, memory and will – and the internal relations of the Trinity of Persons. Whereas in chapter 4 Bonaventure turns to the power to image God which is found in the *anima reformata*, and the distinction is made transparently clear in the same terms in which the distinction between image and likeness is made in the *Commentary on the Sentences*:

we can understand how we are guided to things divine through the rational soul itself and its naturally implanted faculties, considered in their activities, their relationships and their possession of the sciences. This is apparent from the explanation of the third step. We are also guided by the reformed faculties of the soul itself. This takes place with the help of the freely given virtues, spiritual senses and spiritual transports. And this becomes clear in the fourth step.[22]

The 'image' and 'likeness' distinction, implied though not made in so many words in the *Itinerarium*, therefore provides a second principle of division within the structure of the soul's ascent to God; but it is not the one we want which distinguishes the last two steps from the previous four. Rather, it gives us a way of dividing the scale into two halves at mid-point between the third and the fourth: to put it with a preliminary imprecision, it is here that the distinction between 'nature' and 'grace' becomes an operative structural principle of the *Itinerarium*.

Now here it is important to tread carefully. It would be perfectly possible to read Bonaventure as having divided his six-step ladder

---

[21] Who is once again following Hugh, see *De Sacramentis*, I, 6, 2, PL 176, 264C–D.
[22] *Itin.*, 4, 7.

into two halves, the first corresponding to Hugh's *simulacra naturae*, but subdivided, in a way that Hugh does not, into *per vestigia*, *in vestigiis* and *per imaginem*, the second, corresponding to Hugh's *simulacra gratiae*, subdivided into *in imagine*, and the two direct contemplations of the divine properties, being and goodness – hence, into two broad categories of natural and supernatural contemplation. It would be possible to do this and right, but this reading would tell only half the story. For though Bonaventure does distinguish between natural and supernatural contemplations, and though on the ladder of contemplation the point of distinction between them does occur at the point of distinction between steps three and four, it is only from one point of view that we can distinguish between natural and supernatural contemplations at all.

For it is necessary to distinguish. If one looks at the hierarchy of this ascent as a series of *successive* steps, then certainly the soul moves further 'upwards' and further 'within' in so far as it moves beyond the mere recognition of the formal analogy by which the soul's powers naturally imitate the Trinity (chapter 3) to the achievement, through the infusion of the theological virtues, of an actual participation in the Trinitarian life which it naturally images (chapter 4). For

no matter how enlightened one may be by the light coming from nature and from acquired knowledge, he cannot enter into himself to delight in the Lord except through the mediation of Christ...The image of our soul must be clothed over with the three theological virtues, by which the soul is purified, enlightened and perfected. In this way the image is reformed and made conformable to the heavenly Jerusalem...[23]

But on the other hand, a purely linear and successive reading of Bonaventure's hierarchy would lead to the misleading conclusion that the first three steps of the ladder are meant to describe purely natural activities of the soul employing its purely natural powers independently of grace and faith. If from one point of view – as it were, viewed from 'below' – the articulation of the steps is successive and exclusive – that is to say, what is achieved at step one falls below what is achieved at step two and so on – from another point of view – as it were, viewed from 'above' – the relation of the steps is inclusive and, we might say, 'totalising'.

From this latter point of view the metaphor of a ladder misconstrues something essential to the mediaeval conception of hierarchy. For on a ladder not only is to be on a lower step not to be on a higher, to be on a higher is not to be on a lower which has been left behind. If one reads Bonaventure's hierarchy of ascent literally in the light of the ladder metaphor we will get the misleading conclusions first, that there is a 'purely natural' set of steps, one to three, which contain no element of grace, and a supernatural set of steps, four to six, which involve no engagement of the soul's natural powers. And both conclusions misconstrue the structure of Bonaventure's 'ascent' for the same reason. They both misconstrue Bonaventure's conception of hierarchy.

For, in the first place, if we must pursue the ladder metaphor, we will have to conceive of it not as a rigid structure of successive steps, but as a rope ladder which the climber pulls up with herself as she climbs. At every stage she has not only passed through the preceding steps but has brought them along with her, for every higher step contains within it all that is contained in the lower. Thus, at the fourth step, the natural image in the soul is not *displaced* by the theological virtues as the image of the Trinity; rather the infused grace of those virtues brings the natural image participatively into the Trinitarian life which it naturally images. And if that is how the fourth step 'contains' the third, it is also how the fourth step 'contains' the second and the first. That is to say, the *vestigia* of the Trinity which are known naturally at steps one and two are incorporated into the life of faith, hope and charity of the *anima reformata* of the fourth step. It follows, *ex hypothesi*, that the fifth and sixth steps are in the same way arranged, in inclusive hierarchy with each other and with all the steps below them.

Thus, it is possible to read a hierarchical structure either from below or from above. And it is fair to say that throughout the *Itinerarium* Bonaventure reads his scalar metaphor in both ways simultaneously. In so far as the steps are distinguished, they are read from below. But at each step the progress of the soul is understood to be inclusive, as containing all that precedes that step and, in the last resort, the whole ascent is properly seen only from the standpoint of its summit. For this reason, although it is certainly true that the distinction between the third and the fourth steps is decisive, seen as dividing the step of natural image from that of grace, or the step of 'image' from that of 'likeness', nonetheless, the dominating perspective of the whole journey and of all its steps is that of its end point: the soul transformed by grace and taken up

into God in the *excessus* of love. It is in and for such a soul that the
vestigia of nature or the *imago* of interiority have the power to lead
the soul to God.

With this qualification, therefore, the 'image/likeness' distinction
does help to clarify the distinction between steps three and four of
Bonaventure's ladder of ascent. But if it does so, then for that very
reason it serves no purpose of clarifying the distinction between
steps three and four taken together and steps five and six. What,
then governs the latter distinction?

A clue as to how Bonaventure makes this distinction is provided
by the unmistakably Dionysian sound of the titles to chapters 5 and
6 of the *Itinerarium*, for they correspond, in reverse order, to chapters 5 and 4 of Denys' *Divine Names*. And I suggest an implied
Dionysian source which not only explains the distinction between
the contemplations of chapters 5 and 6 and those of 3 and 4, but
also overdetermines and reinforces the threefold structure of the
Itinerarium as a whole.

For in Denys' account of them, 'Goodness' and 'Being' are
the highest 'conceptual' names of God, the most 'similar' of the
similarities of God. The study of them[24] constitutes the apex
of Denys' threefold classification of those 'affirmative' theologies
which he outlines in his *Mystical Theology* 3: 'symbolic', 'representational' and 'conceptual'. It seems reasonable to suggest that
in Bonaventure's ascending scale of contemplations the 'direct'
contemplations of the divine properties of 'Being' and 'Goodness'
are distinguished from the contemplations through and in the
image of God, as Denys' 'conceptual' theology is distinguished
from his 'representational' theology. For as Denys says in
both the *Mystical Theology* and the *Divine Names*, his *Theological
Representations* studied the Trinitarian nature of God through the
best human analogies, and this is what Bonaventure does in
chapters 3 and 4 of the *Itinerarium*. And if this is plausible, then it
seems equally plausible to suggest that Bonaventure's steps one and
two, on which God is contemplated through and in the vestiges
of the external world, correspond with Denys' *Symbolic Theology*
which is constructed out of the most 'dissimilar', material, 'similarities'.[25]

[24] Together with many others, of course: see the chapter titles of the *DN* for a complete list.
[25] *MT*, 1033A–B.

On this account of the organization of Bonaventure's ascending scale of contemplations, we have, then, a third principle governing the structure of the work, which is that of the Dionysian epistemological hierarchy of affirmative theologies. And this Dionysian principle, as I say, overlaps with and reinforces the first, based on Hugh's 'Augustinian' principle of the articulations of 'without', 'within' and 'above' and with the second, between 'image' and 'likeness'. It would be incautious to make too much of this correspondence. After all, we do not possess either Denys' *Theological Representations* or his *Symbolic Theology*, if he ever wrote them. Nor did Bonaventure. Nonetheless it is of the utmost consequence for an understanding of the *Itinerarium* as a whole that we should recognize the significance of this *theological–epistemological* emphasis of Bonaventure's work. To ignore it is to run the risk of an unbalanced and too 'spiritual' a reading of the *Itinerarium*, it is to ignore one of its chief intellectual purposes, which is to demonstrate the coincidence of the hierarchy of theological knowledge with that of the soul's personal ascent into God.

And it is easy for us to discount this aspect of the *Itinerarium*, our interest in it being predominantly as a work of what we call 'spirituality', though it is hard to know what Bonaventure himself could have made of this notion in so far as it is contradistinguished from theological study. It is fair to say that if in so many other ways Bonaventure is an 'Augustinian' theologian, in this respect too he is reworking the theology of his master: it is proper to see the *Itinerarium* as being, among the many other things that it is, a thirteenth-century rewriting of Augustine's *De Doctrina Christiana*, which was Augustine's survey of the breadth and divisions of the whole of Christian *learning* as serving the ends of Christian *charity*.

At each of Bonaventure's 'steps' on the ladder of contemplations to God, Bonaventure's contemplations draw on that part of the academic curriculum which contributes to it. It is true that he provides no formal classification of the branches of academic study. His purpose is not taxonomical. His purpose is rather to demonstrate in what way all the learned sciences serve the purpose of leading the soul to God, beginning from the sciences of the natural properties of things (chapter 1), through the 'practical' and aesthetic arts (chapter 2), the principles of natural philosophy, logic, ethics and the natural science of the soul (chapter 3), transformed by grace into a personalised love of God (chapter 4), to the contemplations of God in his primary metaphysical descriptions of the being of God in his oneness (chapter 5) and of the goodness of God in Trinity (chapter 6). These academic disciplines are therefore an intrinsic part of theology, and in this respect the divisions of the learned sciences correspond with Denys' threefold articulation of 'theologies': the 'symbolic', which for Bonaventure consists in the contemplation of *vestigia* (chapters 1 and 2), 'Representational', which for Bonaventure consists in the contemplation of *imagines* (chapters 3 and 4) and 'conceptual', which is the contemplation of the proper names of God, the 'similar similarities' (chapters 5 and 6). In this respect too the *Itinerarium* may be seen as a compendious *Reductio Artium ad Theologiam*. But they are not, as 'theology', to be distinguished from 'contemplation' as the practice of the Christian life, but are to be seen as wholly and unproblematically serving its purposes. In this respect, finally, we can say that Bonaventure's ascent into God is, like Denys', an ascent of the *intellect* to God, though, as we will see, not of intellect to the exclusion of desire and love. What we must say, at any rate, is that it is very far from being an ascent of love to the exclusion of intellect.

Looked at in the formal aspects of its organization, then, the structure of the *Itinerarium* is multiply determined, containing many more structural divisions than the most obvious Augustinian division between 'without', 'within' and 'above'. Moreover, in terms of sources too it draws on a wide variety within the spectrum of Christian Neoplatonism. But even in the very complexity of the structure itself is incarnated a certain unity and synthesis. For if the elements of metaphor determining that structure – and I have greatly simplified it – include the threefold distinction between the 'outer', the 'inner' and the 'above', the hierarchical metaphor of 'ascent' and the Dionysian threefold distinction of theologies,[26] these dominating structural determinants are already, that is to say *structurally*, synthesized into an overdetermined, integrated whole. For the reader it is never difficult to see where Bonaventure is, nor where he is going. The resulting structural complexity has a unity like that of shot silk, providing a kaleidoscope of impressions,

---

[26] Bonaventure outlines a great variety of further structuring triadic images: the three days' journey into the desert, 'evening, morning, noonday'; the threefold existence of things in matter, understanding and in the Eternal Art; and the threefold substance of Christ, the corporeal, the spiritual and the divine, *Itin.*, 1, 3. All of these would need to be taken into account in any comprehensive study of the structuring imagery of the *Itinerarium*.

which aspect dominates depending merely on slight shifts in the angle of vision. And so far we have examined only the mechanical principles of this structure without reference to the central theological vision which is the dynamic of that structure's energy and movement.

IV

That central theological vision is Christological. It is with Christ that the *Itinerarium* begins and ends. It is Christ who is the means. It is Christ who is the meaning. It is, however, as Ewart Cousins says in a comment which we will later need to qualify, the 'mystical' Christ, more than the historical Jesus of the *Lignum Vitae*, who energises the *Itinerarium*.[27] The Christ of the *Itinerarium* is not the poor Christ whose life is the object of an almost visual, empathetic meditation in the *Lignum Vitae*, it is the cosmic Christ who is the summation of Bonaventure's exemplarism, the human Christ who, like Hugh of St Victor's, is the 'supreme Hierarch',[28] in whom is incarnated and recapitulated all the power of the created order to make visible the invisible and so is the ladder of ascent to the invisible and unknowable Godhead.[29]

There is in this emphasis on the human nature of Christ something quite distinctively Bonaventurean; and since it is quite impossible to make significant distinctions between them this emphasis is a characteristic equally of his theology and of his spirituality. As the person of Christ informs his personal spirituality, so Christology informs every aspect of his systematic theology. As Christ is the origin, meaning, goal and means of the soul's ascent to God, so is his Christology the point at which converge and are reconciled the various streams of theological influence which feed into his thought. Bonaventure's is a Christocentric spirituality and theology.

---

[27] Introduction to Bonaventure, *The Soul's Journey Into God, the Tree of Life, The Life of St Francis*, trans. Ewart Cousins, New York: Paulist Press, 1978, p. 35.

[28] *Itin.*, 4, 5.

[29] We should not exaggerate the differences between the Christ of the *Itinerarium* and the Christ of the *Lignum Vitae*. It is the human Christ, indeed it is the humiliated, crucified Christ who is the starting point, the route, the goal and the means of the soul's itinerary. The 'exemplary' Christ of the *Itinerarium* likewise is not in any way to be opposed to the 'historical' Christ of the *Lignum Vitae*. For Bonaventure *the best* possible simulacrum of the Godhead is the crucified Christ, see *Itin.*, prologue, 3 and 7, 6. In this, once again, Bonaventure has Hugh to follow, see *In Hier.*, I, 1, PL, 175, 925A. And see the further discussion of this point below pp. 129–33.

His Christocentrism provides him with a distinctive solution to that problem which all Christian Neoplatonism must expect to face, the problem of how to reconcile the implications of an *hierarchical* ontology with the key Christian instinct of the immediacy of all things in their relations with their Creator. In chapter 2 we saw that the form in which that problem arose for Denys was that of a prima facie conflict between the hierarchical gradation of 'distances' in which the different orders of creation stand to their origin, and the Christian belief in the immediacy of the relation of created dependence. But there is no doubt that this is a problem which is not unique to Denys' theology and is one which will arise for any Neoplatonic theology. McEvoy is therefore right to generalize, but more particularly in connection with Bonaventure, to see the problem as having especial importance in connection with the place of the human within the hierarchy of all things:

The Latin theological tradition had to struggle against the anthropological consequences of [Neoplatonic] subordinationism [of men to angels, for]…Neoplatonism in almost all its Greek and Arabic forms from Proclus onward was an angelology rather than an anthropology in its central interest. The intelligences emanate from the principle more immediately than does man who is always…lower and further removed from God.[30]

Bonaventure's Christology may very well be the context in which the solution to that problem is eventually found, but in the first instance it is in a Christological context that the problem arises. The problem is, as I say, quite general. As Bonaventure faced it, it was the problem that the objective hierarchy of creation places the human at a point of not very particular eminence, as a middle-ranking link in the chain of beings, far 'below' the highest angels. This was a problem not, as it might be for us today, because of some sensibility of an anthropocentric kind which is offended by this relatively poor hierarchical ranking. The problem arose for Bonaventure out of the central Christian fact: that the second Person of the Trinity had, mysteriously, assumed the nature not of the highest being on the hierarchical scale, but of this middle-ranking being, the human. And this fact appears to disrupt the ordered seemliness (*convenientia*) of the hierarchy itself.

---

[30] J. McEvoy, 'Microcosm and Macrocosm in the Writings of St Bonaventure', *S. Bonaventura*, II, p. 342.

Hence, in a clear acknowledgement of the problem caused for a Christology by the 'angelological' implications of hierarchy, Bonaventure asks why it would not have been more appropriate had the second Person of the Trinity assumed an angelic nature rather than become incarnate in a human, since, among other reasons, the angelic nature is higher, and so nearer in kind, to the divine nature than is the human.[31] After all, he says,

God is spirit, as it is said in John, 4: and so that creature which has more of the character of the spiritual shares more with God; and what shares more with God is more capable of being united in the unity of Person; therefore, since the angelic nature is more spiritual than the human, it follows...[32]

His response to this argument takes us back in a series of stages into the fundamentals of his theological position as a whole. It takes us back to a starting point in that overarching 'world-view' which we have seen that he shares with Hugh of St Victor, according to which the whole of creation is, in different ways and with different degrees of capacity, a simulacrum of the creator. Now those capabilities of reflecting the Creator are ranked in a hierarchy of degrees of expressiveness, as we have seen, and because this is so the problem arises in the form he has stated it: since angels are more expressive of the divine nature than are humans, would it not have been more apt for the Second Person to have assumed the angelic nature than the human?

But the second stage of the response to this argument turns the implications of Neoplatonic hierarchicalism against itself, or at least it has a powerfully *revisionary* consequence for that hierarchicalism. The human is, certainly, speaking ontologically, no higher than at the mid-point on the ascending scale of beings ranked below God, standing between the animals and the angels. But on the other hand in that existence at mid-point on the hierarchy lies the advantage, indeed the superiority, of the human above all other beings, angels included, in its *representational* capacity.

The first reason for this is the most fundamental. It is that only a being which shares both the nature of the angels in being intellectual and the nature of animals in being embodied, is capable of perceiving the symbolic at all. Animals cannot own symbols, angels

---

[31]   *Utrum maior sit congruitas ad unionem in humana natura quam in Angelo, an e converso. III Sent.*, d.2, a.1, q.2.
[32]   *III Sent.*, d.2, a.1, q.2, obj.1.

need not; indeed angels both need not and cannot, for lacking any sensuous power they can no more own symbols than animals can, though for the opposite reason; and being pure intellect they have direct, if still only limited, access to the divine light and so do not need symbols. Precisely *because of* their position in the hierarchy, human beings are uniquely placed to respond to the world's representational capacity, since symbols can *only* exist *for* human beings.

The second reason derives from an Aristotelian source concerning the nature of human knowledge as such. 'The human soul', Aristotle had said, 'is in some way all things',[33] for, Aristotle thought, the knower, in knowing an object, *becomes* what he *knows*. Obviously, Aristotle had argued, the knower does not 'become' the thing known in the manner of existence which that thing possesses *in re*, for that would not be to know it at all. To know a material object is not to become that thing materially. A cow's recognition of grass cannot be that kind of becoming in the cow that being reduced to cud is in the grass. Likewise, the act of perceiving a red object is not itself a red-coloured act of perceiving. Otherwise, having once known a red object I could not know a green object, for, as when seeing things through rose-coloured spectacles, the red perception would have us see green things yellow. Nonetheless, the perception of a red object is, Aristotle thought, properly characterized as a 'change', but one by which I become *intentionally* or immaterially what the object is *materially*. Now there is nothing which, in principle, is unknowable by the human mind. Consequently, there is nothing at all which human beings cannot, through the intentionality of knowledge, become. 'The human soul is in some way all things.'

That being so, in the order of knowledge human beings may be said to be a sort of microcosm of the macrocosm. For, as Bonaventure puts it – in this following Aristotle – all things in the Book of creation can be written on the mind by means of their likenesses, that is to say, by means of their existent forms possessed intentionally by the mind. Since, therefore, the totality of the created universe represents the creator, the mind contains the whole extent of the expressive capacity of that universe in microcosm. The human mind *is* what it *knows* and so is, microcosmically – as a *minor mundus* – what the universe – the *maior mundus*[34] – is writ large.

---

[33] *De Anima*, III, 8, 431 b20.   [34] *Itin.*, 2, 3.

Therefore Bonaventure exclaims: 'What a great thing is the soul! For in the soul may the whole world be described'.[35]

If this 'microcosmic' character of the human is found at the level of human cognition, it is found also in the very constitution of human nature as such, in the fact that only in the human are all created natures present. In the human body as material are found all the elements of which any material thing is composed; in the human body as alive are found all the powers of living, non-sentient beings. In the human person as sentient are found all the powers of the animal world. In the human person as rational are found not only the distinctively human powers of rationality, but also, at the summit of the human *mens*, the intellectual capacity which exists in pure form in the angels. The human being is, there-fore, the cosmic hierarchy in small, containing within her nature all that the universe of beings contains but, as it were, miniaturised and interiorised.

Moreover, these powers are ranked within human nature in the same relations of subordination and inclusion which govern the cos-mic hierarchy itself. For just as, for Denys, each rank of a hierarchy 'contains' in a higher way all that is contained in those ranks below it, so each level of existence within the human contains in a higher way that which is subordinate to it: the sentience of a rational being is a 'higher' kind of sentience than that which animals possess, the vegetative nature of a rational being is a higher form of life than it is in either an animal or in a mere vegetable, and so on. So that in the very constitution of human nature all the world of the human, the animal, the vegetative and the purely material is contained in a manner capable of being more expressive of the Creator than are any of those natures in their separate existence.

Nor does the human contain merely all those natures which are 'below' it, for at its 'highest' point, at the *apex mentis*, it overlaps, as it were, with the angelic nature which is above it. For the human *mens* is not only rational and discursive; indeed, it is very much a consideration of the Augustinian element in Bonaventure's thought, that the human *mens* could not be *just* discursive, for in order to exercise the discursive powers of judgement at all, it has to be *more than* discursive. The argument is the familiar Augustinian case for saying that the human mind could not make even the

---

[35]   *In Hexaem.*, 22, 24.

characteristically *human*, i.e. *rational*, judgments which it makes about the changeable things of this world, if it did not do so in that light which is not itself the object of rational judgement, the eternal Truth known only to the power of *intellect*. In short, to be rational is necessarily to be more than rational, it is to share in some way in the intellectual powers of the angelic nature. For

since our mind is itself changeable, it could not see...truth shining in so changeless a manner were it not for some other light absolutely and unchangeably resplendent; nor can this light possibly be a created light subject to change. The intellect, therefore, knows in the light *that enlightens every man who comes into the world*, which is the *true light*, and *the Word in the beginning with God* (Jn., 1, 1 and 9).[36]

Moreover, there is a second respect in which the human can in some way 'overlap' with the angelic nature so as even in a certain way to achieve equality with it. For not only in its objective constitution does human nature 'contain' all the natures below it, not only does it in some way participate, through its intellectual powers, in the angelic natures 'above' it, for the human *mens* can also, through grace, 'interiorise' the whole angelic hierarchy itself: the *anima reformata* can become an *anima hierarchizata*. This is a theme which undoubtedly Bonaventure borrowed from the thirteenth-century Victorine Thomas Gallus of Vercelli, as any even superficial comparison of texts will reveal.[37] Both Gallus and Bonaventure in turn rely heavily upon Denys' *Celestial Hierarchy* for the characterization of the nine different orders and ranks of angels, but what is distinctive about their adaptation of this angelic hierarchy is the way in which they transpose and interiorise the objective hierarchy of angelic natures into yet another account of the structures of interiority themselves.

These things attained, our spirit, inasmuch as it is in conformity with the heavenly Jerusalem, is made hierarchic in order to mount upward...Thus our spirit is sealed with the nine degrees of orders, when in its inner depths the following are arranged in due order: announcing, dictating, guiding, ordering, strengthening, commanding, receiving, revealing, and anointing, and these correspond, step by step, to the nine orders of angels...Having obtained these, the soul, entering into itself, enters into

---

[36] *Itin.*, 3, 3.
[37] See his second *Expositio in Canticum Canticorum*, Latin text in *Thomas Gualterius, Abbas Vercellensis, Commentaires du Cantique de Cantiques*, ed. Jeanne Barbet, Textes Philosophiques du Moyen Age, n. 14, Paris: 1967, and my translation of the prologue in *Eros and Allegory*, pp. 317–339.

the heavenly Jerusalem, where, considering the order of the angels, it sees in them God, who dwells in them and performs all their works.[38]

It is not, of course, that Bonaventure abandons the angelic hierarchy in its objective existence as the highest part of the created order. To interiorise the angelic hierarchy is not to deny its objective reality. It is rather that, in this connection too, the human has the power to make its own microcosmically that which has an objective, macrocosmic existence in itself. In short, the human may by grace 'interiorise' the objective orders 'above' it in the same way that by nature it 'interiorises' the orders of creation 'below' it. Thus truly does the human soul contain all natures and so resume all the representative capacity of the universe.

There is a third reason why the human is a more powerfully *representative* nature than is the angelic; and this, like the second reason, has to do with the distinctiveness of human nature, but this time deriving from the essentially embodied character of human beings. For human nature is a composite of soul and body in which the soul is the principle of the whole life of the body, omnipresent in it, informing the organism with all its living, sentient and rational powers. Once again, in this respect human nature is a microcosm of the whole created order except that in this connection it is a summary not merely of creation itself, but also of the relation of God to creation. For just as the soul animates the body throughout its extent, sustaining it in all the levels of life and existence of the human, so God sustains the whole universe in existence in each of its characteristic modes. Summarizing his reply to the problem of why the Word should have assumed the human rather than the angelic nature, Bonaventure therefore says:

> The...reason is the greater representational [power of human nature] by reason of which man is said to be a 'smaller world'. The rational soul not only in itself represents God, but also in so far as it is united with a body, which it governs and indwells throughout its extent, as God does the 'greater world'; and Augustine mentions this on many occasions.[39] By virtue of this greater degree of conformity there is a stronger reason for [human nature] being united [with the Word].
>
> The [next] reason is the complexity of the human make-up. For man is made up of a bodily and a spiritual nature and in some way shares with every creature, as Gregory says;[40] consequently, since it is human nature

[38] *Itin.*, 4, 4.
[39] See, e.g., *De Spiritu et Anima*, c.18, PL, 40, 794.
[40] See, e.g., *VI Moralia in Job*, 16, 20, *CCSL*, CXLII, Turnholt: Brepols, 1979.

which is assumed and made God-like, in a certain way all nature is raised up by being united to God through its own likeness. And that is why the assumption of human nature achieves more by way of the perfection of the whole universe than [the assumption of] the angelic nature [would have achieved].[41]

We might with some reason doubt if what Bonaventure achieves through the introduction of this 'microcosmism' is any very real conciliation of the opposed pressures of the hierarchical metaphor of 'distance' and that of the 'immediacy' of the human soul's relation with God. For, after all, there are real tensions here, and it is hard to see how a strategy merely of placing the doctrine of microcosmism alongside the metaphor of hierarchy by itself does anything to resolve them. At one level this strategy could, perhaps, be conceded to work. For there is no contradiction in saying that though *ontologically* the human exists at a lower point on the scale than do angels, *representationally* the human has the greater power to reflect the divine, since it contains microcosmically, in a way that angels do not, the representational power of the whole universe. Moreover, there is a certain common-sense logic in Bonaventure's argument. In an intuitively obvious way it is a perfectly sound claim that a world would not be the richer by being limited to a population only of its best components. For a world populated only by angels would not, by virtue of their being the highest natures possible, be a better world than the world we have got, which is populated by many kinds of being inferior to them as well. And if our universe is such as to embrace all the possible varieties of creation, then there is much to be said for the view that it is not the 'highest' beings in our universe which are most *representative* of it, but those beings in whose nature is contained elements of all its variety and complexity. What one wants in a good meal is not a diet restricted to just the one dish, even of caviar, but a menu of some variety, even if made up of many dishes of which the potato is one.

Since human beings resume microcosmically all the variety of the created macrocosm there is therefore no inconsistency in maintaining that they are both ontologically lower than the angels and higher than them in their representational capacity. But that is not where the tensions end. For they appear to persist even as between

---

[41]   *III Sent.*, d.2, a.1, q.2, concl.

the different things which Bonaventure says about the *representa-tional* character of the human. On the one hand, in a convention-ally Augustinian spirit, Bonaventure finds the true image of God in the soul's highest powers, the powers of the human spirit, intellect, memory and will and, though also like Augustine, he concedes that there are 'trinities' in the lower, sensory powers of the soul, he denies that in them can be found any true 'image' of the Trinity. For, as we have seen, both for Augustine and for Bonaventure, the image of the Trinity is to be found only in those powers of the soul which, through grace, are capable of being engaged participatively in the actual life of the Trinity: and none but the soul's spiritual powers are capable of that.

That on the one hand. On the other, and apparently in conflict with traditional Augustinian orthodoxy, is Bonaventure's novel doctrine of microcosmism.[42] According to this, as we have seen, it is in the integral complexity of human nature that the superior rep-resentational capacity of the human is to be found, not merely in that part of that complexity which is ontologically 'nearer to', and so more 'like' the divine. On the one criterion, therefore, the hier-archical metaphor of 'superiority' and corresponding 'nearness' to God is what dominates, and it brings with it the attendant dangers of an angelological anthropology: for on this account the capacity of the human to image the divine will be in direct proportion to the similarity of humans to the angels. On the other criterion, the metaphor of the 'centrality' of the human within the created order is what dominates, for it is that position of being at the centre of all creation in which lies its power as a résumé of all created simulacra of the divine. The two criteria push against one another. We *might* say that they are 'mutually correcting', complementary metaphors. It is easier, perhaps, to see them as unreconciled and opposed ten-dencies of thought.

Where they are reconciled is in Christ. For Christ is at once the 'supreme Hierarch' and, through the assumption of that human nature which is the résumé of all creation, the true 'centre'. In Christ is all creation, drawn, through his human nature, into the nature of the divine; he is at once, therefore, the 'centre' and 'sum-

---

[42] It is, of course, not a doctrine unique to Bonaventure, nor one original in his theology. It is found inchoately, as he himself acknowledges, as early as Gregory the Great, in the twelfth century in Isaac of Stella and also in Grosseteste in the thirteenth century, to mention just three precedents.

mit' of the universe. In the human the whole book of creation is written. Through the assumption of the human in Christ, the book of creation becomes the Book of Life

in which God the Father has *hidden all the treasures of the wisdom and knowledge of God* (Col. 2, 3). Therefore, the only-begotten Son of God, as the uncreated Word, is the book of wisdom and the light that is full of living eternal principles in the mind of the supreme Craftsman, as the inspired Word in the angelic intellects and the blessed, as the incarnate Word in rational minds united with the flesh. Thus through the entire kingdom *the manifest wisdom of God* (Eph. 3, 10) shines forth from him and in him, as in a mirror containing the beauty of all the forms and lights and as in a book in which all things are written according to the deep secrets of God.[43]

However, to say that the tensions between the hierarchical and the anthropocentric metaphors are reconciled 'in Christ' is but to say *where* they are reconciled, not *how*. Let us note once again the possibility of being satisfied – it amounts to a real temptation – with a merely rhetorical harmonisation of what are objective tensions of thought. It is not as if the hierarchical language of the *Itinerarium* were in that sense 'merely' metaphorical in that it might represent a simple literary choice on Bonaventure's part, one which he could therefore correct the tendencies of by placing along with it the rival metaphors of a microcosmism, equally chosen *ad placitum*. The hierarchical is a metaphor for the inner ordering of the *anima reformata* and for the soul's journey into God because, for Bonaventure, the world *is* hierarchical. The metaphor derives from the way the world is; it is not just a particularly illuminating way of looking at the world which, its purpose being served, could be dropped in favour of alternative metaphors. And the same can be said of those alternative metaphors. Bonaventure's microcosmism is not less rooted in the facts of the matter, for it is a metaphor imposed upon the theologian by the utterly surprising fact that the second Person of the Trinity became a man, not an angel.

It is therefore important for us to note just *how* surprising this fact has to be for a mediaeval Platonist – and how difficult it is for a modern mentality to recover that sense of surprise. For we do not think hierarchically. But for Bonaventure the Incarnation cut across and potentially subverted the implications of his cosmic ontology. It simply will not do to suppose that so profound a dis-

---

[43] *The Tree of Life*, in *Bonaventure, The Soul's Journey into God, The Tree of Life, The Life of St Francis*, trans. and intro. Ewart Cousins, New York: Paulist Press, 1978, Fructus 12, 46, p. 170.

ruption of the mediaeval Christian world-view as the Incarnation threatened could have been overcome or 'resolved' in a merely pious metaphor. Nor does it do any justice to the radicalness of Bonaventure's theology to suppose that he thinks the matter can be so easily resolved. What is needed is a conceptually adequate theological solution and it is in the last three chapters of the *Itinerarium* that Bonaventure attempts to work one out.

V

Structurally, chapters 5 and 6 of *Itinerarium* represent the transition from the 'exteriority' of the first two chapters and the 'inwardness' of the next two, to 'ascent', as Bonaventure explains at the opening of chapter 5:

> It is possible to contemplate God not only outside us and within us but also above us: outside, through vestiges of Him; within, through His image; and above, through the light that shines upon our mind.[44]

At this highest level, contemplation of God becomes in a certain sense unmediated and 'direct'; for on these two highest steps God is contemplated through attributes which belong principally to him and only secondarily to created beings. These contemplations therefore differ from the four which precede them, because those first four steps of contemplation were mediated by metaphors, images and analogies derived from created things and applied, in only extended senses, to God. Not so with these two highest contemplations, for the names through which we contemplate God – 'being' and 'goodness' – name God directly, because their proper and primary referend is God. They are therefore applied in only an attenuated sense to creatures. It is in these terms that Bonaventure reads Yahweh's declaration of his name *He who is* in Exodus 25, 28 and the saying of Jesus 'None is good but God alone' in Luke 18, 19.[45]

In these two contemplations, therefore, the mind attends to the pure attributes of being and goodness themselves, not to any particular existent things or instances of goodness. And when the mind attends to existence as such it discovers that it is, and could only be, the name of God: for

---

[44] *Itin.*, 5, 1.   [45] Ibid., 5, 2.

this being is not particular being, which is a limited being, since it is mixed with potentiality; nor is it analogous being, for that has the least of act because it least exists. It remains, therefore, that the being we are considering is the Divine Being.[46]

And in an extension of an Augustinian image, which has significant overtones both of Plato's cave allegory and of the imagery of the *Mystical Theology*, Bonaventure explains why it is so difficult for the human mind to hold its gaze steady upon this name of God. For the created mind, he says, 'being' is normally the light *in which* we see beings just as in human perception the light is normally the medium of our seeing, not its object – for the medium in which things are visible must itself be invisible. In the same way the mind knows 'being' naturally as the medium in which we judge creatures and can only with difficulty and with partial success turn its attention to that medium as object:

Thus our mind, accustomed as it is to the opaqueness in beings and the phantasms of visible things, appears to be seeing nothing when it gazes upon the light of the highest being. It cannot understand that this very darkness is the supreme illumination of our mind, just as when the eye sees pure light, it seems to be seeing nothing.[47]

Behind this Dionysian imagery lies the Dionysian dialectic. For in attempting to construe the simplicity and oneness of God as being we are constrained to use the many opposed names which belong to creatures. We have to say contradictory things of God and the necessity of our affirming contradictions simultaneously 'will lift you up in admiration'.[48] For this being, which at the same time is not *a* being, but Being, is

both the first and last; it is eternal and yet most present; it is most simple and the greatest; it is most actual and most changeless; it is most perfect and immense; it is supremely one and yet omnifarious.[49]

Moreover, God is not just both the one and the other of each of these opposed pairs, but is each of them *because of* the other: present to everything *because* eternal, the end *because* the beginning, omnifarious *because* it is one. The members of each pair are related not just as contradictories but also as entailments. And what else is it to say of God when we say that each name is simultaneously necessary and implicative of its opposite, than to concede that same lan-

---

[46] Ibid., 5, 3.   [47] Ibid., 5, 4.   [48] Ibid., 5, 7.   [49] Ibid.

guage-defeating necessity of speech which Denys had described in chapter 5 of his *Mystical Theology*? For in Bonaventure too there is the same recognition that our language about God, rooted as it necessarily is in the logic of created, finite difference, must transcend all comprehensible, nameable difference in naming God. And how is this to be done in language except by the apophatic procedure of having to name God in all contradictory ways and then by negating the negations? And what is it to do that if not to demonstrate, by means of language, the language-defeating reality of God?

'Take care', Bonaventure therefore warns in chapter 6, 'that you do not believe you can understand the incomprehensible'.[50] Here, in his discussion of the Trinitarian nature of God through the attribute of goodness, the same apophatic logic is applied. For we must also attribute contradictory predicates to the Trinity, both the distinctness and the communicability of the Persons, both their coeternity and their processions, both consubstantiality and multiplicity, and in just the same way these opposites are mutually entailing. Hence the same apophatic outcome is generated by the same inner logic of theological language; and then at yet a higher level still. For the two contemplations of Being and Goodness, represented by the two Cherubim facing each other as they guard the Ark of the Covenant,[51] also face each other in the transcendent unity of their opposition.

But, Bonaventure continues, those Cherubim not only face each other, mysteriously they are also said to face 'towards the Mercy-Seat', which is Jesus Christ. For

we must admire the characteristics of the divine essence and of the divine Persons, not only in themselves, but also in comparison with the most marvelous union of God and man in the unity of the Person of Christ.[52]

For it is in Christ that the unity of opposites is to be found; the first made one with the last, because Jesus was God and man; the eternal with the temporal, because the eternal Word was born in time of a virgin; the most actual, and so impassible, with the man who suffered and died; the utterly simple with the man who was composite; the supremely one with the man who was but one among many; the most immense with the insignificant; Being with *a* being. And in Jesus too is found the unity of the contradictions within the

[50] Ibid., 6, 3.   [51] Ibid., 6, 4.   [52] Ibid.

Trinity, for if those contradictions amaze you, be further amazed that

in Christ a personal unity coexists with a trinity of substances and a dual-ity of natures; that an entire accord coexists with a plurality of wills; that a mutual predication of God and man coexists with a plurality of proper attributes; that co-adoration coexists with a differentiation of eminence; that co-exaltation over all things coexists with a differentiation of digni-ties; and finally that co-domination coexists with a plurality of powers.[53]

In an adequate Christology, then – and of course in the *Itinerarium* Bonaventure presupposes and merely paraphrases one – is found the résumé of every vestige of God, every image of God, every likeness of God and the unity of the differentiated conceptual names of God. Christ is, as it were, the résumé of the cataphatic, for in Christ is all our language of God – indeed Christ *is* the lan-guage of God and in both senses of that ambiguous expression; for Christ is both the Word God speaks to us and the only true word we can speak of God, the Book of Life. It is because the human is the meeting point of all creation that Christ the man is the meeting point of all creation with God and is therefore both the centre, sit-uated at that point in the hierarchy where the human is situated, and the summit to which the human can be raised. The human is therefore both a little less than the angels and raised, through Christ, to the height above them, to an ecstatic oneness with the Godhead, of which the ecstatic love of the Cherubim is but an inadequate metaphor.

It is in this sixth contemplation, therefore, that

consists the perfect illumination of the mind, when, as it were, on the sixth day, it sees man made to the image of God. For if an image is an expressed likeness, then when our mind contemplates in Christ the Son of God, who is by nature the image of the invisible God, our humanity so wonderfully exalted, so ineffably united, and when at the same time it sees united the first and the last, the highest and the lowest, the circum-ference and the centre, the *Alpha* and the *Omega*, the caused and the cause, the Creator and the creature, that is, *the book written within and with-out* (Rev. 1, 8), it has already reached something perfect. Now it arrives at the perfection of its illuminations on the sixth step, as with God on the sixth day. And now nothing further remains but the day of rest on which through transports of the mind the penetrating power of the human mind *rests from all the work that it has done.* (Gen. 2, 2).

53   Ibid., 6, 6.

VI

If in Christ is resumed the full resources of our affirmations of God, so too in Christ are all affirmations transcended. If all creation leads to Christ and finds in Christ the perfect image of God, then Christ leads us to the Father, who is the *Deus absconditus*, hidden in the divine darkness of unknowing.

In the description of that dark ecstasy, Bonaventure is so dependent on Denys as to be satisfied mainly with extended quotation from his *Mystical Theology*. But in two ways Bonaventure effects a radical transformation of his Dionysian source, and the transformation is so effortless as to be almost imperceptible.

The first I will mention only briefly, since it is a matter to be discussed in a later chapter.[54] Both in thought and in imagery Bonaventure's description of the apophatic ecstasy shifts the emphasis from the intellectualism of Denys' mysticism of vision toward the voluntarism of a mysticism of love. Whereas Denys' ecstasy is the *excessus* of self-transcending intellect, Bonaventure's is an ecstasy in which, ultimately, intellect is transcended not by itself but by a transport of desire. The two 'darknesses' therefore differ both as to cause and in the power of the mind in which they occur.

One must be cautious not to overstate this difference. By no means is Bonaventure's mysticism an anti-intellectualism. Boehner is right to say that if Bonaventure is not an intellectual*ist*, he is certainly an intellectual mystic,[55] for, as Bonaventure himself says, the Christian soul deprived of refreshment to the mind is like a body starved of food, 'it fades away and is weakened, becomes deformed and depressed in all its activities: therefore it must be fed'.[56] But in his reading of Denys' *Mystical Theology* he follows rather the revisionary interpretation of Gallus than the text itself, for, like Gallus, he holds that the intellect is engaged in perfect unity with love through every stage of the ascent into God, except when it passes into the final *excessus* into which only love can proceed.[57] When, therefore, Denys says that in the apophatic ecstasy 'all intellectual activities must be relinquished'[58] he means that intellect is transported *as intellect* beyond what it can do by itself into its own daz-

---

[54] See pp. 187–94.   [55] Boehner, *Itin.*, p. 131.
[56] *In Hexaem.*, 17, 6.
[57] See Gallus, *Commentary on the Song of Songs*, in my *Eros and Allegory*, p. 323.
[58] *DN*, 872B.

zling darkness; whereas Bonaventure can quote this same passage and mean: love *takes over from* intellect, leaving it behind.

The second way in which Bonaventure transforms Denys' apophaticism brings us back to the central issues of this chapter, and it consists in the effects on Denys' hierarchicalism of Bonaventure's resolute Christocentrism. For Bonaventure, as we have seen, Christ is the meeting point of all our language about God. But Christ is also the point of juncture of the cataphatic with the apophatic. For if Christ is, on the one hand, the only perfect image of God, he is, on the other, our only access to the unknowability of God. If in Christ is concentrated all our language about God then in Christ is concentrated all the contradictoriness of that language. But if in Christ is found the unity of our language's multiplicity, the reconciliation of its impossible contradictorinesses, it is found there only because in Christ is found the *transitus* from affirmation to negation, from the work of the six days of creation to the silence and the rest of the seventh,[59] from the knowability of the incarnate Son to the unknowability of the Father.

Undoubtedly this Christocentrism is a profound development of the dialectical logic of Denys. But it is not in this, the 'mystical' Christ, that the true radicalness of Bonaventure's transformation of the Dionysian dialectic is to be found. For Bonaventure locates the *transitus* from knowing to unknowing not abstractly in the incarnate Christ as some generalized symbol, for that, after all, is a move at least consistent with Denys' principle that the names of God most aptly representative of the divine transcendence are those which are most 'dissimilar'. More radically still, Bonaventure locates that *transitus* in the broken, crucified Christ, in a 'similarity' so 'dissimilar' as to dramatise with paradoxical intensity the brokeness and failure of all our language and knowledge of God. It is in this, the most radical theological conclusion of his *Itinerarium*, that we find the unity of Bonaventure's Neoplatonic 'exemplarism' with the almost brutal concreteness and historical specificness of his meditations on the life of Christ in the *Lignum Vitae*. For far from their being in any way opposed, the Neoplatonism of the *Itinerarium* is resolved into the historically concrete fact of the Cross, so that the significance of that uniquely individual fact can be opened up into its universal dimensions by the Neoplatonism. No text illuminates

---

[59] *Itin.*, 6, 7.

this thematic and theological unity of his personal love of the human Christ with 'high' Neoplatonic apophaticism more than the words with which Bonaventure closes the *Itinerarium*. It is, he says, necessary that we should

die and enter into this darkness. Let us silence all our care, our desires, and our imaginings. With Christ crucified let us *pass out of this world to the Father* (Jn. 13, 1), so that when the Father is shown to us, we may say with Philip: *It is enough for us* (Jn. 14, 8)...For he who loves this death can see God, for it is absolutely true that *Man shall not see me and live*. (Exod. 33, 20)

VII

I have attended in this chapter principally to the manner in which Bonaventure's mystical theology can be seen as an attempt to harmonise two broad streams of Neoplatonic thought, the Dionysian and the Augustinian. At any rate, the problem which Bonaventure inherited with this double indebtedness was that of the divergent tendencies of an hierarchicalist ontology and of an anthropocentric Christology. And I have suggested that Bonaventure achieves some measure of stability in this synthesis through an adaptation of the Augustinian theme of interiority, a stability which is achieved through his doctrine of the human as microcosm, the human as *minor mundus* in which, through interiorisation, the objective hierarchy of the *maior mundus* is recapitulated.

Nothing in this reading of Bonaventure's *Itinerarium* should be taken as implying that Bonaventure shows the least sign of abandoning the Dionysian hierarchy as ontological. There is simply no evidence of such a tendency of thought. Indeed, as I have argued, if Bonaventure had thought that hierarchy could have been reduced to a metaphor of interiority, then no problem of consistency could have arisen for him which could not have been resolved by means of another metaphor. But Bonaventure does not think of metaphors in these terms as if they were the chosen *devices* of explanation. Hierarchy could function as metaphor through its interiorisation only because hierarchy is the way all things are disposed in the order of the universe.

Moreover, we have seen that in his Christological solution to the problem, the Dionysian dialectics of negativity have a crucial role to play. And those dialectics are, for him, inseparable from hierarchy. Hence, whether one looks at Bonaventure's mysticism from the point of view of its Christological anthropocentrism or from the point of view of his dialectical epistemology, the objective hierarchy of creation is a presupposition.

That having been said, it is also true to say that what predominates in Bonaventure is not hierarchy as objective, but hierarchy interiorised; not the source of the Dionysian dialectics in the hierarchy of creation, but the dialectics applied within the interiorised hierarchy of the soul. Hence, if, penultimately, one wishes to say that Bonaventure's theological achievement lies in the remarkable poise with which he holds together the tensions of the hierarchical and the Christocentric, ultimately one wishes to say that that achievement is also pregnant with another possibility: that the language of interiority and the dialectics of negativity would become detached from their foundations in the Dionysian objective hierarchy of creation. And if Bonaventure himself showed no inclination to exploit this potentiality, there were other, later, Augustinians who most certainly did.

PART TWO

Developments

CHAPTER 6

Eckhart: God and the self

I

Our approach to the development of Western Christian apophatic theology has thus far been severely and narrowly textual, an approach which would have very little justification were our purposes otherwise than with theoretical issues, specifically of the relationship between a metaphorical discourse and the ontological and epistemological conditions of its employment; moreover, with theoretical issues raised by works in the genre of the 'high', technical theological treatise. Had our concerns been with popular piety and spirituality, or with texts written for specific readerships less academically equipped than were their authors, or with texts responsive to immediate and historically specific circumstances, it could not have been seriously proposed to examine them without reference to those historical contingencies. But since Denys and Augustine, Hugh of St Victor, Gallus and Bonaventure wrote their most influential works of spirituality without any *conscious* sense of occasion and as set-pieces intended to stand on their own, it has been at least possible, if not in every way desirable, to consider them in those terms in which they were written.

In the early fourteenth century, however, the apophatic tradition becomes for the first time in its long Christian history embodied in formulations which are regarded with suspicion of heresy. Though it is possible to consider these formulations without regard to their contemporary reception or to the historical conditions which determine it, it is rather less easy to justify doing so. Two cases stand out, those of Marguerite Porete and of Meister Eckhart. On 1 June, 1310, Marguerite Porete, a Beguine of Hainault, was burned at the stake in Paris as a *relapsa* for having continued to possess and to allow the circulation of her work *The Mirror of Simple Souls*.[1] Some years previously, at any rate prior to 1306, the work itself had been consigned to the flames by the Bishop of Cambrai, Guy II, at Valenciennes as containing heretical teaching and Marguerite forbidden to possess or promote it.[2] Doubts about Eckhart's orthodoxy issued in 1329, the year after his death, in Pope John XXII's condemnation of some 27 propositions extracted from his writings. Indeed, it continues to be debated whether the writings of either theologian are capable of an orthodox interpretation.

Having said that it is impossible to ignore contemporary judgements of their heterodoxy − and equally whether those judgements were justified then, or sustainable now − these are questions which will not centrally occupy us in this chapter. Suffice it to say that it is perhaps significant that both wrote in their native vernaculars, Marguerite in Middle French and Eckhart in Middle High German. It is possibly significant too that the one was a woman, and the other fell foul of inquisitors at least partly because his vernacular sermons were preached mainly to women. And it is more than possible that, in particular, the associations both had with the Beguines supplied an *anterior* reason for questioning the orthodoxy of their writings, for the early decades of the fourteenth century was a period of very particular hostility to the Beguine sisterhoods. These possibilities become, finally, something approaching probabilities in view of the evidence that Eckhart knew Marguerite's work[3] and, if he did not wholly approve of it, nonetheless borrowed central ideas and even some characteristic modes of expression from it. In short, the cases of Marguerite and Eckhart may very well be connected not only through their being the common object of a single, concerted anti-Beguine campaign, but internally through a variety of common features of idea and language and conceivably through direct influence of the Beguine upon the Dominican.

[1]   The original French, and the near contemporary Latin texts of the *Mirror* have been edited by Romana Guarnieri and Paul Verdeyen for *Corpus Christianorum, Continuatio Medievalis*, LXIX, Turnholt: Brepols, 1986.

[2]   Guy II was Bishop of Cambrai between 1296 and 1306, so Marguerite's first condemnation must have taken place between those years. We have no date for the writing of the *Mirror* itself.

[3]   Marguerite was burned in 1310. Her inquisitor, the Dominican William Humbert, was living in the Dominican house of St Jacques in Paris in 1311 when Eckhart joined the community upon taking up his second regency in theology at the University. It is impossible that Eckhart could have been ignorant of Marguerite's writing by then, possible that he was acquainted the *Mirror* even before that.

Such aspects of the issue of orthodoxy – though of interest in their own right – concern us only indirectly. For us they arise in a related, but different connection. Both Marguerite and Eckhart situated their *œuvres* firmly within the traditions of apophatic mystical theology whose sources and syntheses we have considered in the first part of this book. We will want to know how far their theologies do in truth 'fit' within those traditions and we must properly begin such an enquiry with the fact that whatever their inquisitors may have thought, or whatever we may now think, both denied that they had departed in any significant way from the mainstream of Dionysian and Augustinian theology.

Yet they did appear to offer a theological challenge to their contemporaries, a challenge which is not to be wholly explained in terms of considerations of ecclesiastical *realpolitik*. And there seems little doubt that what lay at the root of their trouble with inquisitors theologically was not so much the heady mix of mysticism and metaphysics which characterizes them both, as the implications which they appeared to draw from it for ascetical and moral practice. And, for sure, it is here that what is distinctive about the early fourteenth-century development of the apophatic tradition is most easily identified. Contained in the *Mirror* and in some of Eckhart's *German Sermons* is a daring, thoroughly original and often startlingly paradoxical transposition of the dialectics of apophatic theology onto the sphere of ascetical practice, a transposition productive of what may be called an 'apophatic anthropology'. If Eckhart's dialectical theology can be situated recognizably within the continuities of the Augustinian and Dionysian exploitation of the metaphors of 'interiority' and 'ascent', of 'hierarchy' and of 'light' and 'darkness', his ascetical doctrines, at least prima facie, represent a startlingly radical innovation. And not the least startling effect of this transposition is the emergence of a new theme, powerfully introduced by Marguerite and developed systematically by Eckhart, that of 'the self', in particular, that of the 'nothingness' of the self. Indeed, the writings of both are characterized by an idiosyncratic and highly colourful discourse of the soul's identity with the Godhead which, more than anything else, gave theological hostages to contemporary fortune.

Regrettably, space precludes more than cursory comparisons between the manner in which this theme is developed by these two writers; our concerns are principally with Eckhart, and with

Marguerite – who properly deserves a separate study – only in so far as her slightly earlier development of similar themes helps to correct mistaken impressions of Eckhart's uniqueness and originality. It is not clear that either Marguerite Porete or Meister Eckhart would have shared our contemporary perception of them as unique though orthodox any more than they consented to their own contemporaries' judgements of them as unique and therefore heterodox.

II

In the Bull of Condemnation, *In Agro Dominico*,[4] Eckhart is reported as having maintained the startling view

That there is something in the soul that is uncreated and not capable of creation; if the whole soul were such, it would be uncreated and not capable of creation, and this is the intellect.[5]

Curiously, in his defence Eckhart denied having held this view, though the same thought, and virtually the same words, occur in his vernacular sermons with some frequency – a fact which lends credibility to the suspicion that at the time of his trial Eckhart was past his prime intellectually. One sermon recalls the frequency with which he said such things, how

Sometimes I have spoken of a light that is uncreated and not capable of creation and that is in the soul. I always mention this light in my sermons; and this same light comprehends God without a medium, uncovered, naked, as he is in himself.[6]

The metaphor of the 'light of the soul' is at the centre of Eckhart's theology and mysticism. Alternative metaphors proliferate: it is 'a spark of the soul', 'a something', 'the innermost part', the 'fortress of the soul', the 'ground of the soul', a 'refuge of the spirit', a 'silence', a 'desert'. These are the metaphors of what might be called an 'apophatic anthropology', as if to say that there is something unknowable about the self, as much as, in more familiar terms, of an 'apophatic theology', for which God is unknowable. Hence, above all, 'the self' is nameless:

---

[4] The full text of the Bull in English translation is to be found in *The Essential Sermons, Commentaries, Treatises and Defense (Essential Sermons)* trans. and ed. Edmund Colledge and Bernard McGinn, London: SPCK, 1981, pp. 77–81.

[5] Ibid., p. 80. [6] *Sermon 48, Ein Meister Sprichet*, p. 198.

it is neither this nor that, and yet it is something which is higher above this and that than Heaven is above earth. And therefore I give it finer names than I have ever given it before, and yet whatever fine names, whatever words we use, they are telling lies, and it is far above them. It is free of all names, it is bare of all forms, wholly empty and free, as God in himself is empty and free. It is so utterly one and simple, as God is one and simple, that man cannot in any way look into it.[7]

Thus it is nameless with the namelessness of the Godhead itself:

God, who has no name – who is beyond names – is inexpressible and the soul in its ground is also inexpressible, as he is inexpressible.[8]

This light of the soul is an inexhaustible capacity for, and tendency towards, the Godhead itself which, being beyond all names and all distinctions, is beyond even those of the Father, Son and Holy Spirit. Hence, it cannot be satisfied with any image or medium between itself and the Godhead, but must 'break through' into the very ground of God. There,

when all images have departed from the soul and it sees single unity, then the pure being of the soul, passive and resting within itself, encounters the pure formless being of the Divine Unity, which is being beyond all being.[9]

But just there, on 'the simple ground of God', the 'light of the soul' reaches its own ground too, for

there is something which is above the created being of the soul and which is untouched by any createdness, which is to say *nothingness*...It is akin to the divine nature, it is united in itself, it has nothing in common with anything at all...It is a strange land and a desert, and it is more without a name than nameable, more unknown than knowable.[10]

It is notoriously difficult to say how near Eckhart's hyperbolic language drives him to a pantheistic form of identification of the 'ground of God' with the 'ground of the soul'. The Avignon theologians seem to have been in some doubt as to whether Eckhart held such views, for the charge on this score is included in a supplemen-

---

7   *Sermon 2, Intravit Jesus,* ibid., p. 180.
8   Cited in Oliver Davies, *God Within,* London: Darton, Longman and Todd, 1988, p. 50. The source is to be found in J. Quint, ed. and trans. *Meister Eckhart: Deutsche Predigten und Traktate,* München, 1977, pp. 229–30.
9   *Meister Eckhart, Die Deutschen und Lateinischen Werke (DW),* Stuttgart: hrsg. im Auftrage der Deutschen Forschungsgemeinschaft, 1936ff., III, 437-38 (cited in Davies, *God Within,* p. 51). Where I cannot source citations from Eckhart in available English translations I have given their German source, as above (*DW*), in Oliver Davies' translations.
10 Davies, *God Within,* p. 50 (*DW, II,* p. 66).

tary list of two propositions for which, as we have seen, Eckhart disowned responsibility, claiming not to have taught them, and the inquisitors seemed to lack the documentation to disprove Eckhart's contention. Nonetheless, the issue is still alive, since we know that Eckhart did in fact teach them and there can be little doubt that his interrogators held *the propositions* to be unorthodox.

III

Why? For at one level the doctrine that the soul at its highest point touches upon God is, as we have seen, a Christian Neoplatonist commonplace and Eckhart's sources for his own version of it are set firmly within the common mediaeval-Augustinian tradition of divine illumination and Dionysian hierarchy. The soul's powers are in relations of hierarchical subordination to one another, but this

natural order is one in which the highest point of what is inferior touches upon the lowest point of its superior.[11]

At its highest point the soul is intellect and it is this which joins us to God, meeting God in a conversation of erotic mutuality, for it is a 'contact, meeting and union of what is essentially superior with the highest point of its inferior' in which 'both sides kiss each other and embrace in a natural and essential love that is inward and very delightful'.[12]

There is nothing very novel for the Middle Ages, nor even for later traditions, in either the doctrine itself or in the eroticism of the imagery. Apart from Augustine, Eckhart refers to the Jewish theologian, Moses Maimonides, as an authority. But in the sixteenth century Teresa of Avila implies the doctrine that I, in my most interior being, occupy one and the same ground as does the divine being. For Teresa, self-knowledge and the knowledge of God are directly proportional and ultimately are one knowledge in a union in which all distinctions are lost.[13] That, after all, is the implication of the structuring image of the *Interior Castle* itself, for, in the seventh 'dwelling places', where the soul finally rests at its own centre, there is to be found not some substantive 'I' or 'self',

---

[11]   *Parables of Genesis*, 3, 139, Colledge and McGinn, *Essential Sermons*, p. 109.
[12]   *Parables of Genesis*, 3, 146, ibid., p. 113.
[13]   *Interior Castle*, 1.2.8, in *The Collected Works of St Teresa of Avila*, II, trans. Otilio Rodriguez and Kieran Kavanaugh, Washington: ICS, 1980, pp. 291–93.

but the indwelling Trinity of Persons themselves.[14] Thus too, John of the Cross: 'The soul's centre is God', he says baldly[15] and, earlier in the same century, Catherine of Genoa describes how:

Once stripped of all its imperfections, the soul rests in God, *with no characteristics of its own*, since its purification is the stripping away of the lower self in us. *Our being is then God.*[16]

In the fourteenth century, the English anchoress Julian of Norwich spoke of a 'godly wil' which 'never assentid to synne ne never shal',[17] for it is, to use Eckhart's phrase, a 'refuge of the soul', and in Julian's word 'substance', so unbreakably one with God that, she says, 'And I saw no difference atwix God and our substance, but as it were al God.'[18] And in so many words, the theme of the 'deification' of the soul is one on which Eckhart's great Dominican predecessor, Thomas Aquinas, had rung many changes, uniting in so doing the two principal sources on which Eckhart later was to draw, Augustine and Denys.[19] *Some* version of the soul's ultimate identity with God is the common stock in trade of the whole Western mystical tradition, at least until as late as the sixteenth century.

So why was Eckhart's version of it so problematic? The reason was, perhaps, that more often than not he was neglectful of a fundamental qualification of the doctrine of oneness with God which, when added, was permissive of the most hyperbolic language of union, but, when absent, cast into doubt the orthodoxy of the most restrained formulas. When, in the twelfth century, William of St Thierry could speak of the soul's being embraced in the loving embrace of the Persons of the Trinity, united within their love and loving by means of their love, the hyperbole is forgiven – indeed for most of the Middle Ages it is mis-attributed to no less an

---

[14] *Interior Castle*, 7.2.4: 'In the spiritual marriage the union is like what we have when the rain falls from the sky into a river or fount; all is water, for the rain that fell from heaven cannot be divided or separated from the water of the river.'

[15] *The Living Flame of Love*, stanza 1, 12, in *The Collected Works of St John of the Cross*, trans. K. Kavanaugh and O. Rodriguez, Washington: ICS, 1979.

[16] *Purgation and Purgatory*, in *Catherine of Genoa, Purgation and Purgatory, The Spiritual Dialogue*, trans. Serge Hughes, London: SPCK, 1979, p. 80.

[17] For the middle English version I have used *Revelation*, 37, p. 39. For a modern English version, see *Julian of Norwich, Revelations of Divine Love* (Wolters), trans. Clifton Wolters, Harmondsworth: Penguin Books, 1966, p. 118.

[18] *Revelation*, 54, p. 65 (Wolters, p. 157).

[19] '...*necesse est quod solus Deus deificet, communicando consortium divinae naturae per quandam similitudinis participationem...*' *ST*, 1-2ae, q.112, a.1, corp.

authority than Bernard of Clairvaux – but it is forgiven because William was careful to add a precise, and time-worn qualification. 'The man of God', he says,

is found worthy to become not God, but *what God is*, that is to say *man becomes through grace what God is by nature.*[20]

For grace, even the uncreated grace of union, is received by the soul in a created, finite faculty. We are, according to this traditional formula, only as like God as a finite creature can be made to be.

Not so, it seems, for Eckhart. Eckhart's thought seems to burst through the conventional formulas of a William and later of Thomas Aquinas. It is true that in a few places Eckhart does use the same formula.[21] And it is true that in some of the Latin works we find more moderate metaphors of union than those to be found, with such frequency, in the German *Sermons*. Thus, in the *Parables of Genesis* he speaks of the soul's union with God as being like the 'dialogue' between a person and his image in a mirror, which, if it suggests an identity of representation, at least implies a separate identity of image and imaged.[22] And in another metaphor of dialogue he says:

to become, to be created and to be produced by God are the same thing as to hear him commanding and obey, as well as to answer, speak and converse with him when he speaks.[23]

This at least implies the duality of persons in dialogue. But alongside these images we have to place the more formal statements that my ground is so identical with the ground of God that I existed with the Godhead before all creation, and so eternally; and because eternally, I could be said to have assisted with the Godhead in the very generation of the Persons of the Trinity:

I say more: He [the Father] gives birth not only to me, his Son, but he gives birth to me as himself and himself as me and to me as his being and nature. In the innermost source, there I spring out in the Holy Spirit, where there is one life and one being and one work.[24]

[20] William of St Thierry, *The Golden Epistle*, II, xvi, 263, trans. Theodore Berkeley, Kalamazoo: Cistercian Publications, 1980, p. 96. Italics mine.
[21] *On Detachment*, Colledge and McGinn, *Essential Sermons* p. 285. See also *Sermon 6, Intravit Iesus*, in M. O'C. Walshe, *Meister Eckhart: German Sermons and Treatises*, London and Dulverton: Element Books, I, p. 59: 'God alone is free and uncreated, and thus He alone is like the soul in freedom, though not in uncreatedness, for she is created.'
[22] *Parables of Genesis*, 3, 150, Colledge and McGinn, *Essential Sermons*, p. 115.
[23] Ibid., 3, 160, ibid., p. 120.   [24] Davies, *God Within*, p. 57, *DW*, I, p. 109-10.

Here is found no qualifying phrase that my 'divinisation' is of grace, not of nature. And yet, even without the qualification Eckhart feels he can say yet more. For not merely does the Father give birth to me in the Son, before all that I was in the Godhead in its absolute, primitive oneness, a oneness which 'precedes' all the differentiations of the Trinity of Persons, that 'seething and boiling' or *bullitio* as Eckhart calls it.[25] Therefore I was in the Godhead before ever I was created; before I was created I was uncreated. For my existence in the Godhead is beyond all distinctions, in the undifferentiated oneness of the Godhead, it cannot be distinct from the Godhead as such. Therefore I existed in the Godhead *before God*, in God's very 'own ground'. If I was there in that ground at the birth of the Trinity, *a fortiori* I was there before my own creation. 'When', therefore,

I stood in my first cause, then I had no 'God', and then I was my first cause. I wanted nothing, I longed for nothing, for I was an empty being and the only truth I enjoyed was the knowledge of myself...But when I went out from my own free will and received my created being, then I had a 'God', for before there were any creatures God was not 'God', but he was what he was.[26]

These formulas seem reckless and heterodox, taken by themselves – which, Eckhart complained, is how his inquisitors did take them. And no responsible interpreter can justify such a procedure. Alongside the condemned proposition must be placed its context, for in the very same passage in which he speaks of the uncreatedness of the soul's 'ground', Eckhart explicitly denies that the soul as such is *wholly* uncreated. For though, he says, there is a 'place' in the soul which is uncreated and uncreatable, that is to say the intellect; and though it follows that *were* the soul nothing but intellect then the whole soul *would be* uncreated, 'this is not the case. For the rest of the soul is dependent on time, and thus is touched by createdness and is itself created.'[27] Furthermore, in *Sermon* 48, Eckhart resists the apparently dualist implications of this solution, suggesting that the soul is divided into two parts by as radical a division as there could possibly be: the division between the cre-

[25] *Commentary on Exodus*, in *Meister Eckhart, Teacher and Preacher* (*Teacher and Preacher*) ed. Bernard McGinn, Frank Tobin and Elvira Borgstadt, New York: Paulist Press, 1986, p. 46.
[26] *Sermon* 52, *Beati pauperes spiritu*, Colledge and McGinn, *Essential Sermons*, p. 200.
[27] *DW* I, 220, quoted in Davies, *God Within*, p. 49.

ated and the uncreated. For though it is true, he says, that this 'light of the soul' is closer in oneness with God than is any other part of the soul, nonetheless, as one of the soul's powers, this light is no less a created capacity than are any of the soul's other powers, such as 'hearing or sight or anything else which can be affected by hunger or thirst, frost or heat'.[28] And in a tellingly anti-dualist phrase he gives the reason: 'It is the simplicity of my being which is the cause of that'.[29]

In view of these distinct rhetorical emphases, therefore, the one on the uncreatedness of part of the soul (intellect), the other on the unity of the soul as created, it can be difficult to say where Eckhart truly stands. It looks, prima facie, as if Eckhart wants to eat his cake and have it, to say both that I am a created temporal self and that part of me is uncreated and eternal, thereby putting at risk the simplicity and unity of the soul which, nonetheless, he emphatically affirms. For both the created and the uncreated appear to coexist in me, temporal created being as I am. Huston Smith appears to admire this paradox, seeing in it not an unresolved ambiguity but a valuable analysis of the human condition. For on Smith's account, Eckhart holds human beings to be 'divided creatures. A part of ourselves…is continuous with God, while the balance remains categorically distinct from him.'[30] This, however, is a formula, disintegrative of the divine and the human in the human, which Eckhart would most certainly have rejected. It compounds the misinterpretation of Eckhart's intentions to conclude that, for Eckhart, the question which each human being must face is 'With which part do we identify?' And the error is completed if we suppose that there is anything at all Eckhartian in the reply Smith supposes he would have given: 'Mystics are persons who, like Eckhart, identify with the God element in themselves emphatically.'[31]

If it is a puzzle to know how Eckhart means to speak of the intersection of the divine and the human within the human, the one thing that can be said is that, for Eckhart, I could not find my identity *in the choice between them.* Any theological position which requires me to choose between the divine and the human, between my uncreated self and my created, must itself be, for Eckhart, a symptom of the disintegration of the self. Eckhart states clearly that

[28] Sermon 48, *Ein Meister Sprichet,* Colledge and McGinn, *Essential Sermons,* p. 198.
[29] Ibid., p. 198.   [30] Ibid., p. xiv.   [31] Ibid., p. xiv.

the occurrence of the disjunction between the created, temporal, embodied self on the one hand, and the highest part of the soul, its ground, on the other, can only be the result of that fracturing of the intimacy between God and the soul which we call 'sin'. Because sin destroys our union with God it destroys the unity of the soul within itself, it destroys the *persona*. And so he argues in *The Parables of Genesis*:

when the bond and order of the height of the soul to God was dissolved through the injury of sundering sin...it followed that all the powers of the soul, inferior reason and the sensitive faculty as well were separated from contact with the rule of superior reason.[32]

And in a splendidly precise and homely image he illustrates his indebtedness to those Neoplatonic principles of internalised hierarchy which underlie his argument for the simplicity of the soul:

When a magnet is touched by a needle it hands its power over to the needle so that when this needle touches another with its point it attracts it and calls 'come' to it. The second needle adheres to the first with its head, and the same is true in the case of the third and the fourth, as far as the power handed over and absorbed by the magnet reaches.[33]

In short, it is the soul's contact and union in its highest part with God which is the power by which it coheres in the simplicity and unity of all its powers. Consequently, it will be only for that soul which has lost its union with God through sin for whom there could possibly be any *choice* between the divine and the human elements in it. For the soul in union with God, the choice could not arise.

It is, then, very far from being an implication of Eckhart's doctrine of the divine element in the soul that the mystic is required to choose between that divine element and the created human. Indeed, the implication of Eckhart's doctrine as a whole is the reverse: that a spirituality or mysticism constructed upon the necessity of any such choice, whether between spirit and flesh, body and soul, interiority and exteriority, above all between God and creation, is a symptom not of the absoluteness of the claims of the divine over/against the human, but of a sin-induced false-consciousness which is unable to see the divine *except as* over/against the human.

[32] *Parables of Genesis*, 3, 144, ibid., p. 112.
[33] Ibid., 3, 142, p. 111.

And in a supremely pacifying image Eckhart describes the inner harmony and integration of the powers of the soul in union with God, in the language of the Song of Songs, as a 'mutual touch' and a 'kiss'

in which the superior gazes on the inferior and vice-versa. They kiss and embrace each other in this touch and encounter with a love which is natural and essential.[34]

So what are we to say? Merely 'on the one hand this' and 'on the other hand that'? Are we to allow Eckhart to eat his cake and have it? Recent scholars have been no more satisfied to leave the *aporia* unresolved than they ought to be, and various attempts have been made to find a reconciliation of the apparent conflict within the consistencies of Eckhart's own thought.

IV

The proposition that the soul's powers are only truly integrated with one another when its highest power, whether the *apex intellectus* or the *apex affectus*, is in union with God is an innocent enough Augustinian platitude of hierarchy: it is found, as we have seen, not only in Augustine but also in Thomas Gallus and Bonaventure. If the problem of the consistency of Eckhart's theology is to be resolved by requiring either of the conflicting propositions to give ground, it is therefore the proposition that the *apex intellectus* is uncreated which, to a contemporary, would have seemed the obvious one to give way. For his contemporaries it must have sounded as paradoxical a statement as it does to us, risking, as it appeared to do, a blurring of the radical transcendence of God in relation to the human creature.

Is there any way of preserving the essential meaning of Eckhart's statements on the 'uncreated light' while reducing that degree of paradox which threatens the consistency of his position as a whole? The ingenuity of contemporary Eckhart revisionism is impressive, and commonly serves to derive an affirmative answer. It seems worthwhile to explore some of these 'benign' interpretations with a view to achieving a more balanced reading of Eckhart than some of his contemporaries were prepared to permit.

---

[34] Ibid., 3, 146, p. 113.

Oliver Davies notes that much which seems most paradoxical in Eckhart's writing – paradoxical, that is to say, by the standards of formal Christian orthodoxy – appears less so when understood within the context of his preaching work, than it would were it read as an attempt at precise doctrinal statement. Davies speaks, therefore, of Eckhart's 'poeticisation' of theological language and of his preaching discourse as a kind of 'conceptual poetry' in which that which is done by means of a technical vocabulary in a formal treatise is reworked in the preaching context as image and metaphor.[35] Davies notes Eckhart's extensive use of the tropes of a rhetorical genre – paradox, oxymoron, chiasmus, neologism – and, rightly, emphasizes the character of Eckhart's sermons, especially the vernacular sermons, as acts of *communication*, acts which must – and perhaps may legitimately – use almost any devices to stimulate insight, because what matters is the end, not the means, the insight, not the technical accuracy of the linguistic devices. As Davies puts it:

We are justified in calling this process the 'poeticisation' of language because it involves the loosening of the relation between signifier and signified, and thus the foregrounding of language, as bearer of meaning, rather than meaning itself – a phenomenon which is usually judged to be a prime characteristic of poetic texts.[36]

There is, it would seem, some justice in this view. Often Eckhart seems careless of the meaning of what he says in its own right. What appears to matter to him is the meaning which what he says is capable of evoking in the minds of his listeners, as if what mattered to him was not the exactness of *his* meaning, but the exactness with which his language evokes meaning in them. It is language as *doing* something which the preacher attends to; it is language as *meaning* something which is of principal concern to the teacher. Eckhart the preacher, therefore, can judge with precision what his saying *does*, even while Eckhart the teacher recognizes the possible imprecision of what his saying *says*. And at any rate, in certain controlled contexts there is nothing necessarily irresponsible in acknowledging these differences between the discourses of teacher and preacher.

Moreover, there is another consideration, noted by McGinn,[37] which adds to the plausibility of this way of reading Eckhart's more

---

[35] Davies, pp. 180-84.   [36] Ibid., p. 180.
[37] McGinn, Tobin and Borgstadt, *Teacher and Preacher*, p. 15.

'hyperbolic' statements. McGinn notes that for all his dependence on Augustine, Eckhart's apophaticism far outstrips that of Augustine. In what is probably his most outspokenly 'apophatic' statement, Augustine is still relatively moderate:

> Have we spoken or announced anything worthy of God? Rather I have done nothing but wish to speak: if I have spoken, I have not said what I wished to say. Whence do I know this, except because God is ineffable? If what I said were ineffable, it would not be said. And for this reason God should not be said to be ineffable, for when this is said something is said. And a contradiction in terms is created, since if that is ineffable which cannot be spoken, then that is not ineffable which can be called ineffable. This contradiction is to be passed over in silence rather than resolved verbally. For God, although nothing worthy may be spoken of him, has accepted the tribute of human voice and wished us to take joy in praising him with our words.[38]

As McGinn says, Augustine's advice that the necessary contradictoriness of theological language should be 'passed over in silence' was followed neither by him nor by his successors. For sure, we have seen that for the mainstream apophatic tradition in Western Christianity the strategy of the apophatic consisted in a deliberate practice of straining to speak about God, in the purposive stretching of the discourse of theology to those limits at which it snaps, in the contriving of that paradox and contradictoriness on the other side of which there is only silence. Hence, while it is certainly not true that in a Denys or in a *Cloud* Author, contradiction is 'passed over in silence', it is true to say that for both silence is the goal, paradox and contradiction the means to it; ineffability is what is sought, the breakdown of language the route; oxymoron the means, unutterableness what is achieved by it.

In a certain sense, then, the apophatic tradition seeks by means of speech to pass over into silence. And in the course of expounding what one might call the 'classical logic' of this strategy, I have argued that there really is no such thing as 'apophatic' *language* at all. For the 'apophatic' is what is achieved, whether by means of affirmative or by means of negative discourse, when language *breaks down*. The apophatic is the recognition of how this 'silence' lies, as it were, all around the perimeter of language, perhaps in the way that the spaces between the piers of a mediaeval church

---

[38] *De Doctrina Christiana*, 1.6 in *On Christian Doctrine*, trans. D. W. Robertson, New York: Macmillan, 1958, pp. 10-11.

can be seen to shape the solids, as much as the solid piers shape the spaces.

Now what might be said to distinguish the language of Eckhart from that of Denys is that in one way Denys' apophatic strategy is nearer to Augustine's than is Eckhart's. Denys is, as it were, content to let theological language break down under the weight of its internal contradictoriness, and if he does not exactly 'pass over' the contradictions 'in silence', it is his strategy to let *language* pass over into a silence of its own making. Whereas there is in Eckhart a certain rhetorical strenuousness: he twists the discourse, breaks it up, recomposes it. His rhetorical devices are *artifices*. Whereas Denys *lets* language collapse into silence and through the cessation of speech express the apophatic, Eckhart wants to force the imagery to *say* the apophatic. Eckhart cannot let the apophatic be. Hence he is open to the Augustinian objection that he is trying to get the ineffable to mean something, to say what is unsayable about God: or at any rate, he would be open to this objection were it not that he knows perfectly well that the unsayable cannot be placed within the grasp of speech. Yet he will use speech, necessarily broken, contradictory, absurd, paradoxical, conceptually hyperbolic speech, to bring to insight the ineffability of God.

If Eckhart's linguistic ambitions therefore vault over those which the apophatic tradition had accepted as appropriate, the expression of this linguistic 'excessiveness' will be observable in the hyperbolic character of his imagery. The *nimietas* of his language will be seen less as a technical inaccuracy within the composition of scholastic doctrinal formulas, more as a feature of an essentially *rhetorical* discourse, a device of imagery whose strategy is arousal of insight, a feature of his language as speech act, rather than of its semantic character.

As an explanation of the strategy of the vernacular sermons – in which are to be found the most problematic formulations of Eckhart's teaching – this account seems plausible. And it has to be said that Davies does not offer more than an explanation. But if what explains Eckhart's rhetorical hyperbole is incorporated within a *justification* of his strategy, this explanation is more problematic. After all, if a speaker is primarily concerned with what what he says *does*, and only secondarily with what what he says *means*, nonetheless it is only in and through the meaning of what he says that his speech acts. A justification of Eckhart's strategy, on the account just given, would come perilously close to a redescription of a preaching technique less as poetry than as propaganda in which no restrictions on truth or meaning are permitted to inhibit the achievement of belief in the propagandised: and this is propaganda regardless of whether the belief induced is true or false.

Such would be a poor defence of Eckhart's language. Nor may Eckhart properly be charged with having conceded to so extreme a degree of rhetorical licentiousness. When Eckhart says that there is part of the soul which is uncreated, or that there is an uncreated light in the soul and that it is intellect, it is proper to take him as meaning what he says. And what he says means: the intellect is not distinguishable in its character of being a 'nothing' from the divine nature which is 'nothing'. We will attempt some interpretation of what *that* means later in this chapter. For the time being, let us note that Davies' very proper concern to identify the distinct levels at which Eckhart's language works does little to settle questions concerning the coherence of his thought, whether in respect of its internal consistency or in relation to the received theological traditions of his day.

Other lines of reinterpretation are more directly related to his doctrine as such. In the first instance, it seems reasonable to moderate at least some of the paradox of Eckhart's teaching, and so gain for his position a greater degree of consistency, by experimenting with a shift of metaphor. It seems that Eckhart resented his accusers' way of construing his talk of the 'uncreated something' in the soul by means of the metaphors of 'place' and 'piece', since this, McGinn suggests, appeared to imply that 'he held that part of the soul was created and another part uncreated'.[39] If, therefore, there is evidence of Eckhart's unhappiness with spatial metaphors[40] it might help to replace them with an alternative metaphor of two 'dimensions' of a person's being, one created, one uncreated.

From one point of view – or on one axis, or dimension – the soul is uncreated. From another, the soul is created. The human, created, finite subject is not, on this account, a self divided between two parts of itself, the one, uncreated intellect, the rest, the lower

---

[39] Colledge and McGinn, *Essential Sermons*, p. 42. See also his footnote 123, p. 305.
[40] Though he can hardly be excused all responsibility for his accusers' use of it, since perhaps inevitably he himself talked of this light's being 'in' the soul, *Sermon* 48, Colledge and McGinn, *Essential Sermons*, p. 198.

created faculties, so that the person is required to choose, as Huston Smith put it, between which part of herself to identify with. Rather, the finite subject is a point of intersection between two dimensions of itself as a whole, between itself as uncreated and itself as created, an intersection which can be said to occur 'in' the intellect because it is only by means of the intellect that this intersection can be known and, as it were, taken up within the finite createdness of the self.

This shift in interpretation, or something like it, seems to be that which McGinn has in mind when he draws attention to the importance Eckhart attached both in his writings and in his *Defence* to the 'reduplicative *in quantum* principle', that is to say the principle of 'in so far as'.[41] There is no doubt of the importance Eckhart attached to this principle for he makes clear in the *Defence* that an understanding of it is the first of the three technical requirements for an adequate understanding of his whole theological and spiritual project. But it was not unique to Eckhart.

Thomas Aquinas had used the same logical tool to powerful effect in his Christology in order to show the consistency of the variety of things faith, and Chalcedon in particular, required the believer to say about the unity of two natures in the one person of Christ. For, Thomas had argued, 'Christ died on the Cross' is true, 'Christ was God' is true, therefore, 'God died on the Cross' is true. But these three truths taken together cannot be held to entail the truth of 'God died' *simpliciter*. For it was not *in so far as* Christ was God that Christ died on the Cross, for he died on the Cross *in so far as* he was man. And the logic of this argument is sound. For, as Thomas points out, in the subject position, the name 'Christ' refers to the concrete individual Person who was God and man, so that what is predicated of Christ is predicated of the person who was both. But the predicate '...died on the Cross' is reduplicative: it was only in so far as the man Christ (who was God) died that God died; not in so far as the God Christ (who was man) died, that God died.[42]

Eckhart himself explains:

the words 'in so far as', that is, a reduplication, exclude from the term in question everything that is other or foreign to it even according to rea-

---

[41] *Defense*, Colledge and McGinn, *Essential Sermons*, p. 72.
[42] *ST*, 3a, q.16, aa. 11-12.

son...Although in God the Father essence and paternity are the same, he does not generate [the Son] in so far as he is essence, but in so far as he is Father, even though the essence is the root of the generation.[43]

How might the use of this principle help to interpret Eckhart's position? Here again we can take up a suggestion of McGinn's that Eckhart's true intention in speaking of the soul in so far as it is uncreated, was to advert to 'the virtual existence of the ground of the soul in God'.[44]

The proposition that all created beings existed eternally but 'virtually' in the mind of God was a theological truism and it is plausible to suggest that Eckhart's language of uncreatedness in the soul is but a characteristically vigorous and relentless exploitation of this truism. The analogy most prevalent in mediaeval theology was that of the creative artist, especially the architect, whose creative activity, it was supposed, could be conceived of as proceeding from the 'idea' of what he was going to build, through various acts of making, to the finished building which embodied the idea. The building therefore existed 'first', but 'virtually', in the mind of the architect, subsequently in its independent, 'real', existence. 'Virtually', on this account, therefore has the force of 'existing' in the maker's *power (virtus)* to make it. In the same way, God the creator was thought to possess the ideas of all created things prior to making them in her absolute power.

Thus far the analogy was thought to hold. But two features distinguish human creativity from the divine. The first is that in the human case we can make sense of the creative idea's existing 'prior to' the work of art made. In the case of creation we cannot. On this point Eckhart appealed to Augustine's famous discussion of time and creation in *Confessions*, 11.12.14, where Augustine demonstrates that there can be no sense to the question 'what was God doing before he made heaven and earth?' For if time is itself a created thing, there cannot be any time 'preceding' creation and there could have been nothing God was doing 'prior to' creation. 'You made all time; you are before all time; and the "time", if such we may call it, when there was no time was not time at all.'[45]

---

[43] *Defense*, in Colledge and McGinn, *Essential Sermons*, p. 72.
[44] McGinn, Tobin and Borgstadt, *Teacher and Preacher*, p. 42.
[45] *Confessions* 11.13. Pine-Coffin's translation is very free. A more literal rendering might be: 'You made all time and you are before all time, nor was there any time when time was not.'

The second qualification of the architectural analogy has to do with the fact that in the case of a human maker, the mind which devises the 'idea' and the idea devised are distinct identities. Designs come and go, alternatives can be considered and discarded, modified and decided between. The mind which thinks these alternatives must therefore be distinct from the alternatives which it thinks. Moreover, in a human artist the design envisaged and the power to produce a building to that design are unfortunately all too obviously distinct. But in God nothing is distinct from God. God *is* her ideas, and her ideas, even of created things, are nothing other than the self-knowledge of God, in whom the knower and the self known are identical. Nor can God envisage something he cannot produce, for again, the idea and the *virtus* are identical with each other and with God.[46] Therefore, Eckhart concludes, my 'idea', that is to say, my virtual existence in God, was identical with God, and I was everything that God is – eternal, infinite, beyond all description, nameless. Hence, too, in my virtual existence I was there at the generation of the Persons of the Trinity and even, virtually, was present at my own birth in the act of my creation. For it was the eternal 'I', identical with God's thought and power, that God created so as to exist temporally, finitely and contingently.

Construed as amounting to no more than this, Eckhart's doctrine does little more than stretch to its limits, with addition of much poetry and some drama, the language of a conventional mediaeval doctrine. It is in just such a case as this that Davies' description of Eckhart's theology as a species of 'conceptual poetry' is most plausible. But it is in just such a case that one is also inclined to question the implications of that description, since if Eckhart had truly said no more than this – or no more than can be interpreted in this way – then though we cannot imagine his *liking* the poetic hyperbole, it is hard to see how even a Thomas Aquinas could have taken theological exception to his teaching.

But of course no one supposes that Eckhart was merely engaged in a homilectic dressing up of a conventional platitude. In any case, far from its being the case that Eckhart is 'saved' from the most extreme implications of this conclusion by the *in quantum* prin-

---

[46] The famous schoolchild's conundrum 'Can God create a weight heavier than he can lift?' is incoherent. The expression 'a weight greater than God can lift' does not mean anything and so does not describe something God cannot do.

ciple, that principle actually draws his statements into them. His use of the principle in *Sermon* 48 does indeed secure the conclusion that I am not a *wholly* uncreated being, but it nonetheless also entails that I *am now* uncreated not merely that 'before' I was created I *was* uncreated. For the logic of his reduplicative *in quantum* is not that of his counterfactual conditional. Eckhart's conditional 'If I were wholly intellect I would be wholly uncreated' taken together with the counterfactual 'I am not wholly intellect', yields, certainly, the conclusion that I am not wholly uncreated. But the 'in so far as I am intellect I am uncreated' entails that I am uncreated, and whether the 'in so far as' is metaphorised as 'parts' or 'dimensions' can make no difference from this point of view.

Moreover, this is not a case of Eckhart's being forced by logic into a position which he would otherwise have resisted. It would not be enough, for Eckhart, to acknowledge merely his *origins* in the divine creative idea of him. For Eckhart is relentlessly drawing out the implications, as he sees them, of a fully consistent Neoplatonic doctrine: that what I most fully and truly *am*, in my contingent, created existence, is what I *was* in my source. My true being, intellect, is not merely divine but identical with the Godhead in which there can be no possibility of distinctions.

v

We must ask, then, why exactly it is intellect which is the uncreated element in me. The answer to this question may be found, at least partially, in another of Eckhart's many debts to Augustine, and in this connection specifically to Augustine's doctrine of divine illumination. Here again, and again typically, Eckhart derives conclusions from that doctrine which go far beyond any Augustine himself could have envisaged or would have allowed, but it is in Augustine that they have their origin.

For Augustine, as we have seen, the presence in the *mens* of the divine light of eternal Truth is demonstrated by our ordinary secular powers of contingent rational judgement. We could not, Augustine argued, make the judgements which we do about changeable things were it not for the presence within us of that eternal, unchanging Truth. And we can therefore in some way, that is, pre-reflexively, know that Truth itself *in* the finite mutable judgements which we make. But more than that, by a work of critical reflection upon those judgements and their grounds in the Truth itself, we can encounter the presence in us of that Light 'directly' as if 'in a moment of awe' – a possibility which can occur only in the highest part of the soul, the *acies mentis* or *intellectus*, to which that Light is directly present.

That Light, we said, is 'in us but not of us'. That is to say, the divine Light is a necessity for the exercise of our native rational powers in their native rational activities, and so we can say that it is 'in' us. But it is not 'of' us, because it is not itself one of our powers. For which reason the metaphor of 'inwardness' which describes the process of reflection as it reaches back into the deepest recesses of myself, is transformed into the metaphor of 'ascent' just at that point where the divine light and my *intellectus* intersect most intimately. For there, where I am most myself in interiority is where I pass over into that which is not myself, but infinitely 'above' me, the light I am in. Where I end, God begins. But nothing could have induced Augustine to conclude from this that there is any place in me where I am God or that intellect is itself the light by which it is illuminated.

Eckhart, however, does say this. And he makes the move which gets him to his position from Augustine's by means of a characteristic and distinctly non-Augustinian step. In Eckhart's view, for a being which *has* intellect, its existence *is* intellect. For a being capable of knowing, its 'to be' [*esse*] *is* to know. In his early Parisian *Disputed Questions* Eckhart had argued that the highest name of God was *esse* ('existence') *and so* intellect. And this identification of being with knowing was perhaps the most fundamental philosophical prop to the whole Eckhartian theological structure.

Where did he get the idea from? Apart from sources which Oliver Davies has postulated in the work of the thirteenth-century Dominican Dietrich von Frieberg,[47] the identification of being with knowing is most probably the outcome of his own reflections on that Aristotelian doctrine which we saw, in an altogether different connection, was so important to Bonaventure: 'The mind is in some way all things'. What Aristotle meant by this formula was that for the mind to know something was to 'become' it, not of course materially, but intentionally. For me to become a particular known thing in the manner of existence the thing known possesses

---

[47] Davies, *Meister Eckhart*, pp. 91-93.

in re would make it impossible for me to become, and so know, anything else. For if when I perceived a green object my perceiving itself became green, then it would be impossible for me to know a red object as well. Indeed, it would be impossible for me to *know* even the green object.

For on the Aristotelian–Thomist principle that *eadem est scientia oppositorum*, the knowledge of any particular thing is *a fortiori* the knowledge of its contrary. Thus, to perceive a thing as green is necessarily to perceive it in contrast with what is not green, for not to be able to see green's difference from other colours is not to be able to see green as green. Therefore if to know a thing is to become it, then the becoming cannot be the coming to possess that thing's existence *in re*. For nothing can become *in re* simultaneously both a thing and its contrary. It follows that in order to become what I know intentionally, it must be the case that I do not become that thing really.

What Eckhart derives from this Aristotelian argument is one of his more startlingly 'rhetorical' doctrines: 'intellect, as such, is a nothing'. But the fact that it rests on so careful and technical an analysis of the nature of knowledge shows that it is meant as a studied conclusion. Eckhart derives the conclusion from the Aristotelian argument in the following way: if to know a thing is to become it intentionally, and if to become something intentionally is not to become it *in re*; and if the mind can know all things, then it follows that the mind cannot be anything at all *in re*. But to say that there is nothing at all that the mind is, is to say that it is *nothing*. The mind's existence is purely intentional. Its being *is* to know.[48]

In this respect the intellect is therefore indistinguishable from the divine. For no intellect can be of any other nature than identical with its existence. Of course, of no other being can this be said. Of no being except in so far as it is intellect can this be said. But *as* intellect, no distinction can be made between it and God.

---

[48] Of course Aristotle would have considered this argument to be patently fallacious. The mind, for Aristotle, *is* a 'something' *in re*. What his argument proves is not that intellect is no kind of thing at all, for it quite obviously is a thing of a certain kind. The 'nothingness' of intellect refers to its character as intentional, not to its existence *in re*. Eckhart is able to draw the conclusion that intellect is no kind of thing *in re* only because, unlike Aristotle, he holds that the *esse* of intellect consists in its character of being intellect [*esse est intellectus*], so that intellect has no manner of existence except its intentional character. And this doctrine, if Davies is right, Eckhart appears to owe to an arch-Augustinian Dietrich von Frieberg.

Consequently the human intellect, in so far as it is intellect, is for Eckhart what Augustine denied it to be, namely identical with the light by which it knows, the eternal Truth of God. It is a light, moreover, which is a 'nothing', an 'emptiness', a 'desert', it is formless and featureless and it is all these things with the nothingness, the emptiness and the desert-like formlessness and featurelessness of the Godhead. They cannot be distinguished, for 'with this power (intellect)', Eckhart says, 'the soul works in nonbeing and so follows God who works in nonbeing'.[49]

But we might contest: to be 'indistinguishable from' is not the same as to be 'identical with', as two exactly similar coins cannot be told apart, but *a fortiori* are two. Indiscernibles are not necessarily identical. Why could Eckhart not more simply have said, in line with the formula of William of St Thierry, that the intellect is not *God*, but is *what God is*, that the intellect is finitely and in a creaturely way all that God is infinitely and as Creator? Or are we to say, again, that that is all that Eckhart means, and that the rest is hyperbole?

To the last question we must say: scarcely. Eckhart was perfectly familiar with such distinctions and there can only be one reason why, more often than not, he did not make them. They failed to capture the full force of his thought. The answer to the first question is more complex but discoverable from an anachronistic, but still illuminating study of his statements about the identity of the *apex intellectus* with the Godhead alongside those of others, in particular of Julian of Norwich, who is capable of statements subtly close to, but radically different from Eckhart's.

VI

William of St Thierry had maintained, we saw, that the perfected soul is indiscernibly one with God, and is distinct in only one way, as the created is from the uncreated. For what God is by nature we are only by grace. And grace is divinising, divine, but not God. In so far as we are divinised by grace we become indistinguishable in what we are from what God is, but our existence remains radically created. We cannot be, in *any* dimension, God. Hence, in our highest powers, in what Julian calls our 'substance', we can become by

49 *Sermon 9, Quasi stella matutina*, McGinn, Tobin and Borgstadt, *Teacher and Preacher*, p. 258.

grace such that nothing in us serves as a way of distinguishing us from God *except that* we are created and God is not. This is how Julian puts the same thought:

> Our soule is made to be Gods wonyng place and the wonyng place of the soule is God, which is onmade. And hey vnderstondyng it is inwardly to sen and to knowen that God which is our maker wonyth in our soule; and heyer vnderstondyng it is inwardly to sen and to knowen our soule, that is made, wonyth in Gods substance; of which substance, God, we arn that we arn.[50]

The statement that our soul in its substance is what God is in hers, carries no risks for Julian. When she adds, therefore, that she 'saw no difference atwix God and our substance, but as it were al God,'[51] her position remains squarely within the tradition. For to say that there is no difference *to be seen* between our substance and God's is to say that there is no distinction that we can give an account of, not that there is no distinction. Indeed, she goes on to say: 'and yet myn vnderstonding toke that oure substance is in God: that is to sey, that God is God, and our substance *is a creture in God*'.[52]

And Julian does not say that there is no distinction between God and the soul. She says that there is only one thing by which they are distinguished, and that is as created and uncreated beings are distinguished. And if this is true, then of course she is quite right to to say that this not a distinction she was able to 'see'.

Here, we are back in the heartlands of the Neoplatonic dialectics. In our discussion of Denys' *Mystical Theology* we noted how 'distinction' must ultimately fail of God. Distinctions between creatures we can give an account of. We can give an account of the difference between a sheep and a human because they differ as kinds of animal. We know from what sheep are and what humans are how they differ; we know from what red and green are how they differ; and we know from what animals are and what colours are how humans and sheep differ from red and green. And so on: among creatures there are different kinds of difference and our language is a structure of differentiations at a multiplicity of levels. All this we have discussed earlier along with the proposition that, in general, for any difference we can give an account of, there is something that difference is made out in respect of. But that is pre-

---

[50] *Revelation*, 54, p. 65 (Wolters, p. 157).   [51] Ibid.

[52] Ibid. (Wolters, p. 157).

cisely the reason why we cannot make out the difference between the created and the uncreated.

For the predicate '...is a created X' marks no distinction *in kind* from '...is an X'. There is no difference in kind between a tree, a created tree and an uncreated tree, any more than there is a difference in kind between an existent tree and a non-existent tree. If there were such differences in kind, as McCabe points out, then God could not create a tree; he could create only a different kind of thing, namely a created tree.[53] For the tree God was going to create would be one kind of tree – being as yet not created – and the tree God does create would be another, that is, not the tree he was going to create.

From the fact that our language gives us no hold on the distinction between the created and the uncreated, it does not follow that there is no distinction. Language fails to mark the distinction not because there is none but because the gulf is too wide. It is because there cannot be anything to distinguish the created and the uncreated *as*, it is because there is no conceivable standard of comparison to measure the created and the uncreated against, that we cannot utter the contrast between them. The distinction is unutterably great. Hence, Julian cannot 'see' it.

On the other hand, Julian's language of the oneness of the soul's substance with God's substance is rather reinforced than thereby undermined. For Julian, we remind ourselves, the soul's substance differs from the divine substance *only* as created from uncreated. In our 'substance' we are in a created way all that God is in an uncreated way. There is therefore *no* way in which we can utter the distinction between God's substance and ours. We cannot distinguish between God and the soul as kinds of thing, for though our soul is a thing of a kind, God is not. Nor can we distinguish between God and the soul as individuals; for though my soul is one and distinct numerically from yours (your soul plus my soul equals two souls) God is not 'one' in the sense that my soul plus God equals two anything at all, even individuals. For, not being a kind of thing God is not and cannot be an *additional* anything. God is *absolutely* unique. There is not any collectivity to which God could be added as a further item. Hence, God and I are not distinct as individuals are distinct from one another.

---

[53] Herbert McCabe, *God Matters*, London: Chapman, 1987, pp. 70–71.

This, of course, does not and cannot imply that we are *the same* individual – either that God is the same individual that I am or that I am the same individual that God is. For God is not an individual. Nor, in turn, does that entail that God is a multiplicity. God is neither one thing nor three things, because God is not a thing. The language of number fails of God.

The precision of Julian's language cannot be said to rest explicitly upon this Neoplatonic dialectics, for she nowhere gives an account in so many terms of the epistemological assumptions on which her theology draws. Yet the sure-footed control which she exercises over her theological insights reveals that she had absorbed the implications of that dialectic in practice. And the reason for this anachronistic excursus out of Eckhart's time is to illustrate why it is that Julian can confidently play with formulas little short of Eckhart's in audacity while remaining firmly within the common Neoplatonic tradition, while Eckhart's version of them departs from that tradition. At any rate, the precise point of divergence between them is now clear: if, for Julian, the only way in which God and I can be said to be distinct is as the uncreated and created are distinct, then for Eckhart that is the one way in which God and I are *not* distinct.

It is not, of course, that for Eckhart there is no distinction between the uncreated and the created. Indeed, Eckhart was in trouble with the inquisitors of Avignon not for having failed to make that distinction sharply enough but for appearing to have exaggerated it. For he was accused of having held that created things are so sharply to be distinguished from the Creator as to be 'nothing' in relation to the Creator's existence, for holding that 'All creatures are one pure nothing. I do not say that they are a little something or anything, but that they are pure nothing.'[54] Moreover, Eckhart not only admitted that this was his view, he turned to the offensive and tartly accused his accusers of blasphemy for denying it: 'to say that the world is not nothing in itself and from itself, but is some slight bit of existence is open blasphemy.'[55]

Now the propositions that there is an uncreated 'something' in the soul and that created beings are 'nothing at all' both derive from the same underlying metaphysical conviction announced in

[54] *In Agro Dominico*, Article 26, Colledge and McGinn, *Essential Sermons*, p. 80.
[55] *Defense*, ibid., p. 75.

the Prologue to his *Work of Propositions*: *Esse est Deus* – 'to exist is God'. Note that to say this is not the same as saying *Deus est esse*, which, as a way of speaking about God, would have been happily accepted by Thomas Aquinas. The formula is not a characterization of God, but a definition of existence. And in this Eckhart is closer to Bonaventure who, as we have seen, similarly held that the 'conceptual' names of God, such as existence and goodness, are properly predicated of God and in only an attenuated sense of creatures – differing in this from the 'metaphorical' names of God which are properly predicated of creatures and only by extension of God. In saying that creatures are 'nothing at all' Eckhart is merely drawing out one of the implications of this in a way others had drawn them previously, that implication being that created beings have no claim on existence of their own (are 'nothing *in themselves...*'), as in a sense they might be said to have a claim of their own on their properties. A horse *has* a claim of its own to being a quadruped, for it belongs to its nature to have four legs. But it has no such claim on existence. That it can only owe, directly and without mediation, to God.

Of course, to say that a creature is 'nothing in itself' is not to say that it does not exist. It does exist, but only as 'this or that' (*esse hoc et hoc*), or, as Eckhart otherwise puts it, its existence is an *esse formaliter inhaerens*. What Eckhart appears to mean by this is that the existence of a creature occurs only in a 'manner', that is to say, as being the existence of this or that kind of thing. As Aristotle had once put it, 'for a living thing to exist *is* to be alive',[56] its existence is its being 'this [alive] and not that [inanimate]'. Hence, relatively to this *esse hoc et hoc*, Eckhart notes, in duly apophatic spirit, that in so far as *esse* is predicated of creatures, it is better to say that God does *not* exist, or that God is beyond existence. For God is not a *hoc aliquid*. As Denys put it: 'He does not possess this kind of existence and not that',[57] a phrase which seems unfailingly to resonate in Eckhart's ear.

But *esse* is improperly predicated of creatures, properly predicated only of God. As predicated of creatures, *esse* is *esse distinctum* (this and that). But as predicated of God, *esse* is *esse indistinctum*, by which, again, Eckhart appears to mean what Bonaventure had meant in the *Itinerarium*:

---

[56] *De Anima*, 415b 12.   [57] *DN*, 824B.

if being [*esse*] designates the pure actuality of being, then being is that which first comes into the intellect, and this being is that which is pure act. But this being is not particular being, which is a limited being, since it is mixed with potentiality; nor is it analogous being, for that has the least of act because it least exists. It remains, therefore, that the being [*esse*] which we are considering is the Divine Being.[58]

In so far as we consider existence in itself, therefore, existence is God and creatures are 'nothing'. In so far as we consider the existence of creatures, it is better to say that God is 'nothing', because God is not any kind of thing. But the two 'nothings' are radically distinct from one another, as far apart as the Creator and the creature, and the essence of that distinction lies in the distinction between the *esse distinctum* (being 'this and that') of creatures and the *esse indistinctum* (not being 'this and that') of God.

Now from this position Eckhart is able to draw some of those conclusions which we saw to be implied in the logic of Julian's. God cannot stand in any relation of differentiation from anything else, except as *esse distinctum* is differentiated from *esse indistinctum*. This, for Eckhart, is for the same reason that we have just explained: things can be distinct from one another only in some respect that the things distinguished share with one another. But there is nothing which both God and creatures share. Therefore we cannot say anything about how God is distinct from anything else in any terms which would distinguish one kind of thing from another. In this sense, therefore, God can be said to be absolutely 'One', in that he cannot be one of many because God is not one of a kind. God's 'oneness' consists simply in his *esse indistinctum*, that is to say, not as an 'apartness' or 'separation' from anything else, least of all in any relation of mutual exclusion, but precisely in God's not being one of the kinds of thing that is 'distinct': not in any way whatever.

It follows from this that what marks out God's *esse* from that of creatures is, paradoxically, the utter impossibility of our saying anything at all about God's distinctness from creatures: in this alone is God distinct, that whereas one creature is distinct from another, God is not distinct from any of them. Thus, God's distinctness from creatures consists in something no creatures possess, his 'indistinctness', her not being any kind of thing, so that the distinctness of his *esse* is to be *esse indistinctum*. But another conclusion

---

[58] *Itin.*, 5, 3.

follows: if God's *esse* is to be 'neither this nor that', not a *hoc aliquid*, then Eckhart can also say that God's primary name is 'intellect'. For, as his neo-Aristotelian–Augustinian argument showed, that character of being a 'nothing-in-particular', 'neither this nor that', of being a 'nothing', is precisely that in which is found the character of *intellectus*. A being whose nature is purely intentional has to be none of the things that it knows, so that it can become all things intentionally. That is to say, its 'to be' is 'to be nothing in particular', 'nothing', *esse indistinctum*.

Here, then, Eckhart draws the startling, untraditional conclusion from materials all of which are recognizable within the accepted theological traditions: intellect is God. And from this conclusion we can draw another which closes the circle of argument. If intellect is God and consists in God's *esse indistinctum*; and if intellect as such is *esse indistinctum*; and if the only way in which the Creator is distinct from the creature is as *esse indistinctum* is distinct from *esse distinctum*; then it follows that *in so far as* I am intellect I am *esse indistinctum* and uncreated; hence I am, *qua* intellect, God. It is no qualification of that conclusion to add: in so far as I am not intellect I am created, a this or that, a human being and so *also* created. And so we are back with the question with which we began: is the inconsistency resolved which resided, we saw, in Eckhart's appearing to have to say both that I am a being caught between two dimensions of the self, a created dimension and an uncreated, and that I am a being in which all my powers are integrated within a created, finite subject?

The answer can now be seen clearly to be that it is capable of being resolved. For Eckhart has within his resources the conceptual dialectics to demonstrate that there is not and cannot be any incompatibility between saying of one and the same person that she is both divine and human. This might be said to be just as well, since the possibility of saying this without fear of uttering a self-contradictory nonsense must be a necessity for any Christianity which has not straightforwardly rejected the Council of Chalcedon. And what must be said of Christ cannot be a contradiction to say of any human person.[59] Because to be God is not be exclusive of

---

[59] Which is why Thomas Aquinas argued that there cannot be reasons in logic why there *could only be* just one incarnation of the Second Person of the Trinity: *non est dicendum quod persona divina ita assumpserit unam naturam humanam quod non potuerit assumere aliam* (*Summa Theologiae*, 3a, q.3, a.7, corp.) That he thought there were reasons in faith for denying that there were or will be any others is another matter.

any other kind of being; because God's *esse indistinctum* cannot be distinguished from the *esse distinctum* of the created human by any relation of displacement, so that to be the one *entails* not being the other; therefore, my being God, infinite, uncreated, 'nothing', cannot be exclusive of my being finite, created, a *hoc aliquid*, an *esse distinctum*. And at any rate, to this extent we can agree with McGinn's conclusion as a general characterization of his theology:

> In the last analysis Eckhart's theology is both theocentric and at the same time fully anthropocentric. God is God and man is man and yet God's ground and the soul's ground are one ground.[60]

It is not *inconsistent*, therefore, for Eckhart to say the things which appeared to be incompatible with one another. Whether what he says is *true* is another matter besides. For it is now clear that Eckhart has applied to the human person not just the logic of, but also the claims of, Christian belief about the Incarnate Christ. And it is yet another matter whether Eckhart's doctrine of the divine element in the soul is a development consistent with the Neoplatonic orthodoxies of his day. As to the last question I have tried to show that all the main elements of his theology are to be found in traditional sources, but what he did with them startled his contemporaries with their novelty; perhaps they found his conclusions so perplexing in part because they recognized them to have been drawn merely by a remorseless exploitation of the logic of the familiar, which nonetheless turned that inheritance on its head.

As to the question of his doctrine's truth, my exposition has shown nothing relevant, except perhaps to have indicated at what point in his metaphysics a critical engagement with his theology should be directed: the crucial step, in my view, is the statement, *esse est Deus*. Without that step Eckhart could have derived no conclusions from his Neoplatonic sources, whether in Augustine or Denys or Thomas, which those theologians could not have accepted. With it, the conclusion *intellectus est Deus* follows and with it the 'hyperbolic' distinctiveness of his theology and mysticism.

VII

If, as McGinn points out, Eckhart's theology is as anthropocentric as it is theocentric, this will be because of the distinctiveness of his

---

[60] Colledge and McGinn, *Essential Sermons*, p. 61.

identification of the ground of the soul with the ground of God. If, therefore, his theology and mysticism is markedly apophatic, so too is his anthropology, his teaching that I, in my ground, am a 'nothing'. And if we can say that the hyperbolic nature of his apophatic theology has little direct impact on the subsequent development of Christian mysticism in the West, this will have to be put down to the dampening effects on his reputation of the condemnation of 1329.[61] But it is perhaps less easy to be sure that his anthropology has as little impact. At any rate, certainly themes of Eckhart's 'negative anthropology' do receive a significant development in subsequent mystical doctrines – even if it is hard to establish their direct lineage from Eckhart. It is to this 'negative anthropology' therefore, that we must next turn, but especially to Eckhart's doctrine of 'detachment'.

---

[61] The question of Eckhart's influence on subsequent mysticisms is vexed. Oliver Davies points out that one of the effects, ironically, of the Bull of Condemnation was to suppress more effectively the circulation of his more 'moderate' Latin treatises than that of his more 'exuberant' German sermons (*God Within*, p. 72). For a fuller discussion of Eckhart's influence, see Davies' *Meister Eckhart*, pp. 215–234.

CHAPTER 7

Eckhart: detachment and the critique of desire

I

The last chapter was concerned with one of the great issues of Eckhart's speculative metaphysics and theology. The purpose of this chapter is to approach Eckhart's theology from the ascetical end of the spectrum of his interests and to take up the subject of detachment, that is to say, the *practice* of apophatic anthropology. At any rate, the topics of these chapters are distinguished in so far as it is possible to distinguish between an ascetical topic and a speculatively theological one, for in Eckhart there is reason to doubt the value of this distinction. For my part I am disinclined to view Eckhart's writings, whether in the Latin or in the vernacular, either as those of one of the great practical spiritual teachers of the Western Christian tradition, or, alternatively, as those of a great speculative philosopher-theologian; or finally as writings which severally fall some in one category, some in the other. Rather, he belongs within a tradition which has wholly disappeared since the Middle Ages – indeed, perhaps since Eckhart himself – in which one could talk about all these things at once within a single, unified discourse and so could talk intelligibly about a 'mystical theology'. It is not, however, appropriate yet to comment upon the disappearance of this tradition further than to recall how, in our meanings of the terms, the words 'mystical' and 'theology' pull apart from one another in opposed directions; and to guess that, as often as not, those directions appear to be as opposed as the 'experiential' and 'speculative' are: and that opposition increasingly concerns us in the rest of this book.

Nor is this the appropriate place to comment on how, by contrast with our tendency to construe these things as opposed, Eckhart 'puts them together'. It seems doubtful if he shared our assumptions of disjunction even to the extent of supposing that they *have* to be put together. He seems to have been incapable of being troubled by this categorical distinction between the experiential and the speculative because he would not have admitted it. Hence, not sharing our problem, it is perhaps a mistake for us to see him as having, of set purpose, solved it. On the other hand, the fourteenth-century English Author of *The Cloud of Unknowing* does seem to have been familiar with and troubled by something like our difficulty, as, in the fifteenth century was Denys the Carthusian, which is a reason for continuing the discussion of this theme in the ensuing chapters.

But what is this problem about the relationship between the 'experiential' and the 'speculative'? We can begin the process of clarifying this question, in so far as it is raised for us by Eckhart and the *Cloud* Author, by returning to some of the issues which had already been raised for them by the tradition. One version of the question was raised by that curious mix of the 'experiential' and the 'epistemological' which is found in Augustine's employment of the metaphor of 'interiority' in *Confessions*. We saw that there was a question to be raised as to whether the path to greater 'interiority' was best understood as consisting in psychological acts of turning the mind in some way 'within' upon itself, there to encounter 'experientially' the divine Light within, or whether it was better to read this language as principally that of an epistemological critique of human knowledge which demonstrates all judgement to have its foundations in the objective presence to the mind of the divine Light – a presence which is demonstrable whether or not we have any experience of it.

We saw that the language of *Confessions*, is, seen from the point of view of any sharp division between the experiential and the epistemological, hybrid; but that this very hybridity leads us to question the value of any such sharp division in Augustine's thought. Certainly it would seem that to raise the question of Augustine's credentials as a 'mystic' as if it turned upon the question of whether Augustine was a critical epistemologist in the 'Platonic' tradition or rather was reporting upon some high 'experiences' is to presuppose that other questions have been settled which, in relation to any writer between Augustine and Eckhart, need to be debated and clarified, rather than begged.[1] What is the meaning of

---

[1] As does Dom Cuthbert Butler in his *Western Mysticism: The Teaching of Sts Augustine, Gregory and Bernard on Contemplation and the Contemplative Life*, New York: Dutton, pp. 58 ff.

'experience' in its application to medieval theology? What (different?) meanings would different mediaeval theologians have given to this term? In any case, which contrasts, if any, would they have allowed between the 'experiential' and the 'speculative' in theology? And as far as Augustine's *Confessions* was concerned, I concluded that there was little value in, and little justice done to his complex discussions by, an exegesis which relied upon *any* sharp contrast between the 'experiential' and the 'systematic'.

But we left our discussion of Augustine's *De Trinitate* with a question which does have a bearing on a version of this issue which will increasingly preoccupy us in the rest of this essay. We had seen that, for Augustine, the crucial point of division between 'exteriority' and 'interiority' lay in 'imagination'. A mind which sees the world and the self within 'imagination' is living 'outside' itself and in so far as it cannot raise itself above this level, the mind remains trapped within corporeal images of both God and the self. Whether one sees this process as one of epistemological critique or as the achievement of 'higher', more 'inward' experiences, or both, the acts by which the mind moves further inward to itself and then above to its own source of Truth are essentially acts which liberate it from the limitedness of the corporeal image. And yet our question was: is there not an unresolvable paradox in the fact that that whole process of transcending imagination has to be described in metaphors of inwardness and ascent, since such metaphors are themselves paradigmatically the products of imagination?

In the last chapter we saw that Augustine was not unaware of the paradox of having to speak the ineffable, but was happy to leave it unresolved. Others were less happy to do so. The same question which arose for Augustine arises for Bonaventure – or at least, it is one which we can raise *of* Bonaventure. For in Bonaventure too the mind rises on a ladder of ascent from vestiges to images and from images to conceptual names and beyond them to the divine darkness of unknowing into which the death of Christ draws it. But this, like Augustine's, is a process leading beyond image which has nonetheless to be described in terms of vestiges, metaphors of 'inwardness' and 'ascent', which are derived from material things.

Whether consciously as a solution to this problem, or not, the problem is met in Bonaventure's thought by means of a more positive philosophy and theology of 'vestige' and 'image' than any to be found in Augustine. Images, for Bonaventure, can trap us into a merely corporeal understanding of world, self and God. But it is in the essential nature of the image to lead beyond itself. It is only a mind unrestored by grace which will become lost in the corporeality of the image. But it cannot be in the nature of imagination as such to limit the mind to the corporeal, for it is only by means of images of *visibilia* that *invisibilia* can be known at all.

An alternative approach to the same problem can be broadly described both as 'Dionysian' and 'dialectical', working by means of what I have described as the 'self-subverting image', the essential method by which the cataphatic effects the transition to the apophatic. We saw this dialectic at work in Denys' account of the apophatic progress of the mind from the 'perceptual' names of God to the 'conceptual' and beyond. And we saw this dialectic in operation in Eckhart, though we noted there also a certain rhetorical strenuousness with which he seeks to push imagery beyond the limits of contradiction itself – as if to get the image actually to say the unsayable, rather than, as Augustine thought wiser, to leave its unsayability unsaid.

'Imagination' is in a human the faculty of 'experience'. Until the late fourteenth century I doubt if there is any other sense to the English word 'experience' than those contained in the various meanings of the word *imaginatio*. If, therefore, a twentieth-century reader proposes to raise the question of a Christian author prior to the later fourteenth century in terms of the question of 'mystical experiences', one will want to know what that reader has in mind to ask about which the mediaeval writer could have understood otherwise than as a question about the place of *imaginatio* within the ascent of mind and heart to God. On the whole, the theologians in the more 'negative' traditions of Christian mysticism, before the century of Eckhart and the *Cloud* Author, treat imagination with a kind of controlled ambiguity: it is a step on a ladder which ultimately has to be thrown away.

But in the fourteenth century, and in Eckhart and the *Cloud* Author particularly, is found a less nuanced, more openly hostile, account of imagination. In both authors is found the attempt to counter a very specific form of the 'experientialisation' of the way of the Christian soul towards union with God. This 'experientialism' consists, in one of its manifestations, in what they perceived to be a damaging, because distorting, account of the 'way' to God which one-sidedly translates the discourse of 'interiority' into essentially psychological categories; that is to say into *experiences of inwardness*, which it is the purpose of the Christian practices of asceticism and prayer to cultivate. And both saw these phenomena of 'spirituality' as deriving from an inadequate critique of the role of imagination in the soul's ascent to God. It is, I will argue, fair to see Eckhart's profound meditations on detachment as having the purpose of a critique of such 'experientialism'; and it is impossible to read the *Cloud* Author's intentions in any other way, so clearly are his purposes spelt out.

II

So what does Eckhart say about detachment? First, that it is a more fundamental virtue than love:

> so far as my reason can lead me and instruct me, I find no other virtue better than a pure detachment from all things...The teachers have great things to say in praise of love, as had St Paul, who says: 'Whatever I may practice, if I do not have love, I am worth nothing at all' (1 Cor., 13, 1–2). And yet I praise detachment above all love.[2]

Not very helpfully he adds the reason: detachment 'approaches so closely to nothingness that there can be nothing between perfect detachment and nothingness'.[3] Detachment is complete self-emptying: it is the digging out of a void, an abyss within the self, a vacuum into which God is inevitably drawn. God cannot resist the detached soul, for 'everything longs to achieve its natural place' and 'God's natural place is unity and purity and that comes from detachment'.[4] Consequently, detachment is a higher virtue than love, for

> the very best thing about love is that it compels me to love God, yet detachment compels God to love me. Now it is far greater for me to compel God to come to me than to compel myself to come to God; and that is because God is able to conform himself, far better and with more suppleness, and to unite himself with me than I could unite myself with God.[5]

The goal of detachment, then, is 'that a man should be so free of all things and of all works, interior and exterior, that he might

---

[2] *On Detachment*, in Colledge and McGinn, *Essential Sermons*, pp. 285–86.
[3] Ibid., p. 286.   [4] Ibid., p. 286.   [5] Ibid., p. 286.

become a place only for God, in which God could work'.[6] Detachment, moreover, makes a person free not only 'from all created things', but from anything less than the uncreated silence, unity and emptiness of the Godhead, even from God-the-Creator:

Therefore I pray to God that he may make me free of God, for my real being is above God if we take 'God' to be the beginning of all created things. For in the same being of God where God is above being and above distinction, there I myself was...[7]

We are therefore back with the familiar Eckhartian theme of the identity of my ground with the ground of God: and because they are the same 'ground', the names with which the Godhead may be described are also the names of that ground of my being which is identical with it: 'desert', 'silence', 'nothingness'. Detachment is the way of achieving that nameless, featureless depth within the self which is identical with the Godhead and which is, also, in another way, my own identity. Detachment displaces all in the self which would fill that void, all naming, all mediations, whether by created material realities or by spiritual realities. A detached person is dispossessed of all images and concepts of God, and wills nothing for herself, not even to do the will of God, for

So long as a man has this as his will, that he wants to fulfil God's dearest will, he has not the poverty about which we want to talk. Such a person has a will with which he wants to fulfil God's will, and that is not true poverty.[8]

To this detachment, therefore, the more common paths of spirituality and prayer are potential obstacles. If detachment is the way to God, it is so only because it is the way of being detached from ways to God. John of the Cross said no less, describing the terrain of the spirit as a 'land without ways',[9] but Eckhart is the more graphic:

truly, when people think that they are acquiring more of God in inwardness, in sweetness and in various approaches than they do by the fireside or in the stable, you are acting just as if you took God and muffled his head up in a cloak and pushed him under a bench. Whoever is seeking God in ways is finding ways and losing God, who in ways is hidden.[10]

---

[6] *Sermon* 52, *Beati Pauperes Spiritu*, Colledge and McGinn, *Essential Sermons*, p. 202.
[7] Ibid., p. 202.   [8] Ibid., p. 200.
[9] *The Dark Night of the Soul*, I. 12.6, *Collected Works* (*CW*), p. 323.
[10] *Sermon* 5b, *In hoc apparuit*, Colledge and McGinn, *Essential Sermons*, p. 183.

Here, then, we find the outline of a familiar Eckhartian paradox: God is most intimate, the most completely interior to my being, more interior than I am. Yet we can find that God and that self-hood only by detachment from 'ways', including the 'way' of seeking that inwardness. And so the detached person wants nothing, wants no 'experience', even of God's presence in the soul: 'rather should he be so free of all knowing that he does not know or experience or grasp that God lives in him'.[11] That is why he asks for nothing but that 'he might become a place only for God, in which God could work'.[12] Consequently, as the soul attains this complete emptiness of self 'it loses its name and it draws God into itself so that it becomes nothing, as the sun draws up the red dawn into itself so that it becomes nothing'.[13]

III

We wish to consider the question of how far the categories of Eckhart's thought can be appropriated by, and for, a corresponding account of religious or 'mystical' experience. My answer has to be pessimistic: at first blush Eckhart's prescriptions for Christian living seem relentlessly anti-experientialist. For his own part we may notice that, much as he owes to Augustine theologically, Eckhart is no autobiographer; and if, for that matter, neither is any other mediaeval theologian, mystic or not, the reasons in Eckhart's case seem more than incidental and to do with more than a cultural inheritance of autobiographical reticence. Eckhart no more argues from experience than he argues to experience, his own or anyone else's. In any case, the doctrine of detachment so far resists translation into experiential categories as to seem, prima facie, uncompromisingly to exclude any role for them: we get no feel from Eckhart of the experiential profile of the detached person and this seems to be because detachment appears to imply the irrelevance of any kind of 'mystical' or 'spiritual' experiences.

And we may detect a further, more revealing, reason for scepticism about an experientialist reading of Eckhart, a reason which transpires from a comparison between Eckhart's asceticism and the asceticism of that other great exponent of detachment, John of the Cross.

[11]   *Sermon* 52, ibid., p. 201.   [12]   Ibid., p. 202.
[13]   *On Detachment*, ibid., p. 292.

In chapter three I suggested that in Augustine's thought it is possible to identify two broadly distinct approaches to the 'self', on the one hand the approach of 'self-discovery', on the other of 'self-making'. There is something to be said for the view that this distinction has its counterparts in subsequent Western theologies, though I should not wish to defend this sweeping categorisation as complete and exhaustive, nor even fully clarify the distinction itself. Nor do I think it especially useful as a way of classifying mystics, as if it were helpful to describe each as belonging more or less exclusively to one category or the other. It is meant for the purpose of distinguishing between tendencies of thought and between families of metaphors for the self: both may be present in the same mystical writer, though the emphases of some may be such as to permit their identification with the one tendency and metaphorical family more than with the other. In this rather loose way I distinguish between Eckhart and John of the Cross as mystics respectively of 'self-discovery' and of 'self-making'.

In the tradition of self-discovery, the self, in its ultimate and highest form is, as it were, a pre-existing fact, it is there, albeit hidden from the view of most; but it is there whether or not I achieve the capacity to appropriate that hidden self within my conscious self. My true self is continuous with me and is there for me to discover.

Some such partiality for the metaphors of self-discovery is evident in Julian of Norwich, who wrote of the 'godly wyl' which 'never assentid to synne ne never shal'.[14] This 'wyl' is our 'substance' and 'our essential being' and it is there that God dwells intimately, inseparably from our substance, for 'he is with us in our soule endlesly wonand, us reuland and yemand'.[15] And 'ilke kind that hevyn shall be fulfilled with behoveth nedes, of Gods rythfulhede, so to be knitt and onyd to him that therein were kept a substance which myte never, ne should be, partid from him.'[16] And so, in an echo of Augustine's dialectics of interiority and exteriority, Julian can say, 'Peas and love arn ever in us, beand and werkand, but we be not always in pese and in love.'[17]

If only as a matter of emphasis there is no doubt that Eckhart falls within this tradition of self-discovery, for that is the meaning

---

[14] *Revelations*, 37 (Wolters p. 118).
[15] Ibid., 52, (Wolters, p. 152).
[16] Ibid., 53, (Wolters, p. 155).
[17] Ibid., 39, (Wolters, p. 121).

of his central doctrine of the 'spark of the soul', that eternal presence of God in the soul's depths where it is most itself. It is necessary to add to this only that for Eckhart it is detachment which is the strategy of the uncovering and revealing of the spark of the soul, so it is by detachment that we discover our true selves. Eckhart's detachment is not the mechanism whereby space is *made* for God to occupy; it is rather, the process whereby space is recovered from the infilling of attachments. Eckhart's detachment, we might say, is archaeological rather than architectural.

In this Eckhart's asceticism differs in tendency from that of John of the Cross, the radicalness of the difference being partly disguised by the fact that Eckhart and John share a common language of 'centring' and 'depth'. Nonetheless, John's exploitation of this imagery is to a quite different effect. 'The soul's centre is God',[18] he declares; and

when it has reached God with all the capacity of its being and the strength of its operation and inclination, it will have attained to its final and deepest centre in God...love is the soul's inclination and strength and power in making its way to God, for love unites it with God. The more degrees of love it has the more deeply it enters into God and centres itself in Him. We can say that there are as many centres in God possible to the soul, each deeper than the other, as there are degrees of love possible to it.[19]

It is not just the stronger sense of dynamic progression which distinguishes John's from Eckhart's imagery. There is in addition the implication, elsewhere made explicit, that for John God *makes* the space in the soul, creates the depths which he occupies. For John the undetached person is not one who is out of touch with the already existent depths of the self: the undetached person is one who lacks the depths of the self necessary for God to occupy, so that detachment is the strategy of self-making, not one of self-discovery.

This distinction between Eckhart's relatively static account of detachment as self-discovery and John's relatively more dynamic account as divine self-making also, in my view, explains a further distinction between the two ascetical paths. This further difference brings us back to the original difficulty of translating Eckhart's ascetical discourse of detachment into experiential categories. It is evident that this translation is more easily done in John's case for he himself makes it. It is fair to say that no work of Christian

---

[18] *The Living Flame of Love*, CW, stanza 1.12, p. 583.
[19] Ibid., stanza 1.12, p. 583.

asceticism, until the Spanish sixteenth century, can rival Augustine's *Confessions* on the score of psychological insight into the lived experience of the ascetical path; but it is also true that in that century John's *Ascent of Mount Carmel* and *The Dark Night of the Soul* do rival it in a way which, in turn, has scarcely been rivalled since.

It is but a symptom of the facility with which John moves between ascetical and psychological categories that he has the greatest difficulty in distinguishing the lived experience of the famous 'dark nights of the soul' from the lived experience of depression – or 'melancholia' as he calls it.[20] Phenomenologically they are identical. No matter that John is at pains to distinguish them, though it is of the utmost importance to him that they be not confused. The point is that they *can* be confused and this is because, for John, the cataloguing of the experiential detail of the way of detachment requires an acute sensitivity to the inner feel of the process.

Not so for Eckhart. Though Eckhart knows and occasionally describes the dizzying sense of vertigo which the soul experiences as it hangs over the abyss of its own emptiness, the descriptions are perfunctory, relatively colourless, conventional. In any case the feel of the mystical way of self-discovery is, of its nature, the feel of the return to familiar ground, not that of a crisis of the unexpected. It is the feel of a home-coming, it is a mysticism suffused with the sense of the Platonic recollection, the recovery of a once known, only more recently lost, identity. In Eckhart's mysticism the discovery of the self is, as in Augustine, essentially an achievement of memory. His *dis*covery of the self turns out, in the end, to be a *re*covery of broken lines of continuity with the pre-existent self in God.

With John the atmosphere could not be more different. It is true to say, I concede, that John's too is a mysticism of memory, but in his case detachment is the annihilation of memory as the source of our sense of continuing identity. John's mysticism is therefore a way of identity-loss, of discontinuities and breaks, it is a way of experienced catastrophe for the self. When, therefore, in the outcome the soul finds God at the centre, it is with a sense of radical novelty that that centre is encountered. And the encounter of the self with its true centre is paid for at the price of the displacement of all that the person was able previously to call a self.

[20] See chapter 10 below.

Consequently there is present in John and absent from Eckhart a high drama of the soul's journey to God; in Eckhart's scheme detachment is the achievement of a kind of invulnerability, a security in the soul's ever-present ground where the dramas of sin, weakness and suffering can have no place. In John's too invulnerability is an ultimate achievement, but on the way all is risk, heightened sensitivity and so enhanced vulnerability. For John there are indeed securities, but they are found not within the Platonic memory of identity restored, but in the future-oriented, risk-laden transformation of memory into hope. For Eckhart, I am most truly what I once was in my source. For John, I am what I can hope for.

Because, therefore, John's mysticism generates a phenomenology of felt experience, it readily translates into a psychologistic reading in terms of equivalent, secular experience – and Eckhart's does not. This is not to say that Eckhart's mysticism is irrelevant to an experiential psychology of self-discovery, still less that it excludes the possibility of one. On the contrary, it may be possible to make the case that within his understanding of detachment there is implicit the conceptual framework for a psychology of considerable interest and power. It remains true, however, that if he does not exclude a psychology Eckhart does not give us one; and that there is, moreover, a double risk in reading Eckhart as if he did. Those risks are that we will give a distorted account of what he does say and at the same time misread what his mysticism truly implies for a psychology.

IV

I propose, therefore, to venture a speculation about the nature of that relation between detachment and experience. Without question the controlling categories of Eckhart's mysticism are those of detachment and interiority. I propose to say, however, that these are 'categories' in at least a semi-technical sense, meaning that they are, as it were, *schemata* for a possible experience but that they are not themselves experiences. I therefore mean that, relative to all the unlimited possibilities of human desire, feeling and emotion, relative to human fear, anxiety, guilt, love, hate and hope, to the possibilities of self-awareness and self-ignorance, of self-love and self-hate, of love of God and indifference, of human solidarity and alienation; relative to all these secular possibilities of desire, detachment and interiority stand not as alternative experiences, worse still as 'higher' experiences, worst of all as 'religious' experiences, but as form to content, as shapers to experience shaped. As categories, detachment and interiority are, for Eckhart, experientially empty. Detachment is not itself an experience alongside all the rest, no more is interiority. But as categories also, their relevance to secular experience lies in the way in which they shape, transform and give purpose to human experience. For empty they may be *of* experience, but they are not abstract in relation to lived experience, inert, merely explanatory categories, as are those of a theory. Detachment and interiority are, for Eckhart, not so much the names of experiences as *practices for the transformation of experience*; or, we can say, they are the critical practices of an apophatic theology in their application to human desire. 'Detachment', in short, is the ascetical practice of the apophatic.

It is as understood in this way that some of Eckhart's most problematic statements about detachment are perhaps most sympathetically, and fairly, to be interpreted. Again and again Eckhart appears to speak of the 'way' of detachment as if it required the annihilation of all desire. 'For I tell you', he says,

by the truth that is eternal, so long as you have a will to fulfill God's will, and a longing for God and eternity, then you are not poor; for a poor man is one who has a will and a longing for nothing.[21]

Nor is it simply a matter of the detached person no longer seeking God but seeking rather the 'Godhead' beyond God. To desire anything at all, he says, even to be a 'place' in which God can work, is to fail to be the 'nothing' in which God alone can work. It is as if desire as such, being a 'something', constitutes a state of being undetached in itself, and there is no doubt that his Avignon accusers thought Eckhart had moved too close for comfort to an absolute 'quietism' of desire, to an account of detachment as a condition desireless of all 'means'. Contained in the first list of fifteen articles, admitted by Eckhart and condemned as containing 'the error or stain of heresy',[22] is the eighth:

All those who are not desiring possessions, or honors, or gain, or internal devotion, or holiness, or reward or the kingdom of heaven, but who have renounced all this, even what is theirs, these people pay honour to God.[23]

---

[21] *Sermon* 52, Colledge and McGinn, *Essential Sermons*, p. 200.
[22] *In Agro Dominico*, ibid., p. 80.   [23] Ibid., p. 78.

Such statements immediately alert us to the possibility of Marguerite Porete's influence. The annihilated soul, she says,

does not seek God through penance, nor through any of the Church's sacraments, nor through meditations, nor through words, nor through works, nor through any higher creature, nor through justice, nor through mercy, nor through the glory of glory, nor through divine knowledge, nor through divine love, nor through divine praise.[24]

And Eckhart in turn even seemed to have denied that we should pray to God for anything at all, for he was condemned for having written:

recently I considered whether there was anything I would take or ask from God. I shall take careful thought about this, because if I were accepting anything from God, I should be subject to him or below him as a servant or slave, and he in giving would be as master. We shall not be so in life everlasting.[25]

And, indeed, Eckhart had said these things.[26] But how are they to be interpreted?

The first point to be made is that there is in Eckhart's doctrine of detachment what I have said may be called an 'apophaticism of desire' which parallels his apophaticism of intellect. As intellect is a 'nothing' and is nameless, so the will must be a 'nothing' and motiveless. To have a reason, a motive or an explanation as to *why* one should love God, for there to be something one loved God *for*, would be a form of attachment. Such a person would be one for whom God was a 'something'; and in so far as God is a God 'for me', God is not God. And in so far as I am a 'something' for which God is, I am not the nothing which God is. But the spirit which exists in 'oneness and freedom' is a spirit which

has no why [and] the person who has abandoned himself and all things, who seeks nothing for himself in things and performs all his works without

---

[24] *Mirror*, 85, 16–21.

[25] *In Agro Dominico*, Colledge and McGinn, *Essential Sermons*, p. 78. Cp Marguerite:
...those souls which are driven by the purest love, hold it to be all the same to them and desire equally shame as honour and honour as shame, poverty as much as riches, riches as much as poverty, to be tried by God and his creatures as much as to be consoled by them, and they desire as much to be hated as loved, loved as hated, hell as much as heaven, heaven as much as hell, a lowly condition and humble as much as a high and exalted one...these souls neither desire nor do not desire anything of these eventualities, whether of good or ill fortune, for these souls have no will, except that God should will in them. (*Mirror*, 13, 51–67.)

[26] See *Sermon* 6, *Justi vivent in aeternum*, Colledge and McGinn, *Essential Sermons*, pp. 185, 188.

a why and out of love, such a person is dead to the whole world and lives in God and God in him.[27]

But is Eckhart therefore commending detachment as the psychological condition of desirelessness? The answer to that must be an unambiguous negative, if only for the reason that his doctrine of detachment is, among other things, a critique of the very presuppositions which underlie that way of interpreting what he says.

Sermons 29 and 52 are at least clear about one thing. Detachment does not consist simply in an act of transferring our human created desires for created objects from those objects on to an alternative, *un*created object, God. This, for Eckhart, would amount to the strategy of being detached from every desire bar one, a strategy which could have had only one conceivable outcome: that of reducing God to the status of an object of human created desire. This is what it would be to have a God 'for me', a created God, a 'God' interposed between me and that Godhead which stands alone in its pure, free, imageless, uncreated ground of unity and undifferentiation. This is also what it would be for me to be a being *other than* God – and so it is for me to be a 'something', a *hoc aliquid* who stands in relation to God not in a dialectic of oneness in indistinction, but in an opposition of exclusiveness. This 'detachment' is not the breakthrough into the ground of God where I stand in my ground as an uncreated nothingness. True detachment, on the contrary, is my becoming in desire what I am in myself: nothing, an *unum indistinctum*.

It is at this point that it might seem natural to read the consequence of this critique of a false detachment to be that we should not desire even God and so should, in detachment, become entirely desireless. But this is not what Eckhart says. Here, as in so many of his most paradoxical statements, we will be misled if we forget that most of Eckhart's descriptions are of the *logic* of an ideal where we might have supposed him to be describing concrete, imperfect *processes*. What he says of the *ideal* of detachment, when thought of as the process of acquiring detachment, turns into the paradox that we cannot desire even detachment itself except in an attached way, since if we desire detachment for a reason, or with a 'why' (for myself, or so as to be closer to God) then my wanting itself stands

---

[27] *Sermon* 29, *Convescens precepit eis*, McGinn, Tobin and Borgstadt, *Teacher and Preacher*, p. 288.

between me and detachment, and so between me and God. But this is a point, merely, in the logic of detachment. For if I desire detachment this is because I do not possess it. And if I desire detachment in an attached way, it is not truly detachment I desire, but something for myself. Whereas if I truly possess detachment, then there is nothing which I desire, not even God, in that way in which the attached person desires anything. I will desire nothing for myself, not even to be close to God, not even to be a place in which God acts. For between God and detachment, as Eckhart had said, lies nothing at all. But from none of this does it follow that I should not desire detachment in order to achieve it, even if, necessarily, my desire for it is an undetached desire. For what else can I do but desire it and pray for it and work for it? The point in logic, therefore, has no bearing on the process of becoming detached – as if to imply absurdly that one should not, until detached enough to seek it, seek detachment. The logical point has a bearing only on what it is to say of someone that she is detached, not on how an undetached person might or might not set about acquiring detachment.

And to say that someone is detached is to say this: that her desire and God's will are identical. She would then not desire God out of any motivation, or for any reason or with any intention, because any of those can govern her desire only in so far as it is *not* identical with God's will. In the nothingness of detachment there is nothing in my desire which answers the question why I should love God, any more than there can be in God any reason why God should love God. To be detached is to live 'without a why'. It is to love God with an uncreated, undifferentiated love. It is not to be a being without desire.

In this detachment alone, therefore, is there any sense in which a person can be said truly to love himself. For a person will love himself as God loves himself, not in the manner of a false self-love, as an *object of desire*, but, we might say, in sheer delight at his own goodness. Only such a person can truly love another:

Those who are equal to nothing, they alone are equal to God. The divine being is equal to nothing, and in it there is neither image nor form. To the souls who are equal, the Father gives equally, and he holds nothing at all from them. Whatever the Father can achieve, that he gives equally to this soul, yes, if it no longer equals itself more than anything else, and it should not be closer to itself than to anything else. It should desire or heed its own honor, its profit and whatever may be its own, no more than what is a stranger's. Whatever belongs to anyone should not be distant or strange to the soul, whether this be evil or good. All the love of this world is founded on self-love. If you had forsaken that, you would have forsaken the whole world.[28]

V

What, then, is the practice of detachment? I think that as we can say that detachment is the solution, so the problem is not human desire itself, but its possessiveness. The strategy of detachment is the strategy of dispossessing desire of its desire to possess its objects, and so to destroy them. For Eckhart it is not just that, in addition to our other desires, we also desire to possess; as for John of the Cross, possessiveness for Eckhart is pandemic; *all* our desires are infected by it, all that we desire we desire *qua* object of possession; no matter how unpossessible an object may be in itself, possessiveness will convert it into a possible object of possession, will make a property of it, will 'privatise' it, as it were. It is for this reason that the undetached person denatures her world and cannot even properly enjoy it. She cannot meet with reality on its own terms, but only on her own. Detachment, for Eckhart, is not the severing of desire's relation with its object, but the restoration of desire to a proper relation of objectivity; as we might say, of reverence for its object. Detachment is therefore the basis of the true possibility of love, which is why, for Eckhart, it is more fundamental than love, being the condition of its possibility.

After all, as the *Cloud* Author puts it, anyone can love God 'for what he can get out of him'. But such a 'God' is not God. Any 'God' we could possibly love without detachment is not the true God badly loved, but not God at all, the mere godlet of our own invention. What is more, because possessive desire is a form of dependence on its object, the God of our own desire is a form of ego-need, a God on whom we depend not in freedom but in servility, one for whom, therefore, God would have to be master. For possessive desires at

---

[28] *Sermon 6, Justi vivent in aeternum,* Colledge and McGinn, *Essential Sermons,* p. 185. Cp Marguerite:

> 'If [the annihilated soul] does anything outside herself, this will always be not of her. If God does his work in her, this is of him in her, for his own purpose, and not of her...And so what she does which is not of her no more burdens her than if she were to do nothing at all, for she has nothing of herself, having given it all freely without asking any 'why?' (*Mirror,* 81, 18–27 (my translation).)

once destroy what they desire and are enslaved to what they destroy. The gods of the undetached may be poor diminished little things: but they are, for all that, poor diminished little *tyrants*.

Possessiveness is, therefore, the principle of destruction of nature and creation and so of God. But at the root of all other possessiveness is the ultimately possessive desire to be a self: the desire that there should be at my centre not that unnameable abyss into which, as into a vacuum, the nameless Godhead is inevitably drawn, but an identity I can own, an identity which is defined by my ownership of it. That is the ultimately destructive form that attachment can take, for it is an attachment which seeks to infill that nothingness with images of self and with 'ways' to God. Such an identity must necessarily expel God from the place which it occupies, for a God which is thus made a *hoc aliquid* is a rival to the self which is thus made into a *hoc aliud*. Consequently, any God it does affirm it must affirm in exclusion of the I which affirms it. These are the perverse, inverted dialectics of the undetached, the dialectics of the 'exterior' person who is trapped in the polarisations of interiority and exteriority so as to seek God 'within' *rather than* 'without'. For the truly detached person there can be no such distinction, which is why Eckhart is able to resist the conventional polarisation of the active and the contemplative lives and to insist upon the unity of Martha and Mary.[29] That is also why Eckhart is so insistent upon the absolute transcendence equally of God and the self, beings beyond every possibility of being appropriated within some intelligible, meaningful, desirable, possessible structure of selfhood. That is why, for Eckhart, 'my' self is not in the last resort *mine* at all. And any self which I can call my own is a false self, a self of possessive imagination. To be a self I must retain within myself the void and the desert of detachment. To live by detachment is to live without an explanation, without rationale, namelessly one with the nameless God.

Hence, the strategy of detachment is not that of focusing created desires upon God *rather than* creatures: for that in itself is but to make God a creaturely object of created desire. It is, rather, the apophatic critique of desire, corresponding in every detail of its structure and dynamic with the apophaticism of intellect. Just as the dialectics of apophaticism are those of the negation of the negation, so the practice of detachment is that of *opposing oppositions*

---

[29] *Sermon* 86, *Intravit Jesus*, McGinn, Tobin and Borgstadt, *Teacher and Preacher*, pp. 338–44.

between one desire and another, between the desire for God and the desire for created things, as if the desire for God was just another created desire for another created object. It is only for the undetached person that that opposition could exist. To be detached is not therefore to be desireless of creation in order to desire only God, nor is it to desire nothing at all, even God. Rather, it is to desire out of that nothingness of self and God, so that, from the security of this 'fortress of the soul' which nothing created can enter, we can desire all things with a desire truly divine, because it is desire 'without a why'.

There is, in Eckhart's doctrine of detachment the potential for the critique of an ego-serving spirituality, a spirituality of 'ways to God', which finds 'ways' even in detachment, and so loses God. If there was any kind of undetachment which Eckhart feared above all others for its spiritually distorting potential, it was that of the 'spiritual' for whom means displaced goals. This, among other reasons, should have us pause before answering the question 'What is Eckhart's way?' For his is the way of no ways – or rather, it is the way of any way whatsoever, so long as it is submitted to the critical practice of detachment, the apophaticism of desire. This is not so much a 'spirituality' as the critique of spirituality. It is practised upon the ordinary 'ways' and means of the Christian life, for there were no others for Eckhart. But without that critique of detachment, even the ordinary ways of Christians can become a deformed, monstrous anthropomorphic caricature. For which reason Eckhart concludes one of his most spectacularly paradoxical Sermons with the question:

Then how should I love God? You should love God unspiritually, that is, your soul should be unspiritual and stripped of all spirituality, for so long as your soul has a spirit's form, it has images, and so long as it has images, it has a medium, and so long as it has a medium, it is not unity or simplicity. Therefore your soul must be unspiritual, free of all spirit, and must remain spiritless; for if you love God as he is God, as he is spirit, as he is person and as he is image – all this must go! 'Then how should I love him?' You should love him as he is nonGod, a nonspirit, a nonperson, a nonimage, but as he is pure, unmixed, bright 'One', separated from all duality; and in that One we should eternally sink down, out of 'something' into 'nothing'.[30]

That is the meaning and practice of Eckhart's detachment.

[30] *Sermon 83, Renovamini spiritu,* Colledge and McGinn, *Essential Sermons,* p. 208.

CHAPTER 8

The Cloud of Unknowing *and the*
critique of interiority

I

This writyng that next foloweth is the Inglische of a book that
Seynte Denys wrote unto Thimothe, the whiche is clepid
[called] in Latyn tonge Mistica Theologia. Of the whiche
book, forthi that it is mad minde [referred to] in the 70
chapter of a book wretin before (the whiche is clepid the
Cloude of Vnknowing) how that Denis sentence [opinion] wol
cleerli afferme al that is wretyn in that same book; therefore,
in translacioun of it, I have not onliche folowed the nakyd
lettre of the text, bot for to declare the hardnes of it [clarify its
difficulties], I have moche folowed the sentence
[interpretation] of the Abbot of Seint Victore, a noble &
worthi expositour of this same book.[1]

In this, his prologue to a translation of Denys' *Mystical Theology*, the
Cloud Author rather puzzlingly claims both to have made a close
rendering, following 'the nakyd lettre of the text' (which is far from
true) and to have done so in accordance with the 'sentence' of
Thomas Gallus, the thirteenth-century Abbot of St Andrew at
Vercelli (which, for sure, he has). The *Cloud* Author thus at once
makes clear that his indebtedness to Denys has been acquired
through personal acquaintance with his writings and concedes that
his reading of them is filtered through at least the century of
Victorine interpretation which fed into Gallus, if not through the

---

[1] *Dionise Hid Divinite*, prologue, in Phyllis Hodgson, *The Cloud of Unknowing and Related
Treatises (Cloud)*, Salzburg: Institute für Anglistik und Amerikanistik, 1982. p. 119. The
passage referred to in the *Cloud* reads: '& trewly, whoso wil loke Denis bookes, he schal
fynde that his wordes wilen cleerly aferme al that I haue seyde or schal sey, fro the
beginnyng of this tretis to the ende'. *Cloud*, 70, p. 70, 7–9. For the *Cloud* I have used
Hodgson's edition in the same volume. References give the chapter, page and line num-
bers of her edition. I have slightly modernised Hodgson's orthography.

influence of others since that time.[2] As Minnis has pointed out, the contrast between 'nakyd lettre' and 'sentence' is an English rendering of the technical Latin terms *littera* and *sententia* which, in mediaeval biblical exegesis, referred to the domain of the grammar and the obvious surface meaning of a text on the one hand, and to the deeper meaning of the text on the other.[3] This may be so. But in any case it will have to be said that the *Cloud* Author's rendering of the *Mystical Theology* owes much to Gallus that is not found in Denys, both as to *littera* and *sententia*. For the *Cloud* Author has made significant, if small, alterations to the *littera* of *Mystical Theology*.[4] And it cannot escape our notice that all those minor alterations serve only one purpose: to further the interests of Gallus' version of the *sententia* of Denys' mysticism. Specifically, the variants of *Dionise Hid Divinite* reinforce Gallus' shift of emphasis from the intellectualism of Denys' 'mysticism of vision' towards the voluntarism of his own 'mysticism of affectivity'.

It is worth noting this transformation of Denys' apophaticism at the outset – and equally worthwhile spelling out some of the textual detail, as we will do shortly – because together with what amounts to a sustained critique of the role of imagination in the spiritual life, this transformation contributes much to the distinctiveness of the *Cloud* Author's spirituality. We will now consider these two elements of that distinctiveness in turn.

II

Minnis has established authoritatively both the fact of the *Cloud* Author's dependence on Gallus' reading of Denys and that the main respect in which he so depends is in this shift of emphasis, from the supremacy of *intellectus* to that of *affectus*.[5] In summary, the

---

[2] Claims have been made, by Hodgson and others, for Carthusian influence on the *Cloud*, in particular of Hugh of Balma and Guigo da Ponte. These claims are discussed by Alastair Minnis in his article 'Affection and Imagination in *The Cloud of Unknowing* and Hilton's *Scale of Perfection*', *Traditio*, XXXIX (1983) 323–66.   [3] Ibid., p. 326.

[4] And has added one major interpolation, owing nothing to Gallus and incidental to our concerns: most of the paragraph on p. 124, lines 10-22 and all of that of p. 124 lines 23–38 and p. 125 lines 1–5 of Hodgson are an explanatory gloss of *Mystical Theology* chapter 2, 1025 B lines 1–3 in Luibheid, *Pseudo-Dionysius*.

[5] There is no good English translation of the Latin word *affectus*. 'Want' is a word of parallel generality, except that ancient connections of that word with 'lack' skew the meaning in favour of those forms of wanting which arise from need, which will not do for either the Latin *caritas* or *dilectio*, neither of which are 'need' forms of wanting, though both would be included within the mediaeval idea of *affectus*. So in the end, perhaps we will have to make do with 'love' as the best translation.

argument is this: the *Cloud* Author acknowledges few sources explicitly. Among those he does acknowledge are Denys, Richard of St Victor and Gallus. The emphasis on the priority of *affectus* could not have been derived from Richard of St Victor, for it has no parallel in him. Other possible sources, such as Hugh of Balma, contain little that is not either a commonplace of the literature or else is found more explicitly in Gallus. When the *Cloud* Author acknowledges his indebtedness to Gallus it is in the translation of a text of Denys which he has modified according to the *sententia* of Gallus. Hence it is in Gallus principally that the *Cloud* Author finds support for that switch in priority to *affectus*. The case is convincing.

But there is more going on in both Gallus' and the *Cloud* Author's transformation of Denys than consists in this shift towards affectivity – and this is because the effect of that shift is to transform the structure and balance of the apophaticism itself. Both Gallus and the *Cloud* make their own additions as to *littera*. Minor as these are, they disguise a truly radical departure from the dialectical negativity of the intellectualist apophatic tradition.

Gallus' apophaticism is already quite significantly different from Denys'. In the preface to his second *Commentary on the Song of Songs*, Gallus distinguishes the knowledge of God into two kinds:

> the first is intellectual, this being acquired by the contemplation of the created order...This kind of knowledge of God is a kind of abstract reflection [*speculativa*] and is dark and obscure, is spoken of and taught to all and sundry, through meditation, hearing and reading. The pagan philosophers are able to achieve only (knowledge) of this kind. That is why the Apostle says in Romans 1, 19, *what is known of God is plain to them*. That is known which may be gleaned from prior knowledge of the things of the sensible world.[6]

But the second kind of knowledge of God

> exceeds the first beyond all possibility of comparison and the great Denys describes it in *Divine Names* 7 as *the most divine knowledge of God...which comes through unknowing...*This is *the wisdom of Christians which is from above* (James, 3, 17) and it *descends from the Father of Lights* (James, 1, 17), for this wisdom

---

6 *Super Cantica Canticorum Hierarchice Exposita Secundum Dominum T. Abbatem Vercellensem, Prohemium* (Second Commentary), in *Thomas Gualterius, Abbas Vercellensis, Commentaires du Cantique des Cantiques*, Textes Philosophiques du Moyen Age, n. 14, ed. Jeanne Barbet, Paris, 1967, p. 65. For a partial translation of this text, see my *Eros and Allegory*, p. 319, no. 1.

exceeds what is in the heart of humans...The intellectual wisdom first referred to does reach up from the level of sense to the intellect. But this higher than intellectual (wisdom) is *a maidservant of the thrones of God* (Wisd. 9, 4)...And drawing on the teaching of the Apostle, the great Denys the Areopagite has written his account of this more than intellectual wisdom, in so far as it is possible to write one down, in his book on *Mystical Theology*...[7]

There are a number of assumptions behind this distinction, and some implications of it, not all of which it is possible to recognize in Denys. The texts from Denys which Gallus cites in amplification of these two kinds of knowledge, serve in Denys to distinguish between his 'symbolic' and 'mystical' theologies, and so between a cataphatic and an apophatic theology. Gallus uses them to support these distinctions of course, but he combines them with a distinction of his own, with little enough foundation in Denys: that between the knowledge of natural reason such as the pagan philosophers are capable of, and the supra-intellectual wisdom of Christians.[8] The result of this overlaying of Denys' distinctions with his own is to identify, first, the knowledge of natural reason with intellectual knowledge as cataphatic; and, second, the supra-rational knowledge of Christians with the non-intellectual and apophatic. And there are two things to note about these identifications.

The first is that in maintaining that intellectual knowledge of God is inherently cataphatic, Gallus appears to be supposing that there can be no apophaticism native to intellect itself, that intellect only affirms – in which view, of course, he differs from Denys. And from this will follow the second point of note: for if it is not within the power of intellect to construct its own *self*-negations, then the apophasis of intellect's affirmations will have to be the act of another power which negates intellect as such. And both points seem to be borne out by the subsequent discussion in the *Commentary on the Song of Songs*.

Gallus notes that where the *Mystical Theology* gives the theory of mysticism, in the Song of Songs 'Solomon gives the practice of this

[7] Barbet, p. 65 (*Eros and Allegory*, p. 320, no. 2).

[8] Gallus' distinction appears to have any such foundation as it has in Denys in a passage in *Letter* 9, where Denys distinguishes between the 'ineffable and mysterious' aspect of theology and its 'more open and evident' on the other, the latter resorting to symbolism, the other to 'demonstration' (1105D, Luibheid, *Pseudo-Dionysius* p. 283). But Denys' distinction is made within revealed theology, as between names in Scripture, not as in Gallus, between the natural knowledge of philosophers and the knowledge of the theologians.

same mystical theology';[9] and he adds that to understand how he proposes to explain the practice of mysticism it is necessary to take on board the ninefold structure of the angelic orders which Denys explains in the *Celestial Hierarchy*. For, he says, the ranks of the celestial hierarchy 'are duplicated in the hierarchies of each individual mind'.[10] This is the 'internalised hierarchy' of spiritual ascent which later, as we have seen, Bonaventure was to borrow for his *Itinerarium*.

The details of what turns out to be a somewhat pedantic and uninspired explication of the Song of Songs in terms of angelic hierarchy need not concern us. What is of interest is that at every stage up to and including the penultimate eighth, the cognitive and the affective powers of the soul proceed, as he puts it 'hand in hand', but that at the eighth, the rank of the Cherubim, the soul has reached the limits of *intellectus*, beyond which *affectus* cannot yet step:

> The eighth rank contains every kind of knowledge of the intellect drawn towards the divine heights, although it is not able to reach them, and of desire similarly drawn, though it may not transcend the height to which intellect is gathered. For they are drawn together, and desire and intellect as it were walk hand in hand up to the point at which intellect finally fails – this, at the supreme apex of this rank, is the Cherub; and intellect, though drawn up to it, can go no further but there achieves the fulfilment of its knowledge and light; hence this rank is called the 'Cherubim'.[11]

But beyond the eighth is the rank of the Seraphim, where *affectus* is at last able to break its partnership with *intellectus* and step out on its own. This rank

> contains the highest aspirations for God, the excesses and inflowings which go beyond understanding, burning brilliance and brilliant burnings; understanding cannot be drawn into the sublime ecstasies and excesses of these lights, but only the supreme love which can unite [*sola principalis affectio unibilis*]...This rank embraces God and is wrapped in the embraces of the bridegroom, this is no knowledge in a mirror, it takes *Mary's part, which will not be taken away* (Lk., 10, 42). In this order the bed is laid for the bridegroom and bride. It is from this order that the torrent of divine light pours down in stages to the lower orders.[12]

---

⁹ Barbet, *Thomas Gualterius*, p. 66 (*Eros and Allegory*, p. 320, no. 3).
¹⁰ Ibid., p. 66 (*Eros and Allegory*, p. 320, no. 3).
¹¹ Ibid., p. 67 (*Eros and Allegory*, p. 322, no. 9).
¹² Ibid., p. 67 (*Eros and Allegory*, p. 323, n. 10).

This 'practical' mystical interpretation of the internalised hierarchy reinforces the formal statements of the opening paragraphs of the preface. Apophasis begins where *intellectus* ends. Not before that point, for at none of the eight steps leading to the last is there any moment of negation. But only at the last is the breakthrough to the 'burning brilliance and brilliant burnings' of apophasis made and that is by means of *affectus* on its own.

This picture is not in all respects consistent with that of Gallus' *Glossa* on the *Mystical Theology*.[13] Perhaps because in the *Glossa* his responsibilities to the *ipsissima verba* of the text were less easily shrugged off, the constraints of a close gloss tie him to more of the detail of Denys' apophaticism. Hence, short of an outright rejection of the argument of chapters 4 and 5 of the *Mystical Theology*, Gallus could hardly have avoided conceding some kind of immanent 'dialectics of denial' to intellect, and so he does: Gallus follows Denys up the ladder of negations one by one from the lowest perceptual attributes to the highest conceptual. But, as in his *Commentary on the Song*, the break-off point which leads to the darkness of the mystical occurs where *intellectus* drops out and *affectus* takes over and we gain the impression that intellect's own denials are, strictly, not essential to the process: for 'Why', he asks,

is this summit of the divine secrets said to be 'unknown above all unknowns', 'brilliant beyond all brilliance', and 'the highest'?

It is said to be 'unknown beyond all unknowns', because rational enquiry falls short of it; it is said to be 'brilliant beyond all brilliance' because understanding fails of it, being overwhelmed by the overflowing outpourings of light; it is said to be 'the highest' because intelligence cannot reach up to it because of its *transcending union of love*...[14]

Rise up to union with God by means of the highest love.[15]

Thus does love firmly shut the door on understanding before it proceeds on to the mystic darkness.

Crucial both to Gallus, and, as we will see, to the *Cloud* Author, is the interpretation of Denys' allegorical retelling of Moses' ascent

---

[13] There are three works of Gallus relating to Denys' *Mystical Theology*: the *Glossa*, a brief commentary, found in PL 122, cols 267–84, where it is attributed to John Scottus; the *Extractio* or paraphrase of *Mystical Theology*, which probably served as the model for the *Cloud* Author's *Dionise Hid Divinite* and is found in the *Opera* of Denys the Carthusian, 16, pp. 444–54 (together with the Carthusian's own *Commentary on the Mystical Theology* and the Latin versions of that work by John Scottus and Marsiglio Ficino); and finally, Gallus' full commentary on the *Mystical Theology*, which as yet has not been published.

[14] *Glossa* on *The Mystical Theology*, PL 122, 271A.   [15] Ibid., 272A.

of Mount Sinai at the end of chapter 1 of *Mystical Theology*. Denys had marked out a clear set of steps and transitions in this ascent which may be summarized as follows:

1. Moses submits to purification and then departs from those who have not been purified and he hears 'the many voiced trumpets. He sees the many lights, pure and with rays streaming abundantly'.[16]

2. Moses pushes on together with the priests towards the summit and next encounters not God himself but 'the place where he dwells'.[17] This Denys interprets as referring to the illuminations, taken collectively, of the cataphatic theologies, which are able to show his 'unimaginable presence, walking the heights of those holy places to which the mind at least can rise'.[18]

3. Moses breaks free both of the priests who had accompanied him this far and of the illuminations of the cataphatic and 'plunges into the truly mysterious darkness of unknowing. Here, renouncing all that the mind may conceive, wrapped entirely in the intangible and the invisible, he belongs completely to him who is beyond everything. Here…one is supremely united by a completely unknowing inactivity of all knowledge, and knows beyond the mind by knowing nothing.'[19]

Here in Denys' transition from stage 2 to 3, it is intellect which, while 'renouncing all it knows', plunges on into its own dialectic of a '*knowing* inactivity of all knowledge'. Not so in Gallus. Both in the *Glossa* and in the *Extractio* Gallus gives the same account. The 'place of God' he explains is to be understood as

the conceptions of all that is below God who surpasses all things and through them God is made present to us cognitively; he pours down upon us from above the most fundamental and highest of those conceptions [*rationes*] which…are capable of being understood by the contemplative mind [*speculative*].[20]

But when Moses leaves the 'place of God' behind he

enters into the cloud of unknowing [*ad caliginem ignorantiae*], that is, he is made one with the incomprehensibility of the Godhead, which intelligence cannot reach into: [and] this [cloud] shuts out all else and encloses

---

16 *MT*, 1000D.   17 Ibid.
18 Ibid., 1001A.   19 Ibid.
20 *Extractio*, in *Opera Divi Dionysii Cartusiensis*, 16, p. 455, col 2C.

within it and hides in the deepest secrecy all those knowings and under-standings as in the first cause of all. And by means of this [cloud] all who are united with God, who is above all things, are confirmed in an emi-nence which no reason is able to explore nor intellect contemplate; and being set apart from all things and in a manner of speaking from itself, it is united with God, who is unknown to intellect, *through a union of love [per unitionem dilectionis]* which is effective of true knowing, far superior to the knowing of intellect; and in so far as it leaves the knowing of intellect behind, it knows God beyond all knowing and mind.[21]

What Gallus has added to Denys' account is a conception of the apophatic 'knowing unknowing' in terms not of intellect's own self-transcendence, but in terms of a higher kind of knowing than that of intellect, the 'knowing of love'. Thus, whereas for Denys both the 'knowing' and the 'unknowing' are contained dialectically within the immanent dynamic of intellect, for Gallus, the 'knowing' of the 'knowing unknowing' is the 'knowing of love' and the 'unknowing' of the 'knowing unknowing' is the simple *rejection* of intellect. Gallus is, of course, picking up on a very ancient theme in the Latin tradition, stretching back at least to Gregory the Great, according to which love is itself a kind of knowing: *amor ipse notitia est*.[22] This is a theme which we will pick up again in the *Cloud*, but for a moment let us pause to register the effect of this reinterpreta-tion of Denys on the dialectics of the apophaticism itself.

We can say, in fact, that those dialectics have disappeared in Gallus, at any rate in any recognizable Dionysian form. Gone is any sense of the importance of the multi-stage hierarchical ascent of *Mystical Theology* 4 and 5, with its complex ascending scale of negativities; what replaces it is a simple two-stage process of intel-lectual affirmation followed by a transcending stage of the knowing of love. Gone, moreover, is every sense that intellect, upon entry to the cloud, negates itself, and so *self*-surpasses into the darkness of unknowing, for intellect is negated by love, not by itself and is sim-ply bundled away at the point at which its affirmations fail. In short, the hierarchical dialectic of negativity found in Denys is replaced by a simple bi-polarity of knowing and love, which is ulti-mately transcended in the knowing *of* love. This is an apophaticism

---

[21] Ibid., p. 455, col 2C-D.
[22] *Homelia in Evangelia* 27.4, PL 76, 1207. For a full discussion of this tradition, but especially in William of St Thierry, see David N. Bell, *The Image and Likeness*, Kalamazoo: Cistercian Publications, 1984, chapter 6.

in which the cloud of unknowing is a metaphor not of self-tran-
scendent intellect but of its simple abandonment. It is therefore an
apophaticism which, unlike Denys', is pregnant with the possibilities of an anti-intellectualism.

III

The *Cloud* Author's relation with the Dionysian dialectics of intellect is more complex than Gallus'. That the *Cloud* Author owes
much to Gallus' reinterpretation is not difficult to establish both in
his own Middle English version of *Mystical Theology* and in *The
Cloud of Unknowing* itself. As far as concerns *Dionise Hid Divinite*, it
would be going too far to say that it is as to *littera* a version of
Gallus' *Extractio* rather than the 'translacioun' of *Mystical Theology*.
But it would be no exaggeration to say that as to *sententia* it is certainly closer to the *Extractio* than to the *Mystical Theology*. Indeed, in
so far as *Dionise Hid Divinite* differs from Gallus' *Extractio* this would
be not because the former is nearer to *Mystical Theology* than the
Extractio but because it interpolates the *littera* of *Mystical Theology* the
more heavily of the two. Moreover, all the *Cloud* Author's interpo-
lations are to the same effect as are Gallus', namely to emphasize
the ultimate priority of love over intellect as the power which leads
into the cloud of unknowing.

When we turn to *The Cloud of Unknowing* itself, what matters is
the total shift of emphasis rather than the details of textual dependence. Unlike *Dionise Hid Divinite*, *The Cloud of Unknowing* is not written with any declared intention of fidelity to the texts of Denys, but
only in a more general way as being supported, 'fro the beginnyng
of this tretis to the ende'[23] by what Denys says. What is obvious,
however, is that even this is far from the truth and misleading. It is
far from the truth, as we will see, for as in Gallus, the balance of
the dialectics of unknowing is struck quite differently from that of
Denys. And it is misleading because in so far as the *Cloud* Author
invites us to test his claim of loyalty to a Dionysian theology we are
led to read him largely through the consequences of the fact that
he fails that test in so many ways. It becomes all too easy, in consequence, to read *The Cloud of Unknowing* principally through the
points of divergence between his voluntarism and the intellectual-

<hr>

[23] *Cloud*, 70, 8–9, p. 70.

ism of Denys. Such a reading would be regrettable – though it is a temptation hard to resist, if only because the *Cloud* Author asks for it. But it would be a pity, since it would do less than justice to the integrity of the *Cloud* Author's own spirituality and to its intrinsic coherence, which can and should be allowed to survive the source-criticism of the scholars. In any case, whether for better or worse, *The Cloud of Unknowing* must be tested on its own merits and in the last resort not in its relations even with those sources its author claims for himself.

Once again, what does need to be said about the voluntaristic shift of the *Cloud* away from the intellectualism of Denys can be said relatively quickly. The *Cloud* Author's is a spirituality in which desire figures not merely as an important emphasis but pretty much as the whole thing – at least as the *unum necessarium*. In a phrase which echoes Bonaventure's *vir desideriorum*,[24] the *Cloud* Author tells his disciple: 'Alle thi liif now behoueth algates to stonde in desire, if thou schalt profite in degre of perfeccioun'.[25] Therefore, he goes on, 'Lift up thin herte unto God with a meek steryng of love', though not until you are ready for what is involved, for the work is hard:

Lette not therfore, bot trauayle therin tyl thou fele lyst. For at the first tyme when thou dost it, thou fyndest bot a derknes, & as it were a cloude of vnknowyng, thou wost neuer what, sauying that thou felist in thi wille a nakid entent vnto God. This derknes & this cloude is, howsoeuer thou dost, bitwix thee & thi God, & letteth the that thou maist not see him cleerly by light of vnderstonding in thi reson, ne fele him in swetnes of loue in thin affeccioun. And therfore schap thee to bide in this derknes as long as thou maist, euermore criing after him that thou louest; for if euer schalt thou fele him or see him, as it may be here, it behoueth alweis be in this cloude & in this derknes.[26]

And if between the disciple's desire and the God desired there stands a cloud of unknowing, between his desire and all the work of mind and imagination there must be placed a 'cloud of forget-ting',[27] a forgetting which will place in oblivion not only all thoughts of creatures, nor only all thoughts of God aroused by creatures, but also all *spiritual* activity which is the work of sense, imagination or reason. In respect of all these ways in which God might be made 'present' to the disciple, God must be made discon-

[24] *Itin.*, Prologue, 3.   [25] *Cloud*, 2, pp. 8, 38–39, 1.
[26] Ibid., 3, p. 9, 28–37.   [27] Ibid., 5, p. 13, 26–27.

certingly 'absent' from him. The *Cloud* Author makes it abundantly
clear that it is not merely 'worldly' thoughts which must thus be
forgotten, but also and perhaps most particularly it is 'spiritual'
thoughts which present a potential obstacle to the disciple's entry
into the cloud of unknowing.

> As ofte as I sey 'alle the creatures that euer ben maad', as ofte I mene, not
> only the self creatures, but also alle werkes & the condicions of the same
> creatures. I outetake [make exception of] not o creature, whether thei ben
> bodily creatures or goostly, ne yit any condicion or werk of any creature,
> whether thei be good or iuel; bot schortly to sey, alle schuld be hid vnder
> the cloude of forgetyng in this caas.[28]

In respect, therefore, of all cognitive activity God must be made
'absent' so that 'the thinketh...that thou arte ful fer fro God',[29] but
in fact he is further from God who has not placed this cloud of forgetting between himself and his cognitions, however much the disciple may think that these cognitions place him in God's presence.
But all this unknowing and forgetting of the familiar 'menes' to
God – so pure and radical a sense of the absence of God – can
cause panic and disorientation and the disciple will ask the *Cloud*
Author:

> 'How schal I think on himself, & what is hee?' & to this I cannot answere
> thee bot thus: 'I wote neuer'.
> For thou hast brought me with thi question into that same derknes, & into
> that same cloude of vnknowyng that I wolde thou were in thiself. For of
> alle other creatures & theire werkes – ye, & of the werkes of God self –
> may a man thorou grace haue fulheed of knowing, & wel to kon thinke on
> hem; bot of God himself can no man thinke. & therfore I wole leue al that
> thing I can think, and chese to my loue that thing that I cannot think. For
> whi he may wel be loued, bot not thought. By loue he may be getyn &
> holden; bot bi thought neither.[30]

So the *Cloud* Author asks the disciple to be resolute in this negation
of all cognitivity; nor is this resolution to be a merely passive deter-
mination to stay fast in it, for it must be an active work of denial
and unknowing. For the *Cloud* Author, 'vnknowing' is an apophatic
strategy, not a mere ignorance; it is an achievement of the work of
'forgetyng', a work which, as we will see, is the normal routine of
the spiritual life, a routine of progressive simplification and attenu-

---

[28]   Ibid., 5, p. 13, 31–37.
[29]   Ibid., 5, p. 13, 27–28.
[30]   Ibid., 6, p. 14, 14–23.

ation of the imagination and reason. To 'unknow' is, for the *Cloud* Author, an active verb-form.

It is not of course that he denies any role at any stage to the work of imagination and thinking on the path to unknowing. An excessive emphasis on the *Cloud* Author's apophaticism could lead to an excessive devaluation of his cataphaticism, both theological and practical. And for sure, the case for saying that, in the end, the *Cloud*'s dialectics have been reduced to a bipolar opposition between the cognitive and the affective could be taken to reinforce a reading of *The Cloud of Unknowing* according to which reason and imagination have no significant role to play. But it should not be so taken. For the *Cloud* Author's dialectics of negation retain some important elements of the hierarchical ascent of affirmations towards God which are undoubtedly Dionysian in language and thought.

There is, he writes, a ladder of 'menes…in the whiche a contemplatiif prentys schuld be ocupyed, the whiche ben theese: Lesson, Meditacion, & Orison'[31] and, perhaps with the Carthusian Guigo's *Scala Claustralium* in mind,[32] he takes the description of the progress of the soul up the ladder of meditative practice to have been adequately given in the traditional literature, so he needs not dwell on it. Nonetheless, the fact that he feels he has little to add to this traditional account of the practices of reading, meditation and prayer can be taken to imply a depreciation of them only if one neglects his stated position on the subject. The aspirant to the highest spiritual achievement of contemplation who believes that he or she can ignore the ordinary means presupposed to that achievement – who precipitately throws away the ladder before climbing it – will end up with a distorted caricature of contemplation, as we will see.

Moreover, the *Cloud* Author does offer his own account of the scale of meditative progress towards contemplation. Meditation will proceed, he says, from many words and many thoughts to few and ultimately to just one; from many requests addressed to God, to just one cry of help, an expressive and compact form of prayer, he says, like that of the person in a situation of extreme danger who cries 'Help!' or 'Get out!'[33] In particular, that devotional prac-

---

[31] Ibid., 35, p. 39, 23–25.
[32] *The Ladder of Monks*, II, in *Guigo* II, *The Ladder of Monks and Twelve Meditations*, trans. and ed. Edmund Colledge and James Walsh, London and Oxford: Mowbray, 1978, p. 81.
[33] *Cloud*, 37, p. 41, 20–21.

tice to which he attaches most importance, the practice of reflecting on one's own sinfulness, will proceed from a maudlin, guilt-ridden picking over of one's many faults one by one[34] to the unified understanding of 'synne conielyd in a lumpe' which is, he says, our sense of 'self'.[35] Progress in the meditative practices, whether of imagination or of discursive reason, therefore leads to simplification and reduction and ultimately to the simplest of prayers, expressive of the disciple's total and immediate dependence upon God; and this work of progressively more 'forgetful' devotion is a permanent task, the normal occupation of the contemplative, 'the whiles thou leuyst in this wrechid liif'.[36]

The continual practice of this simplified meditation and prayer will lead, then, to a stark awareness of an almost 'existential' gulf which stands between the disciple and God, there being nothing else to hold them apart but this stark sense of the self as sinful. The final act of the mind, the act which thrusts the soul into the dizzying, disconcerting, truly contemplative darkness of unknowing, is that by which this 'self-as-sinful' is also placed under the cloud of forgetting and is destroyed.[37] This 'break' by which the practices of prayer and meditation self-destruct is the beginning of a contemplation in which the role of 'menes' finally ceases; but it is not something which we can bring about by ourselves, for it is not the *natural* outcome of the means we have taken to get to the point where it is possible. It is achieved only by the development in the soul of a 'stronge & a deep goostly sorow'[38] which, for the disciple's part, consists in a kind of patient desire that God should offer him 'a ful specyal grace, ful frely goven of God',[39] for nothing he can do can bring it about.

Contemplation, therefore, is a pure grace, a flash of brilliant darkness which intrudes upon the normal, everyday practice of the ordinary, everyday means of reading, meditation and prayer. Contemplation is not, therefore, a 'practice' at all, for it is a grace; nor is it a grace the disciple can count upon as any kind of permanent condition. Moreover it is, in the normal case, a condition which he cannot count on at all except on the strength of many years of effort in meditative practice. Those 'ordinary' means are therefore in no way secondary and dispensable, for they are the

---

34 Ibid., 16, p. 25, 27–35.   35 Ibid., 36, p. 40, 32.
36 Ibid., 40, p. 44, 9.   37 Ibid., 40, p. 46, 10.
38 Ibid., 40, p. 46, 17.   39 Ibid., 44, p. 46, 14.

whole of what the disciple can do and that whole which he can do consists in nothing but the patient desire that God will do the rest. It is only the young, inexperienced and impatient beginner who will try to force the pace and attempt to 'practise' contemplation for himself, with the inevitable result of a weird and stupid caricature.

Hence, at the concrete level of ascetical practice, reading, meditation and prayer form a 'scale' of progressive simplification corresponding with the scale of cataphatic contemplations in Denys. For both, the ascent of this scale is the precondition which leads to true, apophatic, contemplation but for neither is that precondition a mere temporarily prior stage which yields to the apophatic as a second phase leaving the first behind it; for in both the cataphatic is the continuing, permanent condition of the apophatic.

And yet there remains the radical difference. If, for the *Cloud* Author, the apophatic is a moment of 'breakthrough' into the darkness of unknowing, an intervention of grace which irrupts upon the routine devotional practices, that breakthrough is the irruption of love into an ascetical work in which the cognitive powers have been progressively *attenuated* and reduced to a minimum of activity. Hence, at the point of breakthrough love requires the total abandonment of all cognitivity, a cutting of all ties with the safe anchorage of the mind in its familiar images, meditations and narratives of God, leaving all intellectual activity behind, so that the disciple can launch out on to the intellectually uncharted and unchartable seas of the knowing of love. As we have seen, this is not so in Denys.

Consequently, there is not to be found anywhere in the *Cloud* that sophisticated, nuanced, *dialectical* hierarchy of self-negating dissimilar and similar similarities – that 'negation of the negation' – which is what is definitive of Denys' cataphatic ascent. If, on the way to contemplation, the *Cloud* Author admits that there is a hierarchy or scale of ascending affirmations, in the end the logic of the *negations* is not hierarchical, but consists in a simple, uniform, non-dialectical progression towards simplification which is broken off by love's denial of all knowledge *tout court*, to be replaced by the alternative and rival knowing of love. The *Cloud* Author's cataphatic hierarchy is therefore non-dialectical and linear and his apophasis is not immanent within the Dionysian multi-stage hierarchy of denials, but is that, as I have put it, of a two-term polarity of *intellectus* and *affectus*.

IV

It is important to be precise about the nature of the *Cloud* Author's 'voluntarism' and there are two significant comments to be made which will help gain some of the necessary precision for our account of it. The first concerns the imagery of *The Cloud of Unknowing*, the second concerns its dialectics.

If without question the *Cloud* Author inherits and then reinvests the voluntarism of Gallus and thereby transforms into a voluntarism the intellectualist *dialectics* of Denys, nonetheless both he and Gallus retain Denys' predominantly intellectualist *imagery*. Manifestly the *Cloud* Author's image of the 'cloud of unknowing' and Gallus' image of the *caligo ignorantiae* have their origin in that convergence of Hebraic and Platonic sources which flow into Denys. From those sources too derive the complex of images associated with the senses of sight and hearing which so characterize Denys' intellectualist apophaticism, images of 'light' and 'darkness', 'word' and 'silence'. It is surprising to find the *Cloud* Author so loyal to this Dionysian imagery, for it is a distinct feature of the voluntarist traditions of Christian spirituality in the Middle Ages that their imagery is derived not by analogy from the senses of sight and hearing but from those of touch, taste and smell. And there is little trace of such imagery in *The Cloud of Unknowing*.

The habit of deriving imagery for the description of the soul, and of spiritual realities generally, by analogy from the bodily senses is, of course, common to all the patristic and mediaeval traditions.[40] And Augustine, who was unwilling to force issues which seemed so important to later mediaeval theologians about the priorities of intellect and will, was correspondingly free to maximize the diversity of this imagery, employing the language of all five senses in a famous and influential passage:

You called me; you cried aloud to me; you broke my barrier of deafness. You shone upon me; your radiance enveloped me; you put my blindness to flight. You shed your fragrance about me; I drew breath and now I gasp for your sweet odour. I tasted you, and now I hunger and thirst for you. You touched me, and I am inflamed with the love of your peace.[41]

---

[40] See, for example Origen, prologue to *Commentary on the Song of Songs*, in *Origen* (Greer), p. 221; Gregory the Great, *Exposition on the Songs of Songs* in *Eros and Allegory*, p. 217, no. 3, to mention just two early authorities.

[41] *Confessions*, 10. 27. 38.

But in the later mediaeval period the polarisation of voluntarist and intellectualist theologies is most commonly found in conjunction with a corresponding polarisation between imagery of the three lower senses of touch, smell and taste and visual and auditory imagery. The more typical imagery of voluntarism is therefore non-visual, such as is found in the thirteenth-century Augustinian Giles of Rome, whose views on 'contemplation' provide a close parallel with those of Gallus. Like Gallus, Giles divides contemplation into two kinds, that of the philosophers and that of the saints.[42] Like Gallus too, Giles considers the contemplation of the philosophers to be essentially an intellectual activity, expressed in affirmative language, and is a kind of 'seeing' – though unlike Gallus, whose models are always Platonic, Giles' model of the pagan contemplative life is that described by Aristotle in *Nicomachean Ethics*, 10. But the contemplation of the theologian, Giles says, is less a kind of seeing than a kind of tasting – *magis consistit in sapore quam sapere* – and is more a matter of 'loving and sweetness' than of speculation:

Therefore the person who studies in order to know, not to build up and make progress in the love of God, should recognise that he leads the contemplative life as the philosophers describe it, not as theologians do. Hence, if we wish to speak of the contemplative life in terms drawn from the senses we could, in a manner of speaking, adapt the metaphor and say that the contemplation of the philosophers gives delight to hearing and sight; whereas the spiritual contemplation of the theologians gives delight to taste, smell and touch.[43]

Interestingly, Giles bases this allocation of sensory images between intellectual and affective styles of contemplation on a combination of Aristotelian and Dionysian principles. Aristotle had rated sight and hearing as the two highest of the five senses, both absolutely and in respect of their roles in the service of knowledge. Whereas touch, taste and smell are, he thought, more basic, because more 'vital', senses, since they are more closely associated with the body's vital needs.[44] This, taken together with the Dionysian principle that the higher a reality is on the scale of excellence the more appropriate it is to use images of lower things to describe it, gives

---

[42] References to Giles are to his *Commentary on the Song of Songs*, extracts from which are translated in my *Eros and Allegory*, pp. 359–380.

[43] *Eros and Allegory*, p. 363, 14.

[44] *Metaphysics* A 1, 980a–981b.

the result that the higher forms of theological contemplation are best imaged by the three lower senses of touch, taste and smell and the lower, philosophical, contemplation by the higher senses of sight and hearing. Hence,

spiritual contemplation, which consists in tasting – and as such is a more vital activity – has the character rather of pleasing taste, smell and touch, which do more to provide for the means of life. And so, while the happiness of the philosophers is a matter of the intellect, spiritual happiness resides in its fullness and in its highest form in the will...[45]

In this partiality for an imagery of touch, taste and smell by contrast with visual and auditory imagery, Giles is following a long tradition of affectivist piety, in this respect too following Gallus.[46] It is therefore of some significance that not only does the *Cloud* Author uncharacteristically combine a non-Dionysian voluntarism with distinctly Dionysian visual imagery, but that he also positively resists at least some of the manifestations of the affectivist imagery of touch, taste and smell. In a chapter which may with reasonable safety be read as a disparagement of the language of his near contemporary Richard Rolle, the *Cloud* Author warns that the inexperienced person may very well misunderstand what he himself has said about 'depe sorow and desire': he notes that the neophyte may well hear

'how that a man schal lift up his herte vnto God, & vnseesingly desire for to fele the loue of here God. & as fast in a curiosite of witte thei conceyue thees wordes not goostly, as thei ben ment, bot fleschly & bodily, & trauaylen theire fleschly hertes outrageously in theire brestes'.[47]

In this straining of spirit they are liable to fall into 'moche ypocrisie, moche heresye, & moche errour'.[48] There is little doubt that the *Cloud* Author believed the neophyte's error of reading that imagery in too 'fleschly and bodily' a fashion was an unsurprising outcome of the too fleshly nature of the language itself, and not merely to be the result of the neophyte's inexperience. He finds too much danger in the imagery to favour it for himself.

The combination, therefore, of the more astringently negative visual imagery of the Dionysian tradition with its own voluntaristic

---

[45] *Eros and Allegory*, p. 364, 16.
[46] '...the external senses are models of the inner and mental powers; they are in this way models of love because love meets its objects by touching, smelling and tasting', See *Eros and Allegory*, p. 363, n. 14.
[47] *Cloud*, 45, p. 47, 22–26.
[48] Ibid., 45, p. 47, 42–43.

priorities gives a quite distinctive feel to the *Cloud*'s spirituality, though the Dionysian imagery does, initially, play some part in disguising the degree of the *Cloud*'s departure from Denys' intellectualism, perhaps even to the extent of disguising the differences from the *Cloud* Author himself. Of greater consequence, however, is the result – perhaps, even, it is his intention – that the intellectualist imagery highlights the differences between the *Cloud*'s position and that of the more common stream of voluntaristic spiritualities, which its author treats with reserve, and sometimes with outright hostility. Where the *Cloud*'s 'entente' is 'nakyd' – we may say, his account of 'love' is markedly apophatic – he has little sympathy for the emotionalistic varieties of a florid 'affectivist' piety, which, he thought, too much understood the priority of love in terms of actual feelings of desire for God and seemed designed, in the spiritual practices in which it was manifest, for the cultivation of experienced phenomena of affectivity. At their worst, he thought, such forms of piety and devotion could lead to a kind of strenuousness of spirit which was as psychologically as it was spiritually damaging.

Consequently, the *Cloud* Author has particular reason to fear that his own stressing of love will be susceptible to misinterpretation in these terms. For him intellect must indeed be denied in order to leave room for love. But his is no spirituality in which, intellect being negated, undisciplined desire is given free rein. Nor is the discipline of desire a matter simply of loving God *instead of* creatures: we cannot love God as we would love anything else, as if the object of that love could be simply switched from creatures to God. For that would be simply to love God as if she were another creature, as just another object. Therefore,

lift up thin herte vnto God with a meek steryng of love; & mene himself & none of his goodes; and therto loke to thenk on ought bot on hymself, so that nought worche in thi witte ne in thi wille bot only himself. & do that in thee is to forgete all the creatures that euer God maad & the werkes of hem, so that thi thought ne thi desire be not directe ne streche to any of hem, neither in general ne in special. Bot lat hem be, & take no kepe to hem.[49]

We can say, in fact, that for the *Cloud* Author, desire is in itself no more to be trusted than is intellect. If the negative dialectics of

---

[49] Ibid., 3, p. 9, 12–18.

intellect no longer have the determining role in the ascent to God, the discipline and the dialectics of desire take their place. And as in Denys there is an immanent dialectics of intellect which leads to its own self-transcendence, so in the *Cloud* there is an immanent dialectics of desire which leads to its own *excessus*; if intellect is to be denied in the cloud of unknowing, desire is to be disciplined by means of the dialectic of imagination, for imagination is what lies at the root of false desire for God. It is imagination which, damaged by sin, is the source of fantastical and deluded desire and of the fantastical and deluded spiritualities which issue from it. And in a comment ostensibly upon the dangers of an undisciplined imagination in the devotional practices of the immature – though perhaps again an implied criticism of Rolle is intended – the *Cloud* Author says:

before the tyme be that the ymaginacion be in grete partye refreynid by the light of grace in the reson – as it is in contynowel meditacion of goostly thinges, as ben theire wrechidnes, the Passion & the kyndenes of oure Lorde God, with many soche other – thei mowe in no wise put awey the wonderful & the diuerse thoughtes, fantasies & ymages, the whiche ben mynystered & preentid in theire mynde by the lighte & the corioustee of ymaginacyon. & alle this inobedyence is the thyne of the original synne.[50]

V

We are brought by these considerations to the core of the *Cloud* Author's own distinctive version of the apophatic dialectics. These dialectics generate the *Cloud* Author's own version of that 'self-subverting' imagination which we saw at work in Denys. For perhaps no instruction to his disciple is more important to the *Cloud* Author than that he should understand the role of imagination and learn the practice of it in the interior life. If he feared too excessively a materialistic and psychologistic understanding of the love of God – one which simply displaced creatures as its object with a God who is nothing more than a creature of imagination – so, at the second-order level he feared an equivalent 'psychologistic' reduction of the terms descriptive of the spiritual life as such – in particular of the spatial metaphors embedded in those descriptions, of 'above' and 'below', 'within' and 'without'. Chapters 62–69 of the *Cloud* consti-

---

[50] Ibid., 65, p. 65, 34–66, 2.

tute a sustained critique of that traditional language of Christian spirituality, the language of interiority and of ascent.

On the one hand, the *Cloud* Author recognizes the necessity of a 'language of imagination'. And the terms in which he outlines this metaphorical apparatus of spiritual description, as also of the psychological anthropology which underlies it, are broadly in the Augustinian–Bonaventuran tradition. 'Mind', he says, is the name of the collectivity of the human powers including three 'principal' powers, memory, reason and will and two 'secondary' powers, imagination and sensuality. In natural capacity he follows Bonaventure and Aquinas in holding that there are no beings other than God who are superior to human beings, for in the natural order even angels 'ben bot euen with thee'.[51] The higher powers work in spiritual matters independently of the lower and without their help and though the lower powers have some capacity to relate with the physical world in their own right, they do not possess on their own the capacity to know the moral and other conditions of physical creation, 'ne the cause of theire beyngs & theire makyng'.[52]

Following Augustine, the *Cloud* Author takes all physical creation to be 'outside' us and, in consequence, imagination, which is the power of inner reconstruction of 'outer' things, engages us 'outwardly' and 'beneath' us: 'for euer whan the mynde is ocupied with any bodely thing, be it taken to neuer so goode an eende, yit thou arte binethe thiself in this worching, & withouten thi soule'.[53] Self-knowledge and spiritual activities generally, which engage our two main 'worching mightes' – reason and will – upon their own activities draw us 'within' ourselves and upon our own level. But the aspiration of the mind directly to God so that it is 'ocupyed with no maner of thyng that is bodely or goostly, bot only with the self substaunce of God', draws the mind 'above' itself and below only to God.

This familiar three-stage Augustinian pattern of 'without', 'within' and 'above', based in the equally familiar Augustinian threefold division of powers of sensuality, imagination and reason–will, forms the common repertoire of metaphor for the description of spiritual progress. Manifestly the purpose of the *Cloud* Author's rehearsing of this repertoire is so as to prevent what he most fears for his disciple:

---

[51] Ibid., 62, p. 64, 5.   [52] Ibid., 63, p. 64, 32–33.   [53] Ibid., 67, p. 66, 35–37.

that he will 'conseyve bodily that that is mente goostly'.[54] For 'abouen thiself thou arte: for whi thou atteynest to come thedir by grace, wether thou mayest not come by kinde'.[55] For such purposes this language is necessary and desirable. And yet immediately the *Cloud* Author notes a further, subtler temptation to which the disciple may yield: that though the language of 'without', 'within' and 'above' is the necessary instrument whereby he may instruct the disciple to avoid the seductions of imagination and learn to conceive spiritual things spiritually, so powerful is the grip of imagination that it will readily have us conceive that language itself in a 'bodily' fashion. For, of course, that language is itself the work of imagination, which can only think in a bodily way of that which is spiritual; hence, the imagination on which we depend for the description of the 'inner' as distinct from the 'outer' has constructed that imagery from the 'outer' world of spatial relations. Therefore, almost in the very act of distinguishing so carefully between the 'without', the 'within' and the 'above', the *Cloud* Author warns of the dangers of using that language at all:

wher another man wolde bid thee gader thi mightes & thi wittes holiche withinne thiself, & worschip God there − thof al he sey ful wel and ful trewly, ye! & no man trewlier & he be wel conseiuid − yit for feerde of disseite & bodely conceyuyng of his wordes, me list not byd thee do so.[56]

This thought brings the *Cloud* Author back to his earlier invective against the immature disciples who fall into the trap of imagination. Those who seek 'interiority' only to translate it into mental acts of experienced inwardness become entrapped in a vicious circle, for they can only think in an 'outward' way of the distinction between 'inner' and 'outer' and so can only conceive of the 'inner' life materialistically: the consequences for their devotional and ascetical practice are therefore deformative of that true interiority which transcends imagination:

A yonge disciple in Goddes scole, newe turnid from the woreld...whan he redith or hereth spoken of goostly worching, & namely of this worde, how a man schal drawe alle his witte withinne hymself, or how he schal clymbe abouen himself...thei misvnderstonde thees wordes, & wenen, for thei fynden in hem a kyndly couetyse to hid thinges, that thei ben therfore clepid to that werke by grace...& therfore as fast for boldnes & presumpcion of theire corious witte, thei leue meek preier & penaunce ouer-

54 Ibid., 67, p. 67, 28.   55 Ibid., 67, p. 67, 8–9.   56 Ibid., 68, p. 67, 30–34.

sone, & sette hem (thei wene) to a ful goostly werke withinne in here soule…[57]

Such people, he comments, are likely to drive themselves mad by spiritual means, and

on this maner is this woodnes [madness] wrought that I speke of. Thei reden & heren wel sey that thei schuld leue vtward worching with theire wittes, & worche inwardes; & forthi that thei knowe not whiche is inward worchyng, therfore thei worche wronge. For thei turne theire bodily wittes inwardes to theire body agens the cours of kynde; & streyyn hem, as thei wolde see inwardes with theire bodily iyen, & heren inwardes with theire eren, & so forthe of alle theire wittes, smellen, taasten, & felyn inwardes. & thus thei reuerse hem agens the cours of kynde, & with this coriouste thei trauayle theire ymaginacioun so vndiscreetly, that at the laste thei turne here brayne in here hedes.[58]

Moreover, the physical symptoms of this perversity are tragi-comic:

Many wonderful countenances folowen hem that ben disseyuid in this fals werke…For whoso wolde or might behold vnto hem ther thei sitte in this tyme, & it so were that theire iyeliddes were open, he schulde see hem stare as thei were wode, & leiyingly loke as thei sawe the deuil. Sekirly it is good thei be ware; for trewly the feende is not fer. Som sette theire iyen in theire hedes as thei were sturdy scheep betyn in the heed, & as thei schulde diye anone. Some hangen here hedes on syde, as a worme were in theire eres. Some pipyn when thei schuld speke, as ther were no spirit in theire bodies…Some crien & whinen in theire throte…[59]

And so it is, the *Cloud* Author concludes, '[that I] wil…bid thee. Loke on no wyse that thou be withinne thiself. & schortly with-outyn thiself wil I not that thou be, ne yit abouen, ne behynde, ne on o side, ne on other.'[60]

'"Wher than", seist thou, schal I be?', the *Cloud* Author asks rhetorically: '"No where, by thi tale!"' And his answer shows just how sure is his command over the dialectics of interiority: 'Now trewly thou seist wel; for there wolde I haue thee. For whi no where bodely is euerywhere goostly.'[61] It is, he goes on to say, only the 'vtter man', the self who lives by imagination, for whom the life of the spirit is a 'nowhere' and a 'nothing'. This is because the unspiritual person interprets the 'inner life' as a quasi-physical, quasi-psychological place 'inside' consciousness. Consequently, the

---

[57] Ibid., 51, p. 53, 5–22.   [58] Ibid., 52, p. 53, 29–38.
[59] Ibid., 53, p. 54, 9–21.   [60] Ibid., 68, p. 67, 34–36.
[61] Ibid., 68, p. 67, 37–39.

person who, hearing the *Cloud* Author's rejection of this inwardness, supposes that there is no place at all for the spiritual, supposes this only because he cannot think otherwise of the 'interior'
than in terms which, quasi-physically, oppose it to the exterior.
And the person who does that is a person who is still living in
'exteriority': 'What is he pat clepith [calls] it nought? Sekirly it is
oure vtter man, & not oure inner.'[62] On the other hand, for the
'inner' man this 'nowhere' is an 'everywhere', 'all'; 'for of it he is
wel lernid to kon skyle of alle thinges, bodely or goostly'.[63] That is
to say, in the perspective of the 'inner' person there is no distinction at all between 'inner' and 'outer'. The inner self is free, free
from the dualism between 'inner' and 'outer' itself. We may say, in
short, that to be 'within' *psychologically*, is to be 'without' *spiritually*.
To be 'within' spiritually is to be at once 'nowhere' and 'everywhere' psychologically.

This, then, is the *Cloud* Author's paradox, which is none other
than Eckhart's paradox of detachment: that the language of interiority is, as it were, self-subverting, or dialectical. For: (1) that language is needed to state the distinction between the 'inner' and
'outer' self; but (2) only so as then to undermine the very distinction which it marks. For that inner 'space' cannot be approached
by means of any experiential device or technique which would
itself be but a phenomenon of our *exteriority*. It is therefore only for
the 'outer' self that the dualism between 'inner' and 'outer' persists
so as to structure its spiritual experience. But the 'inner' self knows
that there is no 'inner' as against 'outer'. For the 'inner' self possesses an interiority which knows no restrictions of space or place,
no confinement to the 'inner'; for the 'inner' self the interior is a
freedom, a 'nowhere' which is an 'everywhere'.

And we are back again with that string of Eckhartian paradoxes,
identified in the last chapter, which share, within their common
Neoplatonic inheritance of dialectics, the same logic as that of the
Cloud Author's interiority. In Eckhart, we saw, it is the paradox that
a dualism between the divine, uncreated ground of the soul and
the created empirical soul, exists only as a result of the fracturing
of the human psyche by sin. Detachment, far from reinforcing that
dualism of the divine and the human, is the force which heals that
fracturing; it subverts and transcends the dualism. In the *Cloud*, the

---

[62] Ibid., 68, p. 68, 18–19.   [63] Ibid., 68, p. 68, 20–21.

same dialectics are the practical machinery of a critique of 'interiority' whereby the distinction of 'interior' and 'exterior' is at once presupposed and then transcended. The more 'inner' we are the less hold on us has the distinction between 'inner' and 'outer'; the more the desire for God is wrapped in a cloud of unknowing, the less able are we to see that desire as just another, created desire, which, being just *another* desire, could be opposed to our own empirical, historical immanence, to our secular, contingent self. The more we seek our own ground in the ground of God the greater is the power of psychic integration in all the capacities of our persons.

This, then, is the dialectical logic equally of Eckhart's detachment and of the *Cloud* Author's 'interiority'. It is, as I have said, not just a logic, but a practice, a practical critique of desire. As such we can say that it is the strategy of *opposing oppositions*, and with them, of subverting all those pressures, whether secular or spiritual, whether psychological or social, which depend upon these oppositions.

VI

Eckhart's 'detachment', we saw, is the emancipation of all the possibilities of experience; but it is achievable on condition that we do not translate detachment itself into just another experience. The *Cloud* Author's 'interiority', likewise, is the achievement whereby we become detached from, that is liberated from, the very dualism itself between interiority and exteriority in theory and in practice, so that we do not any longer have to see ourselves as caught between their opposed polarities. To see them as opposed, to experience one's experience in terms of their opposition; and worse, to actively seek interiority as opposed to exteriority, *is* to lack interiority. It is, as Eckhart put it, to be attached to a 'way' – perhaps, in one of its forms, it is to be attached to what the *Cloud* Author sees as a 'spirituality'.

For the revenge of the possessive self, the self of 'imagination', threatened by the vacuum of detachment, is to rush to fill the vacuum in by means of a perverted 'spirituality', designed to reproduce the vacuum in a specialized set of 'spiritual' experiences of it: as if the vacuum itself could be made an *object of experience*. But the cultivation of such pseudo-experiences, of inwardness and detachment, can serve only to displace the vacuum by this attempt to reproduce it experientially. This is as self-defeating a procedure as that of trying to reproduce a vacuum in a photograph, for a photograph of a vacuum is itself a plenum, filling the space it is intended to represent. So too with what the *Cloud* Author calls 'imagination' and all its spiritual strategies of prayer, self-denial, repentance and the like; and all its spiritual by-products of a self-absorbed, interiorist piety. And so finally it is for Eckhart – for whom the worst enemy of detachment is its reduction to a psychological act which merely sucks the ego back into the abyss of the self, infilling it with a reassuring possessiveness of the experience of dispossession.

It does not follow from any of this that either Eckhart or the *Cloud* Author deny the importance, indeed the absolute necessity, of the ordinary means of Christian asceticism and prayer. In fact, what their somewhat dauntingly 'pure' negativity seems to demand is precisely the opposite: that the Christian eschew all alternative, extraordinary – should we say 'mystical' – routes to God, such as specialized 'spiritualities' might appear, spuriously, to offer. There is, in fact, a powerful vein of *anti*-mysticism in the astringent negativity of these two fourteenth-century writers, an urge to 'deconstruct' what they think of as a baroque, over-florid, technology of spiritual experientialism. Ordinary means plus detachment are enough for them: all other 'ways' are but diversions.

CHAPTER 9

Denys the Carthusian and the problem of experience

I

In the middle of the fifteenth century, at the very end of the mediaeval period, Denys the Carthusian, a Flemish monk of extraordinary learning and of distinctly conservative theological disposition,
looked back upon the preceding twelve hundred years of theological writing about 'contemplation' and attempted a compendious
survey and an assessment. Denys' *De Contemplatione* is an eclectical
work; it makes few claims to originality, but rather attempts to reconcile conflicting positions within the history of Patristic and mediaeval mystical writing.[1] In particular he is concerned to effect a
reconciliation on the issue which had so often preoccupied late
mediaeval mystics, and as often distracted them from their main
purposes: the issue of 'intellectualist' as against 'voluntarist'
accounts of 'union with God'. For his own part Denys' acknowledged sources of influence are principally his namesake Denys the
Areopagite and his compatriot Jan Van Ruusbroec. But what is of
interest to us in this chapter is less the distinctiveness of Denys'
theology – which admittedly is not great – than the character of *De
Contemplatione* as a survey of the history of Western Christian mysticism in the Middle Ages; and this the more particularly since his
interests, as ours have been, are focused upon the *apophatic* traditions of mediaeval Christian mysticism.

Moreover, the second book of *De Contemplatione* has at least one
claim to uniqueness, though its significance would be easy to miss,
for at first sight this second book consists in little but a series of

---

[1] The modern printed edition (it cannot be called 'critical') is to be found in volume 9 of
the Tournai-Parkminster edition of the *Opera Omnia Divi Dionisii Cartusiensis*, Tournai-
Parkminster, 1912, pp. 135–289. This text is based upon that of the 57 volume edition of
Dirk Loer and others, done for the most part from autograph MSS at the Charterhouse
of St Barbara at Cologne between 1521 and 1538. Subsequent references will be to *De
Cont.*

succinct, if also rather dry, summaries of the major contributions to the subject of contemplation to be found within the traditions of Christian theological writing in the West, from Origen to Ruusbroec. There are, however, two reasons for finding some considerable significance in this survey.

The first is that, as he makes clear in the third book of *De Contemplatione*, the terms 'contemplation' and 'mystical theology' are, for Denys, synonymous.[2] So frequently does he insist upon this synonymity that it is plausible to read some anxiety into his insistence upon it; it is as if he were reacting to a tendency to think of them in different terms. Moreover, for Denys, 'mysticism' itself is simply the apex of the whole theological enterprise, it is not an activity to be pursued independently of theology. Consequently, in Denys' terminology, 'contemplation' is coextensive with 'theology' and 'mysticism' is what theology leads to and, ultimately, is.

In taking this broad view of 'contemplation', Denys the Carthusian is explicitly following the traditional view of Denys the Areopagite. For the Carthusian as for the Areopagite, theology is broadly divided into three kinds, on a rising scale: 'symbolic', 'proper' and 'mystical', – the first two consisting in theology in the affirmative mode, the last in the negative. Theology 'proper', in turn, is of two kinds, the first dealing with the most general and abstract names of God in unity and simplicity, such as the Areopagite treated of in his *Divine Names*, the second dealing with what can be said affirmatively of God as Trinity, dealt with in the lost, or never written, *Divine Characteristics*. The third kind of contemplation, the mystical, is negative, and corresponds with the contemplation of the Areopagite's *Mystical Theology*.[3] Following in the steps of Gallus and Bonaventure in this at least, there is no sense in the Carthusian that this is anything but a continuous scale of 'contemplation', nor that 'contemplation' denotes anything other than theology itself. Moreover, as Denys is careful to explain, there is every good reason to concede the genuineness of the contributions even of pagan Greek, Jewish and Arabic philosophers to the understanding of 'negative' (and so in a sense 'mystical') contemplation: Plato, Aristotle, Alfarabi, Avicenna, Algazali, Proclus

---

[2]   *De Cont.* III, ii, p. 256.
[3]   Ibid., III i, pp. 255–56.

and Apuleius deserving particular mention.[4] All theoretic disciplines are kinds of contemplation. 'Mystical theology' is simply the highest contemplative activity to which the human mind can attain. Denys' conception of contemplation, and so of 'mysticism' as its fulfilment, is thus truly Victorine in its comprehensiveness and is firmly set against what he perceived to be a rising tide of anti-intellectualist mysticisms of his time.

It is clear to Denys, in any case, that this traditional conception of contemplation needs reaffirming. For he is perfectly aware that in his own time, and in the centuries which preceded his, speculative theology and mysticism had not always been seen in this close relationship. Above all, he resists energetically and repeatedly any account either of 'the theological' or of 'the mystical' which would align them with some bifurcation of, respectively, the 'merely speculative' and the 'experiential'.[5] And the first reason for attaching some importance to Denys' list lies in its purpose of reaffirming the tradition to which he sees himself as belonging: if he, Denys, is going to write about 'mysticism', it will be simply as a continuator of this tradition of comprehensiveness for which 'mysticism' is simply the best achievement of the 'contemplative' mind rising to the height of the scale of human theoretic activity, and not conceived narrowly as a particular kind of prayer experience or independent activity of will or love.

The second reason for taking an interest in Denys' survey lies in the fact of the list itself and in the theologians included in it. For in effect Denys' catalogue of contributors to the subject of 'contemplation' is an informal, but significant, canon of 'mystical theologians'. It would be wrong to make too much of this, certainly erroneous to suppose, without more ado, that Denys was self-consciously composing a canon. But he was having to be selective and at least informally some conception of what would and what would not count as a contribution to the subject of 'mystical theology' governs his choices.

Consequently, the membership of his 'canon' seems worth a comment, for, as far as I am aware, it is the first such list in the

---

4 Ibid., III, vii, pp. 262–63. Notably, Denys does not follow Gallus and Giles of Rome in identifying natural with affirmative knowledge, theological with negative. For Denys 'affirmative' and 'negative' divide the contemplations both of the philosophers and of the theologians.

5 *De Cont.*, III, iii, pp. 257–58.

mediaeval period, and I know of no others subsequently in the Middle Ages. The list includes, in his order, Denys the Areopagite,[6] Origen, Augustine, Bernard of Clairvaux, Hugh of St Victor, Richard of St Victor, Bonaventure, Thomas Aquinas, Jan Van Ruusbroec, Thomas Gallus Vercellensis and Guigo da Ponte. In fact we can add to this list, since the chapter on Bernard of Clairvaux includes discussions of several works of William of St Thierry, especially William's *Epistola Aurea* as well as a brief summary of the Carthusian Guigo II's *Scala Claustralium*, works which in Denys' time were commonly attributed to Bernard.[7] There are some surprising omissions even from his standpoint, particularly that of Gregory the Great, whose writings on contemplation were staple food for a mediaeval monk; and it is only a little less surprising that no room is found for Jean Gerson, the late fourteenth- and early fifteenth-century academic theologian and mystic, who shared many preferences with Denys, especially a partiality for Denys the Areopagite. There are some names whose omission might surprise from our standpoint, such as that of Meister Eckhart and of his fellow Dominicans, Tauler and Suso. But of course Eckhart's absence from Denys' list is only to be expected; for Meister Eckhart's writings had been effectively suppressed after the censure of 1329, and a theologian of such rigid orthodoxy as Denys would in any case have treated them with more caution than did his more original and speculatively daring friend and contemporary, Nicholas of Cues, who thought very highly of them.

As it stands, however, Denys' list would bear comparison with any which would be made today, by, say, an academic theologian who was designing a survey course on the history of Western Christian mysticism. What would be notable about any such contemporary list is that until it reached the middle of the fourteenth century the names included would have to be in nearly every case, if not in every case, the same as those included in any list of major systematic theologians, but that from the middle of the fourteenth century the two lists would diverge very considerably. For something happens in the second half of that century as a result of which, from that time until the present day, hardly anyone who would be agreed to be of significance in the history of Western

---

[6] For, of course, Denys believed his 'Areopagite' namesake to be a contemporary of St Paul and so to have preceded Origen historically.

[7] *De Cont.*, II, iv, p. 237.

Christian theology figures at all in a list of 'mystics' and hardly any mystics make a significant contribution to the development of mainstream theology.

On a contemporary list which extended beyond Denys' time this would be more apparent than from Denys' canon. From the middle of the fourteenth century, the figures of the late mediaeval and early modern periods who today would be studied by the historian of mysticism would have to include, on the least controversial criteria possible, at least the following: Tauler, Suso, Ruusbroec, Richard Rolle, Walter Hilton, the *Cloud* Author, Julian of Norwich, Margery Kempe, Jean Gerson, Gert Groote, Nicholas of Cues, Thomas à Kempis, Catherine of Genoa, Teresa of Avila, Luis de Leon and John of the Cross – figures among whom, with the exception of Nicholas of Cues, none is to be found who is of any significance at all in the history of mainstream theology.

And even in Denys' list it is possible to see the signs of this split between the mystical and the theological being read back into the canon even *before* the middle of the fourteenth century. Why include Gallus, a Victorine favoured by Denys because of his fusion of a traditional monastic partiality for scriptural commentary with an enthusiasm for Dionysian apophaticism, and exclude Duns Scotus – if not because Gallus is significant in the history of 'mysticism' but not for his 'theology' and Scotus for his 'theology' but not for his 'mysticism'? We may account for the presence of Guigo da Ponte in the list, indeed for his presence out of historical sequence at the end of it, as an expression of piety towards a favoured Carthusian colleague. But Guigo's pious essays on the theory and practice of contemplative prayer hardly serve to further Denys' polemic on behalf of the unity of speculative and mystical theologies; on the contrary, they rather serve to highlight the problem Denys must have felt there was *especially* with the Carthusian contribution to the subject of 'contemplation', namely that if any tradition had tended to shunt 'theology' and 'contemplation' up different sidings, the Carthusian tradition had tended to do so. And finally, the inclusion of the late fourteenth-century Ruusbroec, the first recognizable 'mystic' in the contemporary sense to be included in Denys' list, may be allowed to tell us something about the state of 'mysticism' in that period. For Ruusbroec engages in no traditional theological pursuits, whether of the monastic scriptural traditions or of the scholastic dialectical traditions, but only in those of the 'spiritual' and 'mystical' writer who is not a theologian. In short, in the first place it seems by the late fourteenth century that there is such a genre as 'spiritual' or 'mystical' writing which is exclusive of more general theological interests, and Ruusbroec's exemplifies this attenuation of the scope of 'mysticism'. Secondly, in Denys the Carthusian that split between the 'mystical' and the 'theological' has begun to be read back into the history of Western Christian theology in a way which is characteristically modern.

Denys' attempt at an historical survey of contributions to the discussion of 'contemplation' therefore to some degree bears out his own conviction of the unity of the 'mystical' with the 'theological', but also offers some evidence of the bifurcation between them which his own theology in principle resists, a gap which he seems to feel has, in his own day, the tendency to widen. Moreover, though, as I say, Denys *in principle* resists this bifurcation, a survey of his enormous *œuvre* as a whole shows an eclecticism which itself confirms the difficulty the late mediaeval theologian had in holding the fissiparous elements of the total theological enterprise together. For Denys is perhaps the last mediaeval theologian to try to do *everything*. He commented, in the traditional manner of the monastic theologian, on every book of Scripture. He composed, as every schoolman was required to, a commentary on the *Sentences* of Peter Lombard, even though as a monk he was under no such obligation. He wrote a précis of Thomas Aquinas' *Summa Theologiae*. He commented, in the manner of a theologian of the Victorine school, on every book of Denys the Areopagite. In addition, he wrote disputations on a great variety of individual topics, pious meditations and systematic treatises on ascetical topics – in addition to his *de Contemplatione* he wrote a *de Meditatione* and a *de Oratione* – homilies, polemics against ecclesiastical abuse, especially among Bishops, many hundreds of letters, mostly now lost, and determinations of questions in canon law. There is no field of mediaeval theological endeavour which Denys leaves untouched.

And yet there is little sense of a synthesis of method or outlook. Denys the monastic exegete owes little to the scholastic theologian; Denys the Dionysian mystic owes little either to Denys the schoolman or to Denys the Carthusian monk; Denys the schoolman and metaphysician owes more to a version of Thomas Aquinas than to the monk or the mystic. The *œuvre* falls apart in too many ways to qualify as a major development in late mediaeval theology or even as a true synthesis of it, partly because he personally lacked the originality of mind to do it, partly perhaps because he was attempting what once had been possible but by the fifteenth century could probably no longer be achieved. What Denys wanted to do, in any case, he was unable to do, which was to restore the unity he senses had too often been fractured between speculative theology and mysticism, between the dialectical work of concepts and the immediacy of experience.

In practice, therefore, he abandoned the task. There is an element of despair in his attitude to 'speculative' theology and its relation with 'mystical'. For sure he rejects a 'voluntarist' account of how they differ, according to which speculative theology is the work of intellect whose object is truth, mystical theology the work of the will, whose object is the good.[8] For Denys is a resolute intellectualist and his mysticism is distinctly a mysticism of vision;[9] he believes that so far as concerns its formal constitution 'mystical theology' is an act of intellect, not of love.[10] But as to what *causes* the union of the mind with God, this cannot, he believes, be the work of intellect, for 'the intellectual power is sometimes hardly at all, or not at all, made one with the good which it sees and at other times burns ardently for it, and is completely taken out of itself by impatient desire',[11] and it is love which makes the difference. Consequently, the fulfilment of mystical theology, what brings about its goal of the intellect's union with God, and moves and stimulates its practice, is to be found in the soul's deepest love.[12]

But even if speculative theology cannot be distinguished from mystical theology on the ground of a voluntarist account of the mystical, Denys is pessimistic about the role of speculative theological disciplines as actually practised in the contemporary schools. Gone from Denys is the relative optimism even of the voluntarist Bonaventure about the share of those speculative disciplines in promoting the ascent of the mind to God – significantly, as we have observed, Bonaventure's voluntarism is not yet an 'anti-intellectualism'. For in Denys' time, things are otherwise. Though

---

[8] In *De Cont.* III, iv, p. 257, he considers this way of making the distinction, but rejects it in III, xiv.
[9] *De Cont.*, III, xiv, p. 270.
[10] Ibid., III xiv, p. 270.
[11] Ibid., III, iii, p. 258.
[12] Ibid., III xiv, p. 270.

Denys himself was far from depreciating the value of scholastic learning, even for the contemplative monk, in this he seems almost alone in his time and he seems to be acutely aware, even personally, of his intellectual isolation.[13] And in his perception the split between the academic and the mystical disciplines has widened too far for him to entertain real hopes of their cooperation within a unity of *mystical theology*, theology as mysticism, mysticism as theology. Augustine's ideal of a *doctrina christiana* serving the purposes of charity no longer seems possible, for, as Denys sees it, 'speculative theology' has become a matter of academic learning merely, whereas mystical theology is available to all the faithful, however uneducated, simple and stupid,[14] so long as they are fervent in love and devotion; mystical theology humbles, whereas speculative theology appears to inflate its practitioners with pride; mystical theology is achievable only by those of reformed character, whereas speculative theology has become such that it can be taught to anyone at all, regardless of the moral quality of their lives, on condition only of sufficient intelligence.[15]

Of course, this scepticism about the value of academic theology is familiar stuff at any time in the Middle Ages, particularly from the pen of a monk, but coming from Denys the Carthusian it is striking. For they appear rather as words of regret that things are not otherwise than a conviction of how things must be in principle. After all, they are the words not of an anti-intellectualist theologian who despises university theology *as such*, but of a man who can defend his interest in scholastic theology, even against his own superiors, in terms as generous to the value of all human learning as anything in a Hugh of St Victor: for truly, he says, writing of the works of the 'philosophers',

they are of no mean benefit to those of a prudent cast of mind, if they are read in an orderly fashion. For the tendency of knowledge and of the real world are in agreement: namely that, in the same manner in which nature

---

[13] Indeed, Denys got into trouble with his monastic superiors and was ordered to cease writing for a period of some years in the 1440s, it seems both because they thought he spent too much time writing and because the range of his theological interests seemed to his superiors to be unsuitable for a monk. The prohibition occasioned a vigorous *Protestatio* in 1441 in which he defends his prolific writing activity and the range of his interests, saying that for him the very laboriousness of his efforts was a kind of ascetical practice and that his studies enabled him to put up with his solitude in greater freedom of spirit: *Protestatio ad superiorem suum, Opera Omnia*, 1, lxxi-lxxii.

[14] *De Cont.* III, iii, p. 257.

[15] Ibid., III iii, p. 258.

serves the Creator, so does natural knowledge serve divine wisdom [*theosophiae*]. And so the contemplation of the natural order of things, as Hugh and Richard say, is a ladder or mode of ascending to the contemplation of the Godhead. For the invisible things of God are known through the visible created character of the world. Therefore they must be most severely rebuked who immoderately inveigh against the study of philosophy, which was so beloved of the most holy people.[16]

It can hardly be said, therefore, that Denys the Carthusian welcomes the disintegrations which he observed the total theological enterprise had fallen into – he is no Thomas à Kempis, grimly delighting in the satire of scholastic academicism. Nor, on the other hand, can it be said that Denys himself was able to reunite the fragments. But if in spite of the generosity and scope of his learning he was unable in practice to restore that total theological unity, he was able to construct an account of 'mystical theology', or 'contemplation', on the principle of its integral unity with all theology. And in this at least he bucks the trend.

The significance of Denys the Carthusian therefore seems to lie in his predicament: temperamentally a synthesizer, he is confronted with fragmentation. Pulled spiritually by the attractions of a pietistic affectivism, his loyalty to his Dionysian apophatic tradition resists a voluntarist anti-intellectualism. In principle yearning for the comprehensiveness of the thirteenth-century syntheses of a Bonaventure or a Thomas, he is faced with the academicism of a speculative theology which could little serve the purpose of the Victorine style of mysticism he so favoured. And perhaps in no connection is this predicament more evident, or striking, than in his attempt to reconcile intellectualist and voluntarist mysticisms, nor is this attempt in any other respect more relevant to our assessment of the late mediaeval developments of 'mysticism' than in his parallel treatment of the relationship between the 'apophatic' and the 'experiential' within mystical theology.

II

As they came down to him, the arguments between the voluntarist and the intellectualist theological traditions appeared to Denys the Carthusian to be inextricably bound up with another issue, that

---

[16] *De Vita et fine solitarii*, 1.a.22, *Opera Omnia*, 38, 288A–B.

between those who saw the uniting of the soul with God as being
in some way an *experiential* act, and those who did not. At any rate,
that is most commonly how those on the voluntarist side perceived
it. But it is important to be cautious about this conflation of what
are distinguishable disagreements, for generally speaking it is
within, and *only* within the voluntarist camp that, first, the distinction itself between an 'experiential' and a 'non-experiential'
description of union with God is made; and, secondly, it is generally voluntarists who maintain that the case for voluntarism is to be
made out on grounds of its better claims to 'experience'. But it is
neither the case that all voluntarists conflate these two claims, nor
is it true that all intellectualists concede the relevance of 'experience' to the issue between them and voluntarists.

There are, of course, mediaeval 'voluntarists' who appeal both
to the priority of love in the formal constitution of union with God
and to the case for that priority on the grounds of love's being
what unites the soul to God in a knowing of experience. Giles of
Rome is one such. Giles, we saw,[17] distinguished sharply between
the contemplation of the philosophers and the contemplation of
the theologians, and he did so on the grounds that the first is a
purely intellectual kind of wisdom, whereas the second is essentially
an act of love and of will: for 'the happiness of the philosophers is a
matter of the intellect, spiritual happiness resides in its fullness and
in its highest form in the will'.[18] And if, as we have seen Giles
maintain, intellectual contemplation is analogous to the senses of
sight and hearing, and the appropriate imagery for it is visual and
auditory, this is because these images are expressive of the intellect's relative degree of distance from its objects, both sight and
hearing standing in a less than completely immediate relation with
them. On the other hand, the more 'vital' senses of taste, smell and
touch (more 'vital' in that they are more immediately bound up
with the needs of the body) provide the imagery for spiritual contemplation because they are the more immediately experiential –
'tasting, smelling and touching…seem…to stand on the side of
will',[19] the side on which spiritual contemplation stands. Therefore,
Giles concludes, 'contemplation as the theologians speak of it is
more a matter of experience than of wisdom's expertise'.[20]

[17]   Above, pp. 201–02.
[18]   *Expositio in Canticum Canticorum*, see my translation in *Eros and Allegory*, n. 16, p. 364.
[19]   Ibid.
[20]   …*magis consistit in sapore quam sapere*, *Expositio*, n. 14, p. 363.

On the other hand, not every theologian who is voluntarist in principle makes the same associations of imagery, nor does every voluntarist mystic in this same way tie in the priority of will with the greater experiential immediacy of affectivity. If the account I have given of the *Cloud* Author's doctrine is correct, he is one in whom these connections are not to be found. For the *Cloud* Author's imagery is consistently visual and his apophaticism is as much an apophaticism of desire as of intellect: he resists, as I have argued, any tendency his voluntarism may have generated towards a voluntarist 'experientialism'. If my account has been correct, therefore, the *Cloud* Author makes no appeal to will as prior to intellect on the grounds of the greater immediacy of the experience of God which it yields.

Denys, by contrast, is, as we have seen, a convinced intellectualist. And yet both on the score of his imagery and on the score of the role of 'experience' he concedes much to the voluntarist position, the first because of the second. As to his imagery, he insists, as does Giles, that the highest forms of true apophatic contemplation are a 'closed book to the philosophers of the world' and even to believers, by whom it cannot 'be known *by experience or inner tasting*', unless they have achieved heroic and perfect virtue and very fervently burn with divine love and are purified.[21]

Nonetheless, it is a knowing, not a loving, which formally constitutes this wisdom and spontaneously Denys combines with the affectivist imagery of 'tasting' and 'burning warmth' the classical Dionysian imagery of a dark cloud of unknowing. For 'through this contemplation...the mind is joined to God as to one beyond our comprehension and unknown, as to an infinite ocean and to a cloud...although in his own being he is exceeding dazzling light'.[22] On the other hand, it is not within the capacity of intellect to achieve this union alone

and therefore [this contemplation] cannot be had primarily by the light of understanding, but is infused by a blazing fire of holy and divinised charity, and is fulfilled and completed in the heat of the love of God; so a burning love takes complete charge [of this contemplation] and it alone is felt, for even the knowledge is said to turn into love and to be somehow transformed into it.[23]

---

[21] *De Cont.* III, ii, p. 256.
[22] Ibid.: *per hanc...contemplationem mens Deo coniungitur tanquam incomprehensibili et ignoto, ac pelago infinito atque caligini...quamvis in sua natura sit supersplendidissimum lumen.* Cp. Thomas Aquinas: *per revelationem gratiae in hac vita non cognoscamus de Deo quid est, et sic ei quasi ignoto coniungamur* in *ST*, I, q. 12, a. 13, corp.   [23] *De Cont.*, III, ii, p. 256.

This contemplation is therefore both 'that supremely *shining* and unique wisdom of Christians',[24] 'a *brilliant* contemplation' and is to be achieved only 'by means of a *burning*, sincere and overflowing love';[25] it is a 'knowledge of God by *experience* consisting in a uniting love...a knowledge of God *by taste*'[26] and yet it is a wisdom which 'leaves all behind it, abandoning the work of sense and understanding, of deliberation and *of love*' of created things, a wisdom which 'plunges the mind into the limitless and unattainable eternal *light*'.[27]

The freedom with which Denys moves between the sensory imagery of the affectivist and the intellectualist traditions reflects his desire to reconcile these positions in a more fully systematic way. When Gregory the Great – and later William of St Thierry – had made the case for a 'knowing of *love*' – *amor ipse notitia est*[28] – they were affirming the ultimate supremacy of love over intellect in the constitution of the soul's union with God; but they were also unconsciously laying the ground for later anti-intellectualisms. For if on the one hand this formula was used by later voluntarists to justify the relegation of intellect's knowing to pre-unitive stages of contemplation, it also served to meet the obvious objection to voluntarist accounts of union that we cannot love what we do not know – love being itself a kind of knowing of which intellect is incapable.

This, as we have seen, is how Gallus understood the proposition. For Gallus allowed the intellect to proceed 'hand in hand' with will at every stage of the soul's ascent to God but the last, the stage of the Seraphim.[29] But for Denys the matter is otherwise and more complex. He resists the implication of the voluntarist position that intellect is in a merely preparatory role to union, and he resists, therefore, that downgrading of intellect to the status of a merely academic, 'scholastic' power of the soul which appeared to be consequent upon that voluntarism. Therefore he insists that intellect is involved in the act itself of union with God in a complex, mutually interacting dialogue with will, which leads all the way to the final achievement of union with God. Therefore, in a passage which it is hard not to read as a deliberate revision of Gallus' view that intellect is finally denied entry into union with God, Denys says:

---

[24] Ibid., III, ii, p. 257.   [25] Ibid.   [26] Ibid.   [27] Ibid.
[28] Gregory the Great, *Homelia in Evangel.* 27.4, PL 76, 1207; William of St Thierry's formula is slightly different: *amor ipse intellectus est*, *Disputatio contra Petrum Abaelardum*, PL 180, 252C.
[29] See pp. 192–93 above.

this contemplation which is mystical insight is the most certain and the most translucent. For it comes about by means of the most limpid and superabundantly ardent fervour of divine love, which gains entry and goes deep within where knowledge is left behind; but having entered deeply and most intimately within, it invites knowledge in also, and joins the mind to God very closely and intimately, in so far as this may be in this life. By this means, in the end, the soul is more intimately transfixed by that light, at once infinite and divine, is marked by it and is made one with it so as to be made the more abundantly radiant, more able to see with added certainty, to contemplate the more lucidly and to become melted almost completely in the fire of love.[30]

Therefore Denys compromises. *Amor ipse notitia est* is true as to love's role of *causing* union by knowledge. But it is not true to say that unitive wisdom *consists in* love's knowing.[31] For in the same way that anger can be said 'to be' the oversupply of blood to the heart (meaning that that is what anger is caused by), so the knowledge which unites with God can be said 'to be' love (meaning that it is by the causality of love that intellect is united with God). But it remains the case that it is intellect which is so united. Certainly, Denys concedes, the authority of Gallus appears to be against this. But he claims that when Gallus says it is the work of *wisdom* to unite the summit of desire to God, Gallus means that this desire springs up from wisdom's work and so follows upon it, the precedence of wisdom, and so of intellect, thereby being confirmed.[32]

To summarize: in Gallus the association of voluntarism with affectivist imagery of union is assumed, as it is in Giles of Rome; in Giles, however, the preference for that imagery is explicitly made out in terms of its greater capacity to express the *experiential* character of the union of love, in which character lies, in turn, the priority of love over knowledge in the formal constitution of union with God. The *Cloud* Author, on the other hand, combines a voluntarism and an *anti*-intellectualism with the visual and auditory imagery more usually found within intellectualist mysticisms and the reason for that seems to lie in the resolute character of his apophaticism. For even if it is will, 'nakyd entente', which unites

---

[30] *De Cont.* III, v, pp. 259–60.
[31] Ibid., III, xiv, p. 270.
[32] Ibid., III, xv, p. 273. Denys' attempt to retrieve Gallus' support for his own position is unconvincing. For even as reinterpreted in this way, Gallus' position amounts to nearly the reversal of Denys', implying that union with God is formally of the will, knowledge being at best a necessary precondition of that union. In any case, even this is not what Gallus maintained.

with God, it does so within the same 'cloud of unknowing' which enshrouds intellect: in the *Cloud* there is no suggestion, I have argued, of that combination of negativity of intellect with a positivism of love which one suspects the presence of in Giles. In Denys, finally, yet another permutation of imagery and doctrine is shown to be possible: for he is at once traditional in his association of affectivist imagery with the greater 'experiential' power of love and of visual imagery with the negativity of intellect, and at the same time at odds with the whole voluntarist tradition in maintaining that it is knowing, not love, which is formally constitutive of the soul's union with God. Clearly, Denys is in search of a synthesis: he wants no affectivist depreciation of intellect, since that would do nothing but reinforce in theory that 'academicisation' of speculative theology which he deplores in practice in the schools; and so he reaffirms the intrinsically intellectual character of mystical contemplation. Nor, on the other hand, does he wish to deny the ultimate causality of love as that which drives the soul up the ascending scale of contemplations towards mystical union; and so he insists upon the role of love in constituting the experiential immediacy of that union. Accepting, therefore, the voluntarist bifurcations of intellect from will and of knowledge from experience, he seeks their recombination in an account of the mystical ascent which acknowledges the mutuality of their dialogue with one another.

And yet for all that, Denys the Carthusian's historical significance lies in the fact that he witnesses more powerfully to what he resists than in the success of his resistance to it. For after all, if he seeks an alliance between intellect and will, knowledge and love, theology and experience, this is because he has in the first instance conceded the bifurcations between them which he so regrets. Therefore, inspite of that conservative instinct which aspires, nostalgically, to a twelfth-century Victorine or a thirteenth-century Bonaventurean ideal-type of a unified 'mystical theology', he witnesses more effectively to a current state of affairs in which 'mysticism' and 'theology' stand visibly in opposition to one another – opposed, moreover, in that manner in which 'experience' and 'speculation' by then appeared to be.

There is, then, something of the character of a 'last stand' about Denys' mystical theology. He wrote at a point very late in the Middle Ages where it was possible to perceive rather clearly what was happening; but it was both too late to prevent it, too early to see that preventing it was no longer possible. What Denys perceived was something about the disintegration of a unified 'mystical theology' into the fragments of a theology which is no longer 'mystical' and a theologically irrelevant 'mysticism'. That is what the evidence of his 'canon' had begun to show, though it is much easier to see what that canon shows from the way it extends into later ages. For, as I have said, those in whom the 'mystical' tradition continues from the fifteenth century to our day can be seen unambiguously to be what in Denys' list few were: 'mystics', no theologians. And, it may be added, it is within the fragmentations of the mystical and the theological, of loving and knowing, of experience and speculation that we today, scholars or practising Christians, generally stand. Where the Middle Ages end, we begin. As Denys the Carthusian was compelled to read the history of medieval mystical theology, *malgré lui*, in terms of these bifurcations, so do we, though, unlike Denys, we need not do so. Nor do we appear to have any conception of why we should resist that reading.

CHAPTER 10

John of the Cross: the dark nights and depression

We have seen in Denys the Carthusian the emergence of what I have called 'experientialism', if only negatively in and through his resistance to it. Denys, however, is not familiar to a contemporary readership, whereas John of the Cross is all too familiar to it, to the point where the history of Western Christian 'mystical theology' is in some ways distorted by his prestige. It is, in any case, all too easy to read John of the Cross exclusively as an 'early modern' writer, to detach his work from its roots in the medieval tradition, and in no respect is this more likely, or more misleading, than in the tendency to characterize John's 'modernity' precisely by its 'experientialism'. It cannot be wrong to see John as an 'early modern'.[1] It cannot be right, however, to neglect those respects in which John is deeply indebted to – that is to say, is thoroughly dependent upon – the mediaeval traditions of apophatic mysticism. And if 'modernity' is to be characterized by a *preoccupation with* the phenomena of the subjective and the experiential, then there is no doubt that in this respect John is a 'modern'. On the other hand, if 'experientialism' is to be characterized by its translation of the dialectical categories of a Neoplatonic theological epistemology into categories of subjective

---

[1] The rich and complex work of Michel de Certeau in *The Mystic Fable* provides a somewhat different emphasis from mine. Michel de Certeau, as I do, places John of the Cross on the dividing line between the mediaeval and the early-modern, seeing him as pre-dating the full reliance on an 'experientialist' mystical epistemology such as is found in Jean-Joseph Surin (1600–1655) and as continuing to owe much to pre-modern epistemologies and cosmologies. Nonetheless, he sees John's autobiographical 'I' – an 'I' at once of 'experience' as found in his poetry and of the 'scientific', self-reflective discourse of his prose commentaries – as ensuring a distinctively modern 'link between "experience" and "science", that is, the very status of [his] entire discourse'. *The Mystic Fable*, Chicago: Chicago University Press, 1992, p. 179. For my part I suspect de Certeau's thesis is overstressed, and I have argued in my *Eros and Allegory* (part I, chapter 7) that John of the Cross can perhaps just as fruitfully be read as linking poetic text and prose *hermeneutic* in the manner of the mediaeval monastic commentator on the Song of Songs.

experience, then it is the argument of this chapter that John of the Cross is distinctly not an 'experientialist'.

For though it is easy to identify in John's writings the dominance of the apophatic metaphors of the mediaeval tradition, above all of 'light' and 'darkness', it would, in my view, be entirely wrong to read these as doing the work of an experientialist psychology. Of course John's 'mystical writings' do in fact contain a psychology of religious experience – often an acute and illuminating one. But his 'dark nights of the soul' are not principally metaphors descriptive of them, but embody, on the contrary, a spiritual temperament resistant to the claims of spiritual 'experiences'. In short, John's 'dark nights' are the metaphors not *of* experience, but of a dialectical *critique* of experientialist tendencies.

I

In this chapter I shall not attempt a compendious survey of John's theological output. Rather I propose to take a close look at the imagery of the 'dark nights' narrowly from the point of view of its potentiality for a psychologistic reading, and nothing focuses that issue more clearly than the question of whether, and if so, how far, John's description of these 'dark nights' of the soul can be related to the undoubtedly psychological and 'experiential' phenomena of depression.

There is, however, a conceptual issue raised by the subject of the 'dark nights' of the soul and depression, and though there is some expository work to be done before confronting it directly, it will be worthwhile providing ourselves first with some clarifications of terminology necessary to the description of what that issue is.

It is obvious that depressions are a very mixed collection of syndromes, varying greatly in cause, course, prognosis and so in treatment. From most points of view it will be important not to ignore these differences and to consider each kind of depression in its own terms. But from the point of view of the issue with which we are concerned in this chapter it is possible, I think, to make a quite general claim. This is that, considered from the point of view of the experience of it, most forms of endogenous depression are in some fashion or other a malaise of the 'self'; or at least that they are the disintegration of an appropriate and healthy *sense of* self. If that is so, then in the first instance what we are to count as depression depends in part on what we think is an appropriate and healthy sense of self. And as for the rest how we are to describe a healthy sense of self depends in turn on what we think the self is. So concepts of the self serve in some way criterially for the description of depression.

We need, it seems, to make some distinctions, and, for the purposes of the discussion of John's account of the 'dark nights of the soul', we will distinguish three languages of 'selfhood'.[2] The first is the language of what I shall call the 'psychological' self, or the self of 'experience'. What we talk about in this language is how a person sees himself, what stories he tells himself about himself, what kind of autobiography he would write, but also what kind of judgements he makes of himself – in short, we talk about his 'self-image'. This language is, therefore, a first-person language which, to put it in Augustinian terms familiar to John of the Cross, is at once a *narrative of a personal past* and as such is the exercise of *memory*; it is the estimation of what that past amounts to by way of its *significance* to me, and so is the exercise of *understanding*; and is the expression of my *present relationship* with that past and its significance in so far as I like and dislike, am happy and unhappy with what I see of myself, and so is a product of *will*. Taken together, then, these acts of memory, intellect and will, as exercised upon my own experience, constitute my *sense of* selfhood, my 'self of experience'.

Now depression is one of the forms which a negative, destructive, sense of self can take. There are many others. I may be a happily self-deceived person, perhaps happy only in so far as I am self-deceived, if I am a person who needs to tell stories about myself which misconstrue my past or present desires or thoughts or doings. And I may need to do that because I cannot be happy with the truth about those desires or thoughts or doings. Or I may be a person who cannot be happy if *others* know the truths about myself which I know all too well, and so need to deceive them, if not myself. Or again, I may be depressed; but depression is a condition which differs from the previous two malaises of selfhood in that whereas they are products, as one might say, of an *over*-constructed selfhood, the constructions merely of fantasy, depression is the

---

[2] I shall make no general case for the theoretical adequacy of this terminology, which is stipulative and designed for the specific purposes of this discussion. Nonetheless, I think that these distinctions are theoretically adequate and defensible and are not *merely* stipulative.

symptom of an *under*-constructed selfhood, of a disintegration of feeling and agency, the collapse of my personal narrative into meaningless segments of event for which I can have no liking or love.

Now in so far as I can perceive myself to be depressed there is implied some understanding of what it would be to possess a more healthy sense of self. And in this understanding is found what I shall call the 'therapeutic' self. It is *possible* to construct theories about this desired condition of selfhood and there are indeed many. But it is not necessary to be in possession of anything very articulate or complete by way of a therapeutic sense of selfhood to know that one is depressed, any more than it is necessary to have a dentist's knowledge of the perfect condition of teeth in order to know that one has a toothache. Nor is the pain of depression any different for the fact that one has an account of a healthier self-image; any more than the dentist experiences the pain of toothache any differently from her patient.

Nonetheless, since depression is experienced as some kind of dislocation of selfhood, it follows that some picture of a therapeutically adequate self-image is playing a role 'implicitly' within that experience. Indeed, one can go further than that, for depression throws into sharp relief what functions within my experience as a therapeutically adequate selfhood, precisely in that sense, albeit only negative, of what has been lost. It is in our 'normal' and non-depressed condition that what we think of as a healthy sense of selfhood is implicit and in depression is made more sharply conscious. For 'normality' is like an answer to an unrecognized question. But depression is a question all too clearly raised about what we *could be* like, accompanied by the despair of ever achieving it.

We must distinguish, further, what may be called the self of 'numerical identity'. A person who suffers from total amnesia has lost her 'self of experience' to some very high degree. But whether or not she can appropriate the fact in conscious self-awareness, she remains one and the same person as she was before her amnesia. For if she did not, then it would not be possible to say that it was *she* who had lost her sense of personal identity; nor would there be any point in trying to restore her memory. And even if, in some technological fantasy, it would be possible to equip her with entirely false 'memories' of her past which she believed to be true – and thus to equip her with a new 'sense of self' – these memories could be said to be 'false' only in so far as she is now numerically one and the same person with that person whose experiences are misremembered. Numerical identity locates the person in whom even the most drastic changes in psychological identity have taken place. If memories, and so *experienced* identities, can be lost, we can still for certain purposes need to know in *whose* memory the experienced identity is lost. If I am depressed, then in one sense my 'selfhood' has disintegrated. But it is still *my* sense of selfhood which has disintegrated and we will need some language in which to handle the force of the conviction that *I* am depressed, that *I* was once not depressed and that *I* could become again undepressed, other than in terms of that selfhood I have lost in my depression.

Philosophers debate with customary intensity what those conditions are which must be met if two experiences of personhood are to be said to be those of numerically one and the same person. It is no purpose of mine to engage in this essay with those debates or do more than stipulate a position. Suffice it to say that the broadly empiricist tradition, according to which the *criteria* of personal identity and continuity are exclusively psychological, seems counterintuitive. For we would not be raising the question of numerical identity of persons were it not for cases where, selfhood on all the psychological criteria being lost, we need some language in which to describe – and criteria for deciding – *whose* identity is lost. Hence, for the purposes of our discussion of John of the Cross' understanding of depression and the self, I shall take it that experienced selfhood is an insufficient condition of numerical identity. And I shall say, without more ado, that for a conceptually adequate account of the numerical identity of persons the material continuity of bodies is at least a necessary condition; and I do so with the greater confidence because, in so far as it is possible to determine the matter, this is John of the Cross' own opinion too.[3]

II

What is the bearing of John of the Cross' 'dark nights' on these conceptual distinctions? The most obvious, and from our point of view the most significant point of contact is that John of the Cross is known best, perhaps, for some very harrowing descriptions of the

---

[3] See pp. 247–48 below.

sufferings which must be undergone by those to whom God comes more than averagely close. Theologically, his account of the cause of those sufferings is familiar to us, for it belongs within that tradition of imagery which conjoins Plato's Allegory with Exodus. Specifically his account arises out of a very typically literalist gloss on Yahweh's warning to Moses 'You cannot see my face..., a man may not see me and live'.[4] From which it follows, according to John, that the life of the Christian who, like the Psalmist, 'seeks the face [of Yahweh]',[5] must be a kind of death in life, for the desire to see the face of God is the desire to meet the condition required. The closer the approach of God, the more the condition of death has to be met. Above all, it has to be met by the self.

Now though, as is obvious, John's theology falls within the long tradition of negative mysticism of the Middle Ages, and dependent as he is entirely upon the Neoplatonic literary and metaphorical conventions of that tradition, John is probably the first in modern times to attach great importance to the lived experience of that purgative suffering, to the extent of mapping out in detail its psychological topography. It matters to John, in a way it appears not to have mattered to any of the preceding authors we have discussed, that he should spell out the *experienced feel* of the deprivations of the clouds of forgetting and of unknowing, that he should detail, in a form which is psychologically recognizable, the experiential feedback of the soul's encounter with God and that those differences of experience should be marked which characterize the different stages of the 'ascent of Mount Carmel'.

We can describe what John is doing, in so meticulously articulating the experience of the ascetical path, in other terms which we have derived from our earlier discussions. John's dependence upon the mediaeval apophatic traditions is most marked, as we will see, in his appropriation of the dialectical and metaphorical apparatus of Neoplatonic mysticism, in other words in his appropriation of the second-order, apophatic *critique* of religious experience. Where he differs most evidently from those traditions is in the exceptionally full and psychologically acute description of the first-order religious experience itself. And the significance of this detailed topographical description lies in the fact that at that first-order level of

---

[4] Exodus, 33, 20. See *The Ascent of Mount Carmel* (*AMC*), II.8.2, in *The Collected Works of St John of the Cross*, trans. Kieran Kavanaugh and Otilio Rodriguez, Washington: ICS, 1992.

[5] Psalm 105, 4.

experiential description John's accounts of the sufferings of the 'dark nights of the soul' are uncannily similar to what a person will give from the inside of the experience of depression.

All the characteristic symptoms are there, from the lowest levels of the physiological – the distaste for food, the gnawings of anxiety in the pit of the stomach – through the disabling of the sensory powers – the dulling of the eye and ear, the souring of taste, the rawness of touch, the rankness in the nose – from all these symptoms in which depression is lived out in the body, to all those symptoms intensified in their metaphorical reference to the emotions and so extended upon the whole power of enjoyment itself; all these experiences parallel and match in detail John's account of what he calls the 'passive night of the senses'. And on top of all these are the generalized and objectless fears, the evacuation of meaning, the collapse of memory into random associations, the sense of the pointlessness of any willed pursuit which, for John, characterize the 'passive night of the spirit'. And above all, perhaps, the parallel is found in the experienced *passivity* of both.

For, of course, John of the Cross distinguished the passive nights, which are brought about directly by the approach of God to the soul, from preliminary stages of active asceticism, whose efficacy can indeed be guaranteed only by grace, but in which we can and must play an active part for ourselves of vigorous self-denial. His recommendations about how we ought to conduct ourselves in this active asceticism can seem to contemporary ears unappealingly negative, requiring variously 'the elimination of appetites',[6] 'their extinction'[7] and 'that we make a complete break with [any] little satisfaction, attachment or affection'.[8]

It is, of course, hard to imagine 'the extinction of appetite' sounding attractive to any ears, and one has to say that there is a problem with John's mode of expression in the *Ascent* which parallels that of Eckhart's language of detachment. For like Eckhart, John appears to say that *any* desire for anything other than God is a desire *opposed* to God. At the very least there is an ambiguity in such asseverations as: 'If anyone is to reach perfect union with God through his will and love, he must obviously be freed from every appetite, however slight.' For though John goes on to explain his meaning to be that 'he must not give the consent of his will know-

---

[6] *AMC*, I.5.6.   [7] Ibid., I.8.3.   [8] Ibid., I.11.4.

ingly to an *imperfection*, and he must have the power and freedom to be able, upon advertence, to refuse this consent',[9] it remains unclear whether he means that any desire for something created *is* an 'imperfection' or whether, more moderately, he means that the will should not knowingly consent to any such desire as *would be* an imperfection. At any rate, it is not so easy to be sure that the moderate interpretation is the correct one in view of statements as blunt and unqualified as: 'By the mere fact that a man loves something, his soul becomes incapable of pure union and transformation in God'.[10]

Nonetheless it seems reasonable to take such unqualified statements as a form of ellipsis and, as in Eckhart, to read John's 'appetite' and 'desire' as referring to *possessive* appetite; for 'possessive' desire is in an 'imperfect' relation with creation and must be an obstacle to 'pure union and transformation in God'. Hence, bearing in mind John's pessimism about the chances of *any* of our desires being free of possessiveness, his demand for the elimination of that possessiveness will have to be unremitting and extend across the whole range of our desires. Ultimately, in any case, the perfectly detached person is not the one in whom desire has been 'extinguished', but is the person who can freely desire 'all'. For, in language and thought which could be mistaken for Eckhart's, John says:

> To reach satisfaction in all, desire its *possession* in nothing
> . . .
> Because if you desire to have something in all
> your treasure in God is not purely your all.
> In this nakedness your spirit finds
> its quietude and rest.
> For in *coveting* nothing,
> nothing raises it up
> and nothing weighs it down,
> because it is in the centre of its humility.
> When it *covets* something
> in this very desire it is wearied.[11]

Nonetheless, no merely *active* ascetical practice could achieve so perfect a state of detachment. Why? Because an active, self-imposed asceticism, by virtue of its being primarily *our* activity of

---

[9] Ibid., I.11.3.   [10] Ibid., I.4.3.
[11] Ibid., I.13.12–13. Italics mine.

imposing our will upon desire, is essentially an indirect reaffirmation of the self in the form of its mastery of desire. On the other hand, with respect to the desire denied, this asceticism is little more than a higher aestheticism, the return in the cash of higher, 'spiritual' pleasures on the ego's investment in short-term pain. Every attachment denied to the senses receives its compensation in a merely more refined satisfaction of a higher sensitivity. For the possessive self, denied the exercise of its possessiveness on external objects, reaffirms that possessiveness in clinging to the me-who-possesses in a kind of literal *self*-indulgence. Paradoxically, this self-indulgence can – and perhaps among 'spiritual' people especially does – find its fulfilment in masochism, the condition of last resort for the pleasure-seeking ego, which is, he says, the asceticism 'of the beast'. For 'like beasts, such people are motivated in [their] penances by an appetite for the pleasure they find in them'.[12]

For John, then, an active asceticism, though very necessary, cannot succeed in its goal of pure detachment and by itself is dangerous. In the very acts in which we deny ourselves satisfaction we reaffirm the egoistic, possessive self which does the denying. Consequently, the beginner very soon needs to be plunged into the passive nights, in which 'an individual does nothing, for God accomplishes the work in him, while he acts as the recipient'.[13] In the passive night of the senses, the power of enjoyment itself, whether of higher or lower pleasures, is disabled as such and not by anything we can do. We are crippled in our power to enjoy, and so also is crippled the normal, routine excercise of agency.

For our power to act in the world rests crucially upon our power to discriminate between objects of pleasure and pain. But in the passive night of the senses that ability is lost. It is the condition of emotional twilight in which, to adapt a *mot* of Schelling's, all cows are grey, for it is an emotional world drained of colour and so of density. 'Thank God for lucidity', said the philosopher, 'for without it we could see nothing'. 'Thank God for opacity', replied his companion, 'for without it there would be nothing to see'. The emotional crisis of the passive night of the senses is like the condition of total transparency, in which nothing can be seen because everything is seen through. It is the emotional equivalent of the perfect cynic who, by virtue of seeing through everything, can do nothing.

[12]   *The Dark Night of the Soul* (*DNS*), I. 6.2.
[13]   *AMC*, I.13.1.

Such, at this low level of experiential description, is the condition also of depression. And John is fully aware of this experiential similarity, for he is at great pains to establish clear criteria by which the two conditions may be distinguished. 'This want of satisfaction in earthly or heavenly things could be the product of some indisposition or melancholic humour',[14] he says, and it often is, for John is conscious that the life conditions of his readers (being in the first instance in enclosed communities of religious) are such as to increase average chances of depression.

III

Given their similarity as experiences, how does John propose to distinguish between depression and the passive nights? Of course, in principle he regards them as being quite distinct in their causes, for the one, melancholia, he assumes to have a physiological cause, the other, the spiritual condition, is brought about by God – or rather inevitably by the closeness of God to the soul. It is here that the influence of Neoplatonism on John's thought is at its most striking, for, following Denys, John describes the whole emotional and cognitive capacity, sensory and intellectual, as being thrown into darkness and pain by an excess of light, just as a flash of lightning first oversaturates the world with light, draining it of colour, only instantly to plunge the eyes into ever deeper obscurity.[15] All well and good, so far as it goes, for their different aetiologies may determine how they differ, but those differences in cause will not, he concedes, enable us to distinguish, for a given experience, which of them it is, since for equal though opposite reasons, the cause of melancholia and the cause of the dark nights are beyond our capacity to experience. Neither comes, as it were, with its cause identified within the experience of it. Not depression, for whenever he speaks of it John seems to have in mind that objectless, non-specific depression which we call 'endogenous' and is not experienced as caused. And as for the action of God in bringing about the dark nights, this is in principle incapable of being experienced, for we

[14] *DNS*, I.9.2.
[15] Other than Scriptural references, John makes very few acknowledgements to theological authorities. Among the few that he does make are four to Denys' *Mystical Theology*, always to the same passage in the opening prayer to the Trinity and always to the same effect: the light of God is a 'dazzling ray of darkness', *MT*, 997B. See *AMC*, II.8.5; *DNS*, II.5.3; *Spiritual Canticle*, stanzas 14 and 15.16; *The Living Flame of Love (LFL)*, 3.49.

can only experience what happens when God does it, not his doing it. The two conditions may therefore be distinct in their causes, but, the causes being both inaccessible to experience, *we* cannot so distinguish them, at least *as experienced*.

In the end, two criteria external to the experience are proposed, only the second of which need concern us.[16] This criterion brings us back to the distinction between the active and the passive nights of the senses. Conceiving as he does of an active asceticism to be by itself but a transfer of egoistic satisfactions from lower to higher, more 'spiritual' levels of self-indulgence, the passive night is needed in order to dismantle the whole apparatus of sensory ego-compensation, and so it dismantles the machinery of agency itself, in so far as our power to act is dependent upon these compensations. So does depression, but depression simply leaves the matter there, for 'if this humour is the entire cause, everything ends in disgust and does harm to one's nature'.[17] But in the case of the dark nights, ego-dependent agency is destroyed as such only to reveal the presence within us of other sources of agency which, without the disablement of our active natural powers, we could not have detected. We discover in ourselves the presence of a purely passive power, a pure capacity to be attracted, a desire for God which, being no longer grounded in the need to possess, to dominate and destroy, can be the desire, as the *Cloud* Author put it, for God 'himself, & none of his goodes'.[18] And in common with a long Latin tradition since Augustine, John regards this pure desire *for* God as possible only in so far as it is also *of* God, not conceivably of anything we could call a 'self' as distinct from God. For, as Simone Weil puts it, 'God alone is capable of loving God'.[19] And, as Thomas Aquinas says, *Solus Deus deificet*.[20] It is therefore only by means of the neutralisation of our active powers in any independent exercise that God can love God in us.

The paralyses of agency which characterize the passive nights are therefore distinguishable from mere 'lukewarmness' by the fact that 'a lukewarm person is very lax and remiss in his will and spirit, and has no solicitude about serving God'[21] whereas the 'person suffering the purgative dryness is ordinarily solicitous, con-

---

[16] *DNS*, I.9.3-7. [17] Ibid., I.9.3. [18] *Cloud*, 3, p. 9, 13.
[19] 'The Love of God and Affliction', in *Waiting on God*, London: Collins, 1951, p. 61.
[20] *ST*, I-2ae, q. 112, a. 1, corp.
[21] *DNS*, I.9.3.

cerned and pained about not serving God'.[22] And this 'purgative dryness' is distinguishable from melancholia on the same grounds, for in the latter case there are none of those desires to serve God which accompany the purgative dryness. 'Even though in this purgative dryness, the sensory part of the soul is very cast down and slack, and feeble in its actions because of the little satisfaction it finds, the spirit is ready and strong'.[23]

It is here that we begin to need some of the terminology of 'self-hood' which I delineated at the beginning of this chapter. For I think we may say, in perfect fidelity with his analysis, that for John both melancholia and the passive nights are destructive of the 'self-hood of experience' and that the distress they cause derives from the sense of loss of normal enjoyment, of normal sensitivity and so of normal agency. Looked at from the standpoint of that lost condition of 'normality' they are identical experiences, for both depression and the dark nights are the experience of that identity loss. But looked at from the standpoint of prognosis they differ in every respect: for what the depressed person hopes for in her depression is the resoration of the lost self-image and its corresponding self-motivating power of agency, whereas the passive nights 'deconstruct' not only the identity we once possessed but also that whole panoply of 'possessiveness' from which derives the need to possess one at all. In short, the passive nights 'deconstruct' not only the given self of experience, but also the 'therapeutic' self, the 'would-be' self, which is implicit in that self of experience.

This means, paradoxically, that what the passive nights deconstruct is precisely the goals and the best results of our active ascetical efforts. For the active nights, the practices of a self-motivated active asceticism, are 'therapeutic' strategies aimed at the construction of a more adequate sense of selfhood and agency, a more autonomous and self-controlled condition of selfhood. As such, therefore, John treats the active ascetical path of the devout, well-intentioned beginner with some degree of ambivalence. For this active asceticism is the process whereby we build up precisely that selfhood which the passive nights demolish. But it needs to be built up before it can be demolished, for the condition of the person who has not yet even begun to practise the active asceticism of the senses is not such that we can ascribe to him any sort of selfhood at

[22] Ibid.   [23] Ibid.

all. The pre-ascetical person is little more than a riot of sensory desire. The active discipline of the senses does something to reduce the riot to some sort of orderly assembly in which there is at least some central core of behavioural consistency and so provides some, at least superficial, coherence to the narrative of experience. It is, nonetheless, a superficial selfhood, because that centre is less a centre of agency than of reaction. The self produced by this active asceticism is but an egoism reconstructed by the discipline of a higher, but still self-interested will. For this reason, such a person is still radically attached, a heteronomous being, a plaything of his own egoisms.

Now for John, any ascetically acquired selfhood has this character of being more or less a construction of egoism and, as I explained earlier, the higher the asceticism the more 'spiritual' the egoism – John's strictures on this evoking a picture of an ascetical cop merely pursuing the robber egoism ever higher up the ladder of the spiritual ascent, the egoism always one step ahead of the ascetical chase. The asceticism can never catch the egoism, for the ascetical 'I' must always reaffirm the egoism it seeks to deny precisely in the acts of its denial.

And so for John there is an 'ascetical self'. It is the product of our best efforts, supported by everything there is in us by way of generosity and goodwill, indeed of love of God. But it is a poor, precarious and self-contradictory structure, built up out of the combination of quasi-moral forces, more or less 'possessive' desires and wishes, bound together by the countervailing force of an ascetically imposed will. And in an attempt to elucidate the dynamics of this ascetical self (and, I should add, with no intention of direct textual fidelity) I shall allegorise these component forces of the moral psychology of the 'ascetical self' with the names of 'feeble moraliser', 'the morally shameless' and 'the moral prig', or, for short, 'Feeble', 'Shameless' and 'Prig'.

IV

Feeble, Shameless and Prig are stereotypes, of course, which I have borrowed, with apologies, from Aristotle's *Nicomachean Ethics*.[24] There Aristotle distinguishes between the *akrates* and the *akolastos* in

---

[24] *Nicomachean Ethics*, VII, 1, 1145a 15–22.

the following terms. The *akrates* is the person who is morally feeble. He knows what he should be doing and does not do it. He does not, therefore, fail of moral perception, for he sees what he is doing, he sees that what he is doing is wrong, and yet, because overwhelmed by desire, he does it. Feeble is a person characterized by his relation to temptation, for his self is, as it were, asserted as over/against temptation. Because of his failures he exists in the form of shame.

The *akolastos*, on the other hand, is incapable of temptation. He differs from Feeble not in what he does, so much as in what he perceives about what he does. The *akolastos*, unlike Feeble, is shameless. He does what Feeble does, but in the *akolastos* it is not a weakness, but a settled disposition. And it is part of the character of such settled dispositions (or as Aristotle called them, 'vices') that they obscure the very perception of the wrongness of what is done. It is not that, having taken rational thought, Shameless disagrees with Feeble about the wrongness of what they both do. It is rather that Shameless takes no thought for and is insensitive to the difference between right and wrong itself, and no longer cares for it. As Aristotle says, a vice always involves a form of moral blindness; Shameless lacks precisely the moral sensitivity which Feeble has to have in order to be morally weak at all.[25] For you are not morally weak unless you *can* see the wrongness of what you do.

Now Aristotle envisages moral decline as the steady descent from moral shame into moral shamelessness, from guilt-ridden self-judgement into a relatively guilt-free but correspondingly passionless form of self-indulgence. There is a very apt term for this state, which has its origins in the thought of Plato, and it is 'dissipation'. Plato sees this dissipation as an attack on moral agency itself. It is the 'I' which is dissipated. For the 'I' whose presence is confirmed by the experience of moral weakness, by the very facts of the conflict between 'me' and 'my desires', is, in the Shameless, dissipated into those desires so as to be indistinguishable from them. Hence the temptationless state of vice, the condition of Aristotle's *akolastos*. Where there is no 'I' which stands out against desire, there is literally nothing to be tempted.

Consequently, it is possible to describe this state of moral shamelessness as a kind of low-grade 'lack of self'. There is no self in

[25] 'The man of vice [*akolastos*]...has no regrets, for he abides by his choice; the weak-willed person [*akrates*]...always regrets his excesses after the event', *Nicomachean Ethics*, VII, 8, 1150b 29–30.

Shameless at least in the sense in which there is one in Feeble, for that contrast between self and temptation which characterizes Feeble's sense of selfhood is, in Shameless, obliterated. And yet, paradoxically, the dissipation of the 'I' into those passions does nothing to reinforce them, for, on the contrary, such a person pursues pleasure, but without any pleasure in the pursuit, out of an empty obsessiveness. As Aristotle characterizes him, Shameless seeks ever to squeeze decreasing amounts of pleasure out of an ever depleted source. In truth he is an *addict*.

There is, however, a third moral character in our stereotype, also found in Aristotle and described as the *enkrates*.[26] This is the morally 'good' person who has dominated desire by the strength of her will.[27] Her name is 'Prig'. Of course she does not really exist, any more than do the pure types of the Feeble and Shameless person. Nonetheless, she is real. She is real especially in the way in which Feeble experiences his moral weakness. Prig is met in Feeble's sense of moral disappointment, in his sense of shame at moral failure. For Prig is the supremo of rectitude who gives shape and form to that sense of shame, for it is she who Feeble is ashamed of *not* being. When Feeble thinks he has failed, the form of his disappointment is given in the ideal of the person who would not have failed, who would have stood her ground against desire. Of course no one would put this person forward as an ideal, for then she would be seen as the grotesque and ugly caricature that she is. Yet Prig is there in that self-judging, self-accusatory spirit in which Feeble judges himself. Prig is Feeble's egoism, an egoism to which Feeble negatively aspires in his sense of the failure to have achieved it.

There is a moral world which is, as I have said, staked out by the boundaries of these three stereotypes, the moral prig, the feeble moraliser and the morally shameless. And there is a moral *persona*, a selfhood, which is constituted out of the interrelations between these elements of moral stereotype. Prig, Feeble and Shameless play their roles in the construction of this self in different ways.

---

[26] Ibid., VII, 4, 1147b 20 ff.

[27] Of course it is essential to an understanding of Aristotle's conception of the moral life not to confuse this *enkrates* with the *virtuous* person. For the *enkrates* is always threatened by irrational desires, even if he has the strength of will to resist them. But, for Aristotle, the virtuous person is the person whose desires are settled dispositions for the good: she *wants* to do what it is good to do and so her will is her desire and her desire her will.

Prig and Shameless are distinguished from Feeble by the fact that only Feeble feels guilt. But Prig and Shameless are distinguished from each other by the differing forms of their lack of guilt. Prig feels no guilt because she controls desire and so has eliminated the discrepancy between self and desire by eliminating discrepant desire; whereas Shameless has eliminated the discrepancy between self and desire by eliminating Feeble's 'self-as-against-desire'. Hence, though Prig and Shameless do in their different ways differ from Feeble they do so within a common perception of selfhood. For Prig and Shameless are in flight from the experience of guilt, and the guilt they flee from is just the same guilt as that which constitutes Feeble's selfhood. All three are dominated by guilt, Feeble by its presence, Prig and Shameless by their need to be rid of it, but in all three cases the 'self' dominates *in the form of anxiety*.

For the relations which I have been describing between the presence and absence of guilt as they exist within these three stereotypes are exactly matched by the presence and absence of the 'I' within them. What all three have in common is their egoism, their self-obsession. Feeble is obsessed by the 'I' he has failed to be, the same 'I' as Prig believes she has successfully constructed and Shameless flees. But of the three, Feeble is central, the most I-obsessed of all. He cannot abandon his guilt-ridden self, which he wishes he could affirm against desire. Nor can he abandon the desires which point up the 'I' which cannot control them. The essence of this 'I' is guilt. Hence, the need to cling to this 'I' brings with it the need to cling to the sense of guilt.

This, then, is the 'ascetical' self. It is a self trapped within the world marked out by these stereotypes and is a structure built out of the materials of them. A more or less stable equilibrium of Feeble, Shameless and Prig represents the best achievement of self which can be obtained by our own efforts. But this is a self which cannot escape from its own egoism, for every move made within this moral game reaffirms it. Every temptation points up the egoistic self which desire clamours to destroy. Every successful resistance to temptation points up the ego which has, for the time being, held at bay the threatening desire. And every act of abandoning the struggle is but the flight from that egoism into its mirror-image, the dissipation of that self into unsatisfied desire. Within this moral world there are the alternatives only of egoism or masochism, self-obsession or self-annihilation.

V

The ascetical self is the best we can hope to achieve by way of our own, albeit grace-assisted efforts: a more or less well-adjusted arrangement of the forces of an elemental egoism. I have not attempted to identify these forces, nor the forms of their reconstruction, in John of the Cross' own terms, but there is little doubt that, for John, little more than some such rearrangement is to be expected from the active nights of sense and spirit.

It may seem surprising that the whole of *The Ascent of Mount Carmel*, with its unremitting insistence on the necessity of active ascetical practices, should be rounded off in the early chapters of *The Dark Night of the Soul* with so down-beat a coda as this:

No matter how much an individual does through his own efforts, he cannot actively purify himself enough to be disposed *in the least degree* for the divine union of the perfection of love.[28]

But the reason is made perfectly clear. Active ascetics are well disposed, generously intentioned, heavily disguised, spiritual egoists. They are still partly Prig, for though 'they are extremely anxious that God remove their faults and imperfections...their motive is personal peace rather than God'.[29] They are still partly Shameless, for even in prayer they spend their time 'looking for sensory satisfaction and devotion. They strive to procure this by their own efforts and tire and weary their heads and their faculties'.[30] And they share Feeble's self-disgust, for 'in becoming aware of their own imperfections, [they] grow angry with themselves in an unhumble impatience', for 'they want to become saints in a day'.[31]

Such is the state of the active ascetic, the 'beginner' as John calls him, who, for all the rigour of his self-denials, 'is not too distant from love of pleasure and of self'.[32] For 'no matter how earnestly the beginner in all his actions and passions practices mortification of self, he will never be able to do so entirely — *far from it...*'.[33]

Now, as I have said, in one way this active asceticism does represent an *achievement*, an achievement of selfhood, which is a genuine moral advance over the dissipated *pre*-selfhood of the pre-ascetical person. But from another point of view this achievement is also ambiguous, it stands at the parting of the ways. Everything

---

[28] *DNS*, I.3.3. Italics mine.　　　[29] Ibid., I.2.5.　　　[30] Ibid., I.6.6.
[31] Ibid., I.5.3.　　　[32] Ibid., I.8.3.　　　[33] Ibid., I.7.5. Italics mine.

depends on what happens next, or rather on what choices are made, indeed on whether any are made at all. For, as John's older contemporary, Teresa of Avila, points out, many people simply stop here in a condition of self-congratulation, thinking they have arrived.[34] Again, in a sense they have arrived: at the beginning, a fact which is disguised from the beginner by the very character of this starting point as an achievement. What such people lack, Teresa says, is self-knowledge, humility. 'With humility present, this stage is a most excellent one. If humility is lacking we will remain here our whole life' in a state of arrested development.[35]

What *can* happen next, to return to John of the Cross, is a crisis of self-knowledge, a crisis which gets its character from the nature of the self whose crisis it is. Depression is one form of that crisis. For in being, as I have said, a self constructed upon anxiety, the ascetical self is especially prone to depression and is demolished by it. Disabled, if only temporarily, by depression, the ascetical 'I', consisting in a moderate degree of smugness holding in precarious equilibrium moderate degrees of self-indulgence and guilt, disintegrates into the warring factions of objectless anxiety and passionless obsession.

Depression, then, is the revolt of this self in despair at its disintegration. The passive nights, on the other hand, are the dawning of a realisation that in this loss of selfhood, nothing is lost; it is the awakening of the capacity to live without the need for it. When the passive nights pass, all is transformed. When depression passes, all is restored, normality is resumed, the emotional life is rehabilitated and so, for all the sufferings of the depressed, which are otherwise indistinguishable from the passive nights, nothing is gained.

Hence, nothing remains to distinguish these two conditions but their causes and their outcomes. It turns out that both the experiential similarities between the dark nights and depression and also the vast gulf which, for John, lies between them, derive from a single fact, namely that they are mirror-images of each other. Every experience in the one is contained in the other, but everything is reversed.

We come, then, to that conceptual issue about the self which, at the beginning of this chapter, I promised we would meet with.

---

[34] *Interior Castle*, III.3.2.1.
[35] Ibid., III.3.2.9.

Depression is *constituted* by the 'therapeutic' self in the form of the sense of its loss; for the depressed person, in so far as she is depressed, the hope is of recovering that selfhood, if not in its *status quo ante*, at best in a more stable, more mature reconstitution. The dark nights on the other hand are *entered into* as loss of that same self, for in that consists their pain, but the hope it acquires is of the *non*-recovery of that selfhood in any form, for what is lost in the passive nights was never the self at all, but only an illusion all along.

But in saying that this conventional self is an 'illusion' it is necessary to warn against an obvious, and tempting, misinterpretation. To say that this self is an illusion is not to say that it is not real, for, on the contrary, it is precisely in terms of such selfhoods that real people really live, most of the time. It is therefore necessary to say that if this self is in some way an illusion, a falsehood, it is nonetheless a lived, *dynamic* falsehood, a falsehood which exerts its force on how a person lives to exactly the degree that that falsehood is needed. In turn, the degree of need for this falsehood is the measure of the severity of the dark nights. For nothing will destroy the illusion of the self which is insufficient to dispel the human need to live by illusions, above all the illusions *of* the self.

The 'problematic' of the passive nights of the spirit is therefore the problematic of possessive selfhood. And a 'possessive selfhood' is that selfhood which I need to possess within my experience. That is why the strategies of the dark nights are the divine strategies of detachment, detachment, that is to say, not merely from a particular self-of-experience, but of the *need* for a self-of-experience of any kind.

VI

The conceptual issue to be raised, then, is: what is the transformation of selfhood which the passive nights achieve? If the passive night of the spirit deconstructs our painfully achieved, 'ascetical' selfhood, with what sense of what selfhood does this passive night leave us? The same question might be asked, of course, of Eckhart. For like John's, Eckhart's detachment requires the dismantling of every sense of created selfhood in the breakthrough of the soul into its own ground; there, where its character of being a 'something' is lost, it finds its own 'nothingness' in identity with the 'nothingness' of the ground of God. Well, then, *what* is this 'I' which thus breaks through to 'my' nothingness? In what experience do I encounter it? For whom is this 'nothing' *his*?

And the first answer which we must give is the answer which the *Cloud* Author gave to his bewildered disciple, who, told not to seek himself in interiority, protested: 'But where shall I be? Nowhere?': 'Now trewly thou seist wel; for there wolde I haue thee'.[36] So, in the first instance, answers Eckhart, but equally John of the Cross. For neither seeks detachment from the self-images of experience only to replace them with others. Both, like the *Cloud* Author, seek the description of that point in the soul at which it is transformed in God, and for both, the language of that description meets with the limits of language itself and then breaks up into the darkness of unknowing. For all three, therefore, the first thing to be said is that we do not have the language in which to describe that transformation of the self, nor the terms in which to answer these questions. And what they will add to this is practical advice: accept the bewilderment of this not-knowing what you are or where to find yourself. Not to see, as Julian had put it, how my 'substance' is different from God's, *is* to see what I truly am, for my true selfhood consists in my transformation in God. I know myself in my not-knowing my difference from God. And 'contemplation' is the power to rest in that not-knowing.

There is no *experience*, then, of which that selfhood is the object. For any selfhood I could experience would not be that selfhood which is transformed in union with God. Therefore, the only experience which will be the product of that union – or strictly, the product of that union's being forged, unilaterally, by the divine initiative of grace – is the experience of the loss of experience of the self: and that experienced loss is what John calls 'the passive night of the spirit'. Herein lies the answer to the question, what is John describing in all that detailed psychology of 'mystical experience'? And the answer must be: he describes no experience *of* anything 'mystical' at all, but only what we might call the 'experiential feedback' of that which is truly 'mystical' – that is to say, 'hidden', 'secret' and utterly beyond experience – the work of grace in the soul. Again and again John places the action of grace itself beyond our power of experience. Faith is an 'obscure habit of union';[37] it is

---

[36] *Cloud*, 68, p. 67, 37-38.   [37] *AMC*, II.3.1.

not an experience; it is an excess of light to the soul, productive in it of the darkness of unknowing, and its presence is known only through what it deprives us of: and we can, and do experience the deprivation.

Faith, for John, is, therefore, the apophatic 'moment' within our religious experience. The pain and bewilderment of that 'negativity' within our experience is as intense as it is in the passive night of the spirit, because in that night of faith is lost all the reassurance of our carefully accumulated religious experience, including the reassurance of our selfhood. And we crave to be a something of ourselves, to be a something with which we can love God, to possess 'means' through which we can approach God, to know ways of our own to God.[38] But John's advice is grim news for this craving selfhood: 'The land of the spirit is a land without ways'.[39] With what sense of selfhood does this passive night leave us, then? With no sense of anything at all, except with the sense of loss.

But am I not 'a self'? Do I not continue to possess my own human powers of sense and imagination, of intellect, memory and will? And if I do, then must I not have some awareness of them as 'mine', of myself as agent? The answer to both of these questions must be yes, for John is the first to say that grace does not destroy nature, but perfects it. But the perfection of those powers is their dispossession, the cessation of their autonomous operation – in so far as their autonomous operation would consist in their being moved by anything other than the divine action of grace. As *intellect* we are dispossessed by faith of our power to construct a meaningful world for ourselves and even a meaningful God, for it 'is a serious imperfection', John says drily, 'and opposed to God's way', to 'desire to feel God and taste of him as if he were comprehensible and accessible'.[40] As *memory* we are dispossessed by hope of any power to construct for ourselves an identity of our own; and in that double dispossession the *will* is set free to be drawn away from its own possessiveness into the incomprehensible darkness of love, there to be transformed by the infinity of what it loves. Intellect, memory and will – our 'selves' as agents – are undoubtedly self-

---

[38] The understudied book III of *The Ascent of Mount Carmel* well repays close attention, for it contains an excoriating critique of the 'ways' of an 'undetached' spirituality, perhaps best exemplified in the contemporary Christian who can only worship God in a liturgy to his personal taste.

[39] *DNS*, I.12.6.   [40] Ibid., I.6.5.

aware, I know them to be 'mine'; but they no longer need to seem to be mine as distinct from the divine power which then moves them, as if their being 'mine' depended upon their not being moved wholly by God. If they are 'my' powers – and they are – and if I freely move them – and I do – I do not do so by way of contrast with God's moving them. For

it is he [God] who divinely moves and commands [these powers] according to his spirit and will. As a result the operations are not different from those of God, but those the soul performs are of God and are divine operations.[41]

But John says nothing about their not being 'mine' just because they are wholly possessed by God, nor of their actions being unfree because it is God 'who divinely moves [them] according to his spirit and will'. For John, like Thomas Aquinas, could not have conceived of the divine action as in some way *interfering* with creation, so as to displace the proper natures of things. As Thomas Aquinas says, God's will is completely efficacious: but 'he wills some things to come about by necessity, and other things contingently',[42] such as the free actions of humans. God's efficaciously bringing it about by grace that I do his will could not be the displacement of my freedom except on some semi-idolatrous notion that God's providence and my freedom are necessarily exclusive of one another. And John could no more have accepted that notion of God than could have Thomas.

For in any case John's doctrine of the soul's union with God is set within that now so familiar dialectic of transcendence which demonstrates the failure of all our language of oneness and distinction. Within that dialectic a dichotomy between grace and freewill is as impossible to construct as any between union with God and distinction. If the soul's union with God, a union which only the passive night of the spirit can make possible, results in its being unable to construe its selfhood except as one with God in agency and identity, so neither can that agency or identity with God be construed by way of exclusion of the soul's own agency or numerical identity. The union of God and the soul is such that they no longer exclude one another *either* way. If I can have no identity as contrasted with God's, then my identity with God cannot be opposed to my identity with *me*.

---

[41] *AMC*, III.2.8.
[42] *Vult autem quaedam fieri Deus necessario, et quaedam contingenter...*, *ST*, I, q. 19, a. 8, corp.

Hence, on John's doctrine, union with God cannot be opposed to his continuing *numerical* identity either. For if John is one with God in 'transforming union' and so is Teresa, then John and Teresa remain numerically distinct from one another on all the standard, secular criteria for the numerical distinctness of persons. But neither John nor Teresa are distinct from God by virtue of *God's* numerical distinctness. For, as Eckhart argued, God is not numerically distinct from anything whatsoever, since, not being any kind of thing, God is not in any way numerable. Therefore, God is distinct from John and God is distinct from Teresa not as one person is distinct from two others, but only as John and Teresa are distinct from one another. For John and Teresa are distinct from one another numerically, whereas, in Eckhart's words, God is distinct from John and Teresa only as *esse indistinctum* is distinct from beings which are *entia distincta*. Hence, John and Teresa can both be identical with God, yet numerically distinct from one another. The doctrine of union with God does not, indeed cannot, require us to say that either John or Teresa lose their numerical identities.

VII

What assessment are we to make of the role of 'experience' in the mysticism of John of the Cross? Apart from the very visible facts of the density and richness of the psychological detail which John provides, what is most evident is that that experiential profusion is provided within the conceptual–theological framework of the continuing tradition of Neoplatonic apophatic dialectics. But, as we have seen, much has happened to those dialectics in the course of their transmission from Denys to John – and much happened that we have not seen.

What we have observed is how the role of the key image of light and darkness became entangled within differences, sometimes of emphasis, sometimes of principle, between the more intellectualist 'mysticisms of vision' of Denys himself and of Eckhart, and the more voluntarist 'mysticisms of love' of Gallus and the *Cloud* Author; and we have seen how each generates its own characteristic apophaticism.

We have seen, secondly, how the ontological hierarchicalism on which Denys' epistemological dialectics depends became increasingly attenuated, first by means of its 'interiorisation' in Hugh of St

Victor, Gallus and Bonaventure and, in a further more radical move of Bonaventure's, by the contrary tendency of an anthropocentric Christology. In consequence, by the time the language of 'ascent' had reached the *Cloud* Author, it was little more than a metaphor of venerable Augustinian provenance, essential, no doubt, as the dialectical counterpart to the imagery of interiority, but detached from its moorings in the Dionysian hierarchical vision of the 'Great Chain of Being'.

And we have observed, thirdly, how that imagery of interiority and ascent – the product of imagination, but also requiring its transcendence – was set within the dialectical logic of transcendence and embodied that dialectic in its character of 'self-subversion'. And we observed, fourthly, how this complex of trope, of light and dark, of exteriority, interiority and ascent, served a double function within the articulation and description of the spiritual path. On the one hand, it had the function of articulating the 'first-order' experience of the spiritual journey, for that journey is experienced *as* an encounter with a 'brilliant darkness', it is a journey 'within'; and, on the other, it served in the role of articulating the 'second-order' moment of negativity within that first-order experience and so it articulated the dynamic of its self-transcendence.

And from all this we were able to observe a possibility – no mere logical possibility either, but a development which the *Cloud* Author feared as a real spiritual deformation: this is the possibility that the constructive *imagery* of an apophatic spirituality should itself become detached from the *dialectics* of that apophaticism and should, in consequence, be non-dialectically cashed out in the first-order values of religious experience itself. This literalism of the spirit could be – for the *Cloud* Author is – a kind of spiritual positivism. I have called it 'experientialism'.

The question which I have sought to answer in this chapter, therefore, is: given the wealth of John's psychological descriptions of the experience of the soul's spiritual journey, is his mysticism an 'experientialism' of this sort? And my answer – admittedly in respect to what is but a single 'test case', depression – is an unambiguous negative. One might have thought that this answer was obvious, except that for every scrap of evidence culled from his texts to show his commitment to a dialectical apophatics, it is possible to cull another revealing of a tendency to think of the dark nights of the soul as being experiences. And because even if, as cannot be denied, John thinks it important to distinguish between the dark nights and psychological conditions such as depression, one might very well ask whether he truly has the conceptual resources with which to do so; indeed we might very well ask *why* he thinks it so important to be able to distinguish them. And because even if John's analytical study of mysticism does imply the distinction which I have made between first-order and second-order language, his imagery of darkness and light blurs that distinction, for he, like the *Cloud* Author, uses the same imagery for both purposes *ad placitum*.

Moreover, though I have no doubt that in the event John's grip on the negative dialectics of apophaticism is every bit as firm as that of Denys himself; and while I have no less doubt of the firmness of his grip on the distinction between the second-order 'negativity of experience' and the first-order 'experience of negativity', I do very much doubt whether we, contemporary readers of the apophatic mystical tradition, have any grip on these things at all. The error of 'experientialism', in fact, is much more likely to be in our reading of John of the Cross than in John of the Cross himself. These are matters properly to be discussed in the last chapter, and not here. In the meantime it is worthwhile noting how John is much less easy to misinterpret when viewed in his continuities with mediaeval apophaticism than when read in the light of contemporary epistemologies, which know little of, and owe nothing to, the classical Dionysian dialectic.

And when read in the light of that mediaeval apophaticism, the answer to our question does clarify. The fullness of John's psychological descriptions is 'first-order'. They describe what I have called the 'experiential feedback' of that which cannot itself be experienced: they do not describe the experience of what causes that feedback. And it is to our purpose to note that if John's intellectual relationship with his older contemporary and mentor, Teresa of Avila, was not always easy, it was very largely on this issue of the role of 'experience' and 'experiences' that the differences between them arose. For in much the same way as the *Cloud* Author's apophaticism can be seen as in part directed against the excessive 'experientialism' of Richard Rolle, so can John's principled scepticism about the significance of 'extraordinary' visions, locutions and raptures be seen as an implied, if rather more tactful, criticism of Teresa. For though Teresa certainly denied that such 'experiences' are constitutive of true contemplation, she was rather more inclined than John liked to distinguish the different stages of spiritual development (the 'Mansions' of her *Interior Castle*) in terms of the 'experiences' which are typically associated with them; if those 'experiences' are not definitive of the 'Mansions' with which they correspond she seems to suggest that they are criterial for them. And, to put John's doubts about this in my terms, this would seem to confuse purely incidental, first-order experiential phenomena with second-order matters of the route of the spiritual path: as if one were to give directions to a place not by means of a map, but by means of anecdotes about what adventures one might have on the way.

For John, in any case, 'interiority' is not an experienced thing. We can be and are much more 'interior' than we can know. To be truly 'interior' is to know, but only in the 'obscure' conviction of faith, that our inwardness is beyond all possible experience, that our agency is moved by that which we cannot incorporate into any experienced selfhood. Of course we can experience that agency and that selfhood *as moved*. But we cannot experience what moves it – God – nor the action – of grace – by which God moves it; nor again can we experience or possess the terms in which to describe how that agency's being 'mine' is to be distinguished from its being God's. This faith is the negativity *of* experience: the *negative experiences* of the dark nights are but the perplexity of the soul and the desolation of desire at the *loss* of its self-of-experience.

Faith, the darkness of unknowing, is the conviction – but also the practice of the Christian life as organized in terms of that conviction – that 'our deepest centre is God'.[43] It is the conviction that our deepest centre, the most intimate source from which our actions flow, our freedom to love, is in us but not of us, is not 'ours' to possess, but ours only to be possessed by. And so faith at once 'decentres' us, for it disintegrates the experiential structures of selfhood on which, in experience, we centre ourselves, and at the same time draws us into the divine love where we are 'recentred' upon a ground beyond any possibility of experience. There is, at the centre of our selfhood, a ground which is unknowable, even to us. Therefore, that ground on which we are centred, which for John is Love, is also for him what it was for Eckhart and the *Cloud* Author: as far as our experience goes, a 'nothing' and a 'nowhere'.

---

[43]   *LFL*, stanza 1.12.

CHAPTER II

From mystical theology to mysticism

I

It is time to calculate what gains have been made from the preceding discussion and to draw some conclusions. They appear to be the following.

First, in every author we have considered, the metaphors of 'exteriority', 'interiority' and 'ascent' are central to the description of the progress of the soul towards God. Moreover, in all of them there is a more or less explicit recognition that that imagery must be employed 'dialectically' or as I have otherwise put it 'self-subvertingly'. And we found that the metaphorical embodiment of that dialectic is most commonly that of the self-subverting imagery of the divine light which, through its very excess, causes darkness and unknowing to the soul; hence, in that most Platonic of images, it is a light which is also a darkness, a 'dazzling darkness', a 'cloud of unknowing'.

Secondly, in the elucidation of the complexities of that dialectic it has seemed to me to be helpful to distinguish, first in Denys the Areopagite and subsequently in the others, between first- and second-order levels of description. Indeed, more than helpful; it seems that this distinction is necessary, and that even if it is not a distinction made *as such* by any of our authors, it is one implied in all the distinctions they do make. We, at least, need it if we are to read the mediaeval apophatic tradition adequately. For without it it seems impossible to make out clearly the distinction between two levels at which the negativity of the apophatic dialectic operates – that is to say, between the cataphatic employment of conflicting negative-and-affirmative images at the first-order level and the apophatic negation of the negation between those first-order descriptions at the second-order level.

Third, that distinction is particularly necessary because the same negative imagery is employed – in different ways, no doubt, but by all equally – at both levels, so that the two distinct purposes which those images serve is not always easy to observe. For the imagery of 'divine darkness' is employed *both* to describe the product of the ascending scales of affirmations and denials as the soul, like Moses, climbs the mountain to God; *and* also to describe the *excessus* by which the soul transcends and surpasses the contradiction between affirmation and denial, and so transcends the distinction between 'similarity and difference' itself, passing beyond all language into oneness with God.

For this reason, fourth, this distinction of levels is needed in the elucidation of the dialectics of 'interiority'. The distinction is implied by the *Cloud* Author, for whom metaphors of 'interiority' serve, at the first-order level, as the language descriptive of the path of spiritual progress, a path which, following Augustine, the *Cloud* Author says must lead progressively from a life lived 'in exteriority' to an 'interior' life. But, at the second-order level, that same language serves as the *critique* of that very distinction itself, which is transcended in the truly 'interior' person for whom there is no longer any distinction at all between the 'exterior' and the 'interior'; such a person lives not 'within' but in a 'nowhere' which is an 'everywhere'.

It is not possible, perhaps, to observe in Augustine a preoccupation with the formal dialectics of the apophatic equal in explicitness with that of a Denys, an Eckhart or a *Cloud* Author. And yet all the problems which that dialectic was designed to accommodate are rehearsed within his own dialectic of 'interiority' and 'image'. The Augustinian emphasis, which we have observed in Augustine himself, but also in Hugh of St Victor and Bonaventure, is upon the power of creation, but very especially on the power of human creation, affirmatively to image God. For as Hugh put it, we have no access to the *invisibilia* of God except through the *visibilia* of creation. Yet if that capacity to image God is in direct proportion to the degree of interiority of the image, nonetheless interiority is itself an image, the product of imagination working on *visibilia* or 'vestiges', and so is a function of our exteriority. Within the dialogue which we may reconstruct between the 'interiorism' of *Confessions* and the 'imagism' of *De Trinitate*, may be found all the resources of the *Cloud* Author's dialectic of interiority. For as in *The*

Cloud of Unknowing, so in Augustine's *De Trinitate*, may be found that dialectical critique of 'imagination' for which the exploitation of imagination's repertoire of imagery leads to the transcendence and critique of imagination itself, in what Minnis has described as the *Cloud*'s 'Imaginative denigration of imagination and symbolic rejection of symbolism'.[1] The words describe as aptly the strategy of the theology of Augustine, but equally that of Bonaventure's.

For if Bonaventure could not in the same way be described as 'denigrating' the imagination – he is far less suspicious of its role in the spiritual life than either Augustine or the *Cloud* Author – nonetheless even for him the best product of 'imagination', the supreme 'image' of God, Jesus Christ, is in the end the doorway through which we step over imagination's threshold into the dark unknowing of the *Deus absconditus*.

Fifth, we have seen that first in Marguerite Porete and then in Eckhart this dialectic takes a new turn. Radical as is their shared theological apophaticism it is complemented by an equally radical apophatic anthropology. In neither is it possible to doubt the distinctiveness of language, or even the novelty of thought. Yet I do not doubt either that this radicalism is but the relentlessly consistent drawing out of the implications of a shared conceptual–theological inheritance, particularly from Augustine. We saw that it is only Eckhart's rhetoric which is hyperbolic: the thought, or much in it that troubled his contemporaries, is traditional. And if we do want to see Eckhart as beating bounds of doctrine somewhere beyond those of a traditional orthodoxy, we will have to acknowledge that Augustine had laid those bounds down in a place where the temptation to step over them was powerfully seductive. After all, it was Augustine for whom the pursuit of interiority led to that point at which selfhood 'opens out', as I put it, into the uncreated light which is above it; and it took only the extreme intellectualism of an Eckhart to *identify*, in a way Augustine did not, that point of deepest 'selfhood' with the uncreated light with which it intersects. Combined with a profoundly Dionysian apophaticism, that identification of selfhood with Godhead generates his 'hardest' *obitera*, those, in particular, which seem to deny the ultimacy of the distinction between the created and the uncreated existence of human *intellectus*.

---

[1]   Minnis, 'Affection and Imagination', p. 346.

And yet Eckhart's position is at least formally saved from the most manifest species of heterodoxy by that same firm commitment to the dialectics of apophaticism. As in Denys, so in Eckhart, the apophatic transcendence of all discourse requires the second-order transcendence of that logic of 'union' and 'distinction' on which all language depends. Hence, for Eckhart, it is impossible to state the ultimate distinctions between the created and the uncreated, between the oneness of union and the distinctness of identities, in terms which set them in opposition with one another. For if we have no language in which to describe the union of the soul with God it follows that we cannot possibly have any language in which to describe that union as *exclusive of* the soul's own created identity within that union.

We have observed, sixth, within Eckhart's exploitation of the common apophaticism of the tradition, the symptoms of what had become, by his time, a progressive attenuation of the Dionysian ontological hierarchy. It is not, indeed, that the *metaphors* of ascent have become any the less necessary in the description of the soul's journey into God, but that their necessity has become less bound up with the Dionysian vision of the created universe as an objective hierarchical ordering of the scale of beings. And we saw how even in Denys that ontological hierarchy stood in tension with the Christian doctrine of creation *ex nihilo*, for the doctrine of creation required that hierarchy to be relativised, at least to the extent of abandoning decisively the Proclan form of it, which understood creation as a *mediated* emanation of plurality from the supreme 'One'.

Bonaventure's anthropocentrism, implied in his Christocentrism, further weakens the hold of ontological hierarchicalism. His residual 'angelology' is, like that of Gallus, interiorised, allowed a role as a metaphor of graduated spiritual ascent, but placed firmly in a position in which the angelic beings can no longer interpose, so as to mediate between, God and the human. In Bonaventure, angels do not any longer occupy with any degree of significance even that role which they have in Denys, of mediating the divine illuminations to the human, still less of mediating *ontologically* between God and the human.

In Bonaventure, as also in Augustine, the important hierarchy is epistemological, it is the ascent from *vestigia*, through 'images', to the conceptual names and beyond into the apophatic darkness. The Dionysian dialectics of negativity thread in and through that

Augustinian cataphatic ascent of interiority, each level self-transcending to the next and ultimately passing beyond all language. In Gallus, and more evidently still in *The Cloud of Unknowing*, we have observed, seventh, a further attenuation of those dialectics of hierarchy, an attenuation which may be attributed to their 'voluntarist turn'. For the crucial 'negativity' in both Gallus and the *Cloud* is reduced to a two-term opposition between the knowing of intellect and the knowing of loving, the Dionysian hierarchical scale of ascending negativities of intellect having a relatively minor significance.

The attenuation of hierarchy in the *Cloud* Author leads him, as it also leads Eckhart, into an almost 'existential' account of the immediacy of the soul's relation with God. Interiorisation, achieved by the negative practice of 'forgetting', leads the soul to an ever greater simplification of the terms in which it relates to God, to the transcending of 'menes' until nothing stands between the soul and God save itself – and then nothing at all. Thus is the immediacy of the relation of creation replicated in the unmediated solitude of the self in the solitude of God, in an unknowing of love, in which all work of intellect is denied. Within the spare, 'reduced' negativity of the *Cloud* Author's spirituality the soul is placed in the bewildering 'nowhere' of interiority; and within that same unmapped territory of the 'nothingness' of self and of God, Eckhart's detachment demands that we should 'live without a why'. In these two authors is found, one could say, the practical apotheosis of Western Christian apophaticism.

Thus within the interplay and cross-patterns of source and influence, do common themes acquire emphases and differences, though not, at any rate as I can perceive, in any usefully describable course of development leading to some determinate outcome. Yet in all this complexity there may be identified a common preoccupation: what we have observed is a one thousand year tradition of seeking the terms in which to state, with a theological precision which alone can sustain an adequate Christian practice, the relation between the apophatic and the cataphatic 'moments' within the trajectory of the Christian *itinerarium in Deum*. This is the common concern of all the authors I have examined and if the superficial differences between an Augustine or a Bonaventure and an Eckhart or a *Cloud* Author are obvious, these differences are, in my view, *only* obvious and, from one point of view, *only* superficial.

Above all those differences are improperly understood as those between 'cataphatic' and 'apophatic' spiritualities. They are more properly understood as expressive of different and freely optional styles available within a common, overarching discourse and practice. In terms of the language which seems so sharply to differentiate the *Cloud* Author from Julian or Bonaventure, the differences of vocabulary and imagery occur at the first-order level; and they are differences of emphasis within a broadly agreed conception of the relation between the cataphatic and the apophatic. For one can, I argued, approach that relation either by the route of the breakdown of discourse through its own excess of affirmations or by the route of the hierarchical ascent of denials. Bonaventure may be said to take the first route, via a resolute Christocentrism, for in Christ is at once concentrated all the affirmative symbolic weight of the universe and thereby the transcendence of all that 'visibility' in the unknowability of the Father. Likewise in Julian, this same unknowability of God is approached through the 'excessive' variety of our language of the Trinity which bursts its own bounds in a kind of self-negating prolixity. Where, therefore, the apophatic is approached in Bonaventure and Julian through the superabundance of affirmations, this same apophatic is approached by Eckhart and the *Cloud* Author through the different route of predominantly negative imagery. But in either case, these qualities of affirmativeness and negativity are first-order qualities, relating to the concrete imagery of a spiritual style and practice of prayer, not to be confused with second-order negations of the negations, which is the truly apophatic dialectic, and is the common possession of them all.

If, in consequence, the differences at the level of language ought not to be seen as anything more than differences of imagery and emphasis, neither ought the practical spiritualities which each generates be set in the wrong relations of contrast with one another. There is no evidence in Eckhart or the *Cloud* Author – or even in Marguerite, when properly understood – of a depreciation of the common practices of reading, meditation and prayer, of the sacraments, liturgical worship, or of visual images. Nor is there any evidence that they thought of the good practice of these things as being very different from the sort of imaginative, empathetic meditations on the life of Christ which are exemplified by Bonaventure's *Lignum Vitae*. The *Cloud* Author, we know, assumes that his disciple is spending most of his time reflecting on his own sinfulness and on the passion of Christ.

Likewise, there is nothing in Bonaventure's *Itinerarium* which conflicts with the *Cloud* Author's expectation that meditative prayer will progressively simplify or that in any case meditation is not in itself the same thing as 'contemplation' – for the complex articulation of the *Itinerarium* is designed precisely on the *Cloud* Author's principle of progressive simplification leading to the *excessus* of contemplative love. Moreover, they are of common mind in believing that that contemplation is not itself a 'practice', that it is something no technique or 'menes' can stage-manage, for it is a pure grace, prepared for by good practice, and by no means guaranteed by it.

Moreover, if Louth is right, a parallel reading even of Denys himself is possible.[2] For Louth has argued persuasively, if too briefly, that the tendency of the Western interpretation of Denys' *Mystical Theology* is unbalanced, favouring excessively the reading of its negative dialectics in terms of the individual experience of Christians and neglecting the roots of those dialectics in the liturgical and sacramental, especially the eucharistic, life of Christians. As Luibheid points out too, the description of Moses' ascent of Mount Sinai in *Mystical Theology*, 1 – that résumé of the high mysticism of the Middle Ages – is couched in terms descriptive of the rhythms of common religious ritual, beginning with the preliminary purifications, proceeding through the dismissal of those not yet fully purified, the approach of the hierarch to the altar in the company of chosen assistants, culminating in the contemplation of the divine mysteries.[3] Even the relation between the cataphatic and the apophatic itself, read in the Latin West as a high dialectical epistemology is, Louth argues, best understood as a reconceptualisation of the liturgical progression which proceeds from the public, verbal symbolisms of the Liturgy of the Word, to the hidden mysteries wrapped in the silence of the *epiclesis*, witnessed only by the few. If Louth is right, therefore, our attention is drawn towards a considerably more exoteric mysticism than Denys is commonly credited with in the classical Western interpretation, one in which the force of the word 'mystical' denotes the 'hiddenness' of the divine transcendent within the public, accessible, common cult, a

---

[2] Andrew Louth, *Denys the Areopagite*, London: Chapman, pp. 101–09.
[3] Luibheid, *Pseudo-Dionysius*, p. 137, note 10.

'moment' of negativity within the affirmative. Denys' 'mysticism' *is* what that common cult gives access to, as, in general, the cataphatic is our access to the apophatic. 'Mysticism' is no more the practice of some esoteric path *alternative* to that common cult than, in general, the apophatic is an epistemic *alternative* to the cataphatic.

Bearing in mind the importance within the dialectics of apophaticism of the distinction between the two levels at which it operates, it is now possible to see more clearly what that deformation of the spiritual life is which the *Cloud* Author was so exercised to denounce. I have called that deformation of the dialectics 'experientialism', for it consists in the practical confusion of these levels so as to translate into the first-order terms of religious *experience* that which in truth is the second-order, apophatic *critique* of that experience. Hence, the deformations of the 'experientialist' derive from the mistake of reinterpreting as a first-order practice *of* Christian piety that which is the second-order dialectic practised upon and *within* that piety; from the error of understanding that which is a 'moment' of reserve, of denial and unknowing within worship, prayer and sacrament as if it were a rival practice which displaces that Christian ordinariness. 'Experientialism' in its most extreme forms is therefore the displacement of a sense of the negativity of all religious experience with the pursuit of some goal of achieving *negative experiences*. Experientialism is, in short, the 'positivism' of Christian spirituality. It abhors the experiential vacuum of the apophatic, rushing to fill it with the plenum of the psychologistic. It resists the deconstructions of the negative way, holding fast to supposititious experiences *of* the negative. It is happy with commendations of the 'interior' so long as it can cash them out in the currency of experienced inwardness and of the practices of prayer which will achieve it. And if the *Cloud* Author's invective against this spirituality of 'imagination' can seem, occasionally, excessively bitter, the hostility is understandable: for he fears experientialism not only for its deformations of the spirit, but perhaps even more for its capacity to stand his own apophaticism on its head, so as to imply the opposite of what it intends.

In the conclusion of this book our attention must turn away from the evidence for this experientialism in the late Middle Ages to its contemporary significance for our reading of mediaeval mystical theologies. If this is to leave the definition of 'experientialism' very

largely unfocused upon the writings and practices in which it is to
be found, this is because the purpose and scope of this work is the
study of an apophatic tradition which, in the later Middle Ages
particularly, increasingly defined its position in opposition to the
psychologistic tendencies of an 'experientialist' spirituality. It is,
therefore, not with 'experientialist' tendencies in themselves that
we are concerned, but with what it was that the apophatic tradition *saw* the need to oppose.

II

It is in connection with these late medieval 'experientialist' developments that the theological predicament of Denys the Carthusian
has its significance for the contemporary reader of the mediaeval
traditions of apophatic mysticism. If there is perceptible in Denys'
canon the beginnings of a disintegration of the synthetic conception of a 'mystical theology', a disintegration which extends to our
own time, then it is not surprising if in the contemporary Christian
reading of the mediaeval traditions of apophaticism there is some
proneness to understand those traditions in the light of these later
disintegrations. Turning, then, from late mediaeval developments
of apophaticism themselves to the perspectives within which we
may tend to read them, we may first remind ourselves of just how
far those perspectives close in on a *canon* of 'mystics' and, secondly,
note how the very existence of that canon provokes the question of
the *criteria* which govern its membership. If 'mystics' are to be identified as composing a distinct theological genre of Christian writing, we must know how to identify that genre; hence, thirdly, we
may note the vast body of contemporary literature which is preoccupied with the question of *definition*: 'what is mysticism?'[4] A canon,
criteria and a definition, these preoccupations dominate contemporary theoretical discussion and betoken the degree to which the
'mystical' has become a specialized theological interest in our time,
focused, moreover, upon some 'essence' of mysticism. But the idea
that there is a 'mysticism' or that there are practitioners of it, 'mystics', is an idea of very recent provenance, perhaps as recently as
our century itself. As McGinn says bluntly, 'No Mystics (at least

---

[4] Some idea of the scale of this literature may be gained from inspection of the concluding
    chapters of Bernard McGinn's *The Presence of God: A History of Western Christian Mysticism*, I,
    New York: Crossroad, 1992, appendix, pp. 265-343.

before the present century) believed in or practiced "mysticism". They believed in and practiced Christianity (or Judaism, or Islam, or Hinduism), that is, religions that contained mystical elements as parts of a wider historical whole'.[5]

We may note, therefore, a fourth characteristic of the contemporary discussion of mysticism, less universally prevailing than the preceding three, but common enough and related sufficiently closely with them to be placed alongside them as a constituent of the contemporary picture: the association of 'mysticism' with 'experientialism'. Again, the late developments of mediaeval apophaticism revealed early signs of this association, particularly where it takes a voluntarist turn, though the signs are fewer than might be supposed by a contemporary mind which unhistorically reads developments in modern Christian thought back into the interpretation of the mediaeval traditions. There was little evidence of an 'experientialism' to be found in the *Cloud* Author, much of a reaction against it; and there is ambiguity in Denys the Carthusian. It remains the case that these authors, and Eckhart before them, detected tendencies which are indicative of the thinking I have defined as 'experientialist' and these late mediaeval tendencies, reinforced progressively by centuries of development in Christian spiritual writing since, are certainly reflected in some important literature on 'mysticism' in the modern period.

No discussion in this century exhibits these linkages more explicitly than Dom Cuthbert Butler's investigation of whether Augustine is to be considered a 'mystic'. Butler's is a criterial question of whether Augustine is to be included in the canon, a question which itself presupposes a definition of 'mysticism'. For Butler, the answer in Augustine's case, turns on the subsidiary question of whether certain passages – namely those (among others) from Augustine's *Confessions* which we discussed in chapter three – may be regarded as reporting 'mystical experiences'.

In the mouth of a later mystic such expressions would rightly be understood of fully religious contemplation and mystical experience; but with Augustine they need mean hardly more than the operations of the speculative intellect, the intellectual apprehension of philosophic or theological truth.[6]

---

5 Ibid., p. xvi.
6 Cuthbert Butler, *Western Christian Mysticism*, New York: Dutton, 1923, p. 58.

As I have argued in chapter three, there is hardly any proposition which could be more disruptive of an adequate understanding of the subtleties of Augustine's thought – or even, if it comes to that, of Christian Platonism generally – than the sort of dichotomizing of 'experience' and 'speculation' which Butler engages in.

For, as I have suggested, there is in the contemporary preoccupation with mysticism as 'experience' an implied theological positivism, not without its parallels in the philosophical positivisms of our own century. For just as the philosophical positivists made a sharp division between the first-order experiential bedrock of 'sense experience' and the second-order theoretical reflection upon the language of experience, so there are those for whom there is, as it were, a 'mystical' equivalent to sense experience – equivalent in its 'immediacy' and subjectivity, equivalent in its foundational character, equivalent in its freedom from theoretical presupposition – in terms of which theological truth is capable of being verified or falsified. Such parallels are not, by any means, always made out explicitly. But in so far as the question can be raised as to whether 'mysticism' is in that way 'experientially immediate' that it can serve in the role of confirming or disconfirming religious belief-claims, the same general epistemic status is implied for the mystical in the theological as for sense experience in the scientific.

McGinn rightly points to the apophatic theological traditions as implying an altogether different epistemic status to the 'mystical' than that of supplying an experiential bedrock to theological belief.[7] He is unhappy with Butler's 'experientialist' criterion if only for the reason that so few Christian writers have ever made any claim to 'experience God' that hardly any could, on that criterion, be claimed to be 'mystics': not Origen, not Gregory of Nyssa, not Augustine, not Denys, not any Victorine, not Bonaventure, not Thomas Aquinas, not Eckhart. Indeed, for McGinn what characterizes the apophatic tradition is precisely the importance it attaches to the experience of the *absence* of God. McGinn concludes that it is not helpful to define 'mysticism' by reference to any kind of experience at all.

Therefore, rather than defining the 'mystical' as consisting in any 'immediate experience of God', he prefers an account of the mystical element in Christianity as 'that part of its belief and prac-

---

[7]   McGinn, I, *The Presence of God*, p. xiv.

tices that concerns the preparation, the consciousness of, and the reaction to what can be described as the immediate or direct presence of God'.[8] But, at any rate prima facie,[9] it is not clear how helpful this alternative definition is, nor how it is any better capable of defence against his own criticisms of the 'experientialist' definition. For 'in preferring to emphasise consciousness rather than experience', McGinn's purpose is to underline 'the necessity for exploring forms of language'[10] expressive of the mystical element in Christianity, subjective 'experience' being inherently inaccessible to the historian. All the same, it is not easy to make out from what he says on the subject how mystical 'consciousness' of the presence of God is supposed to differ from the 'immediate experience of God' claimed by 'experientialists' to be the referend of that language. Nor for that matter is it any easier to see how that 'immediate consciousness' is supposed to be any more accessible to the historian. After all, as McGinn himself puts it:

This experience [of the presence of God] is presented as subjectively different [from ordinary religious consciousness] in so far as it is affirmed as taking place on a level of the personality deeper and more fundamental than that objectifiable through the usual conscious activities of sensing, knowing and loving. There is also an objective difference to the extent that this mode of the divine presence is said to be given in a direct or immediate way, without the usual internal and external mediations found in other types of consciousness.[11]

For history must be one of those 'other types of consciousness' in which this consciousness of the presence of God which characterizes the mystical is not 'said to be given'.

As it stands, therefore, McGinn's alternative definition of 'the mystical element in Christianity' seems not to advance the discussion. And the most fundamental reason why it will not do in this its admittedly provisional form, is best shown from the case he makes for its greater capacity to embody the insights of the apophatic traditions of theology. For if my argument about the nature of the

---

[8] Ibid., p. xvii.

[9] McGinn's definition is, as he makes clear in the general introduction to the complete work, provisional and admittedly in need of amplification. A fair judgement of his preference for the language of 'the immediate consciousness of the presence of God' as against that of 'the immediate experience of God' must await the publication of the fourth volume of his historical survey.

[10] McGinn, *The Presence of God*, I, p. xviii.

[11] Ibid., p. xix.

classical apophatic traditions is correct, then McGinn has situated
the role of the negative, of 'absence', in exactly the wrong place. In
response to the criticism of the language of 'consciousness of presence' that it neglects the apophatic dimension of mysticism,
McGinn comments:

> If everything we experience as real is in some way present to us, is not a
> 'present' God just one more *thing*? This is why many mystics from
> Dionysius on have insisted that it is consciousness of God as negation,
> which is a form of the absence of God, that is the core of the mystic's
> journey.[12]

And he adds a comment of Simone Weil:

> Contact with human creatures is given us through the sense of presence.
> Contact with God is given us through the sense of absence. Compared
> with this absence, presence becomes more absent than absence.[13]

This cannot rightly characterize the negativity of the apophatic
tradition. For manifestly, if a 'present' God were 'just another *thing*'
of which we had 'a sense' (or 'consciousness') then the absence of
God would be nothing more than the absence of *just that thing*, and
the sense of the absence of God but the consciousness of the
absence of just that thing. I have argued that not even in *The Cloud
of Unknowing* (which McGinn also cites in support of his position) is
the apophatic 'unknowing' to be described as the *experience of negativity* (McGinn's 'experience of absence'); rather it is to be understood as the *negativity of experience* (the absence of 'experience'). The
apophatic is not to be described as the 'consciousness of the
absence of God', not, at any rate, as if such a consciousness were
an awareness of *what* is absent. For if we do not know what God is,
and if we cannot be conscious of God's presence, then we do not
know, and cannot be conscious of, what it is that is absent: *eadem est
scientia oppositorum*. Is it not better to say, as expressive of the
apophatic, simply that God is what is on the other side of anything
at all we can be conscious of, whether of its presence or of its
absence? We can, of course, *know* that God is present to us. We can
struggle to say what we mean by this. We can live a life centred
upon that knowledge. We can experience the world in all sorts

12 Ibid., pp. xviii–xix.
13 *The Notebooks of Simone Weil*, trans. Arthur Wills, 2 vols. London: Routledge & Kegan
    Paul, 1976, 1, pp. 239–40.

of ways consequent upon that knowledge, which would not be available to our experience if we lacked the knowledge of God. And so we can, in a sense, be aware of God, even be 'conscious' of God; but only in that sense in which we can be conscious of the *failure* of our knowledge, not knowing what it is that our knowledge fails to reach. This is not the same thing as being conscious of the absence of God in any sense which entails that we are conscious of what it is that is absent. God cannot be the object of any con-sciousness whatever.

That is the understanding of the apophatic which our study has led us to. Moreover, in so far as, in the classical traditions of the Middle Ages, that apophatic element is an essential, not an optional, constituent of theology *as such*, the apophatic may be said to constitute the 'mystical element' in all theology. And the apophatic is not to be understood as functioning in isolation, so that one could construct some such thing as an 'apophatic theol-ogy'. The apophatic, I have argued, is intelligible only as being a moment of negativity within an overall theological strategy which is at once and at every moment both apophatic and cataphatic. If these things are so, then theology in so far as it is theology is 'mys-tical' and in so far as it is 'mystical' it is theology.

For all the value of his breaking the linkage between 'mysticism' and 'mystical experience', McGinn's discussion is nonetheless within the context of the debate as to what *counts as* mysticism, as if there were something about the 'mystical' which distinguishes it as a form of consciousness from ordinary religious experience. At least to this extent, his discussion presupposes the existence of a distinct phenomenon of 'the mystical' and he engages in that dis-cussion with the explicit purpose of defining the precise range of his comprehensive survey of 'Western Christian mysticism'. In short, McGinn's preoccupation is once again with criteria, defini-tion and canon.

III

It may be said that for the historian of mysticism such preoccupa-tions are unavoidably given in those developments in the Western traditions which they reflect. For, after all, there is such a thing as 'mysticism' now and that post-mediaeval genre of distinctively 'mystical' writing is found in texts which form a continuous tradition with medieval apophaticism, for all that no such clear-cut identifications of 'the mystical' can be found in them. Indeed, it might be said that the arguments I have presented in the preceding pages of this book only go to reinforce the evidence of that continuity, precisely in so far as they present evidence for the emergence of a 'mysticism' in the late mediaeval period. But two observations need to be made which throw doubts, of different kinds, on the way in which the history of Western Christian mysticism is studied today.

The first is the more radical and the more speculative. It is not self-evident that the word 'mysticism' illuminatingly names anything at all in the medieval period. And it may very well be doubted that the emergence in the post-mediaeval period of something which by hindsight is identifiable as a 'mysticism', is truly a development of classical mediaeval apophatic theology at all, since it seems plausible to speculate that what emerges is something quite different and in some ways quite opposed to that classical apophaticism. At any rate it is not to be supposed that the undoubted continuities of imagery and vocabulary which unite the *Mystical Theology* of Denys with the common language of 'spiritualities' even today are certain evidence against the hypothesis of a radical break between the mediaeval traditions and today's. Those metaphors of 'interiority' and 'ascent', of 'light' and 'darkness' are, indeed, the common possession of a Denys, a Thérèse of Lisieux and of a contemporary pious Christian. But what could we gain from an Augustine in whom the language of 'interiority' is deprived of its Neoplatonic epistemological content and in whom, therefore, the complex dialectic between the experiential and the a priori is eliminated, except a merely verbal and metaphoric support for a contemporary 'experientialist' prejudice? What, similarly, is to be gained from the contemporary reading of the *Cloud*'s imagery, fashionable as it is today, yet divorced from its author's detailed apophatic critique of the language of interiority, if not some reinforcement of a psychologistic mysticism of 'negative experiences'? What is the contemporary reader going to make of Eckhart's radical doctrines of detachment and of the nothingness of the self if they are ripped up from their roots in the Neoplatonic apophaticism, except some 'mere' metaphors, no doubt satisfyingly redolent of Buddhism? What is to be made today of Bonaventure's metaphor of ascent to God if it is no longer stabilised by the hierarchical ontology of Neoplatonism, except its reduction to a conventional Christocentric piety? No doubt we do retain the verbal imagery of the mediaeval apophatic tradition. But the verbal similarities serve only to reinforce contemporary confidence in the error of supposing that we retain the theology which once sustained it.

There is little basis for such confidence. For while we have retained the discourse of the apophatic we have abandoned the dialectics; while we have retained the metaphors of ascent we have abandoned the ontological hierarchies. And yet when we compose our canons of 'mystical' writers the one thing which characterizes all its members, up to and including John of the Cross, is a commitment to a dialectical critique of the common stock of imagery, and the one thing which characterizes the traditions which develop after John of the Cross is the retention of that imagery in the *absence* of that dialectic. It is for this reason that one may very well ask whether the difference between the mediaeval and the modern 'mysticisms' are not so great as to put in doubt any very genuine, more than merely verbal, continuities between mediaeval and modern conceptions of 'mysticism'.

For what, in the end, characterizes the mystical theology of the Middle Ages is its commitment to the dialectical strategies of Neoplatonism as the epistemic strategies equally of theology as a whole and of Christian life. And the central imagery of that theology and practice, examined in this book, is the metaphoric repertoire of that dialectic, at once embodying it and subject to its negativity. What characterises the practical spiritualities of our times is that same repertoire of imagery evacuated of that dialectic and its corresponding hierarchies and, instead, filled with the stuff of supposititious 'experience'. Between that mediaeval and our modern employment of the imagery there is little case for continuity, other than the merely verbal.

Which is, secondly, why there are risks in reading in the classical tradition as belonging within a single canon of 'mystics' understood in some contemporary subjectivist 'experientialist' sense. So read, we are bound to misread them as merely flattering a contemporary prejudice, whereas it seems to me more likely that, properly understood, mediaeval apophatic theology presents a challenge, at once more demanding and fruitful to respond to, than we are accustomed to find in them.

IV

For the picture of the classical mediaeval apophatic tradition which emerges from our discussion in the preceding pages has a number of strong, distinctive characteristics which may, from the standpoint of contemporary religious sensibilities, seem a little surprising.

First, because our contemporary expectations of the 'mystical' element in Christianity are that it will be an esoteric, subjective and private factor and within the mediaeval traditions it appears to be assumed, and in the fourteenth century explicitly argued, that the 'mystical' is an exoteric dynamic *within* the ordinary, as being the negative dialectics *of* the ordinary. This, it seems, was how best to understand the theology of the founding father of Western Christian apophaticism, Denys the Areopagite, for whom the 'mystical' refers to the moment of unknowing which is discoverable within the discourse of the Church's liturgical action. Denys' elaborate dissection of the *logic* of that discourse is, indeed, capable of being detached from that concrete liturgical contextuality and of being generalized for the whole scope of theological discourse as such – he himself does it in the *Divine Names* and in the *Mystical Theology*. And the Latin tradition took its lead from those writings, rather than from the explicitly liturgical mysticism of the *Ecclesiastical Hierarchy*. But if there is evidence to support Louth's contention of the theological primacy in Denys of the liturgy and so of a 'public', exoteric 'mysticism'; and if it is true that the medieval Latin West detached Denys' dialectics of negativity from that shared commonality of the liturgy and remoulded them within a personal and individualised context, it is not to be derived from this that the Latin tradition typically – at any rate in the period of his greatest influence – 'experientialised' Denys' mystical theology. For what the Latin tradition took from Denys was his epistemology and his ontology whole and entire and with them his conviction that the negative moment of the theological enterprise was intrinsically and 'dialectically' bound up with its affirmative moment, in a rhythm of affirmation, negation and the negation of the negation. And this theology was conceived of principally as the foundation for a theological *critique* of individual religious experience, a critique which was to be practised immanently within it, not, at least until the late Middle Ages, to be translated into the terms of a private, *sui generis* experience *of* 'the mystical'. That rhythm, for the Latinising Dionysians, was, if not as in Denys principally liturgical, nonetheless fully replicated within the ordinariness of the individual Christian life, whether of liturgy, private prayer, ascetical practice, Christian learning and theology, the reading of Scripture or the duties of religious observance.

In a quite independent chain of influence, Augustine receives and passes on from different Neoplatonic sources a comparable, that is to say, logically similar, dialectic of 'imagination' – 'imagination' at once embodying the concreteness of religious experience and at the same time supplying the imagery of 'interiority' and 'ascent' in which is contained the critique of that experience. Through the complexity of this organizing imagery Augustine is, therefore, able to unite comprehensively and in a subtle dialectic both the immediacy of the experiential and the critical negativity of the a priori epistemology, notwithstanding attempts, such as Butler's, to identify these elements separately as expressive, respectively, of the Christian and the Neoplatonic, of the 'mystical' and the conceptual–philosophical.

Bonaventure's *Itinerarium* is a multifaceted work which unites comprehensively the separate influences of Greek and Latin apophatic dialectics. That work is therefore able to demonstrate the immanence of the dialectics of negativity simultaneously at a number of levels. First, in the most general terms, in the Dionysian structuring principle of hierarchy. For this principle is, as Denys had shown, the principle of difference and order, but the structure of 'difference' and negativity which it embodies forms a scale which leads, ultimately, to the disruption of difference as such. And Bonaventure's *Itinerarium* demonstrates the 'self-subverting' character of this hierarchical principle at the level of epistemology, in his conception of all human learning – the *doctrina christiana* – as co-operating in the showing forth of God only so as to lead to an 'unknowing' of all this knowing in the darkness of the the *Deus absconditus*. He demonstrates this same 'self-subverting' character of hierarchy in his conception of the whole universe as a book of signs through which its author may be glimpsed, only so as to reveal the God who, as it were, eludes the meaning of the book he authors. He demonstrates this immanence of the dialectic most concretely of all in the dual nature of his Christology, within which Christ, as perfect man, resumes all the affirmativeness of the human micro-cosm — and so all the symbolic density of the human — and, in the humiliation of the Cross, effects the *transitus* to the hidden Godhead of the Father.

In both Eckhart and in *The Cloud of Unknowing* is found for the first time a conscious employment of the dialectics of negativity in a polemic against an esoteric and psychologically reductionist con-ception of the 'mystical'. For sure, it is possible to identify in the *Cloud* Author's voluntarism a certain theoretical retreat from the hierarchical dialectics of the full-blown Dionysian intellectualist traditions, a certain depreciation of the complex layering of cogni-tive negativities on an ascending scale and a reduction of the dialectic to a bi-polarity of love and knowledge. But at the core of the *Cloud* Author's mystical theology is a profoundly Augustinian dialectic of imagination which retains its grip, as the voluntarisms of Gallus and Giles of Rome do not, on the logic of the Dionysian dialectic, affirmation, negation and the negation of the negation.

I have argued, then, that what is implied by that core dialectic, from Denys the Areopagite to Denys the Carthusian and beyond into John of the Cross, is a sense of the double nature of negation — a sense that negation operates in two roles or at two mutually interacting levels: at a first-order level of experience and at a sec-ond-order level of the critique of experience. At the first of these levels, negation functions as the contradictory opposite of affirma-tion and the interactions of affirmative and negative language in the description of the soul's ascent to God are ranged on an ascending hierarchical scale. In this hierarchy of affirmation and succeeding negation, renewed in yet more affirmation yet again denied, is all the wealth of Christian knowing, ascending towards God in a pattern of simplification, from more words to fewer, from complexity and richness to austerity and simplicity, from speech to silence. Here, in the multiple differentiation of hierarchy is the rule of order, order constituted by difference, difference arranged in hierarchical order. The rule of 'difference' is negation.

But what this first-order complex of theological discourse leads ultimately to is that negation which transcends the opposition of affirmation and negation, the negation *of* negation itself, so that, in this level of second-order 'negation of the negation', we negate but no longer know what our negations do. The principle: *eadem est sci-*

entia oppositorum breaks down. For that principle implies that we know what our negations entail, in so far as to know a negation is to know the affirmation it negates. But the final, apophatic, negations *negate difference itself*, and so negate the negation between sameness and difference, the *eadem scientia* which unites opposites. Consequently, in the highest, apophatic negations, we know only what affirmations we deny; but we know nothing of what our denials affirm. *Et hoc*, as Thomas Aquinas says, *omnes dicunt Deum*.[15]

Order, hierarchy, the due progressions of sameness and difference, structured by first-order relations of affirmation and negation, are, therefore, on this conception of theological knowledge, disrupted and subverted by what they lead to: the negation of its negations. It is not only the metaphors of negativity which are in this way 'self-subversive', for their character of self-subversion derives from the inner dynamic of the orders of knowledge and of creation in which they function as metaphors. For the whole of creation is incomplete, 'self-subverting', centred upon an unknowable reality. Dialectic, ontology and metaphor therefore feed off one another and throughout the classical period of apophaticism, some of the chief exponents of which I have discussed in this book, the three constituents, the metaphoric, the ontological and the dialectical, the imaginative, the metaphysical and the critical–theoretical, the experiential and the epistemic, are quite inseparably united in this rhythmic pattern of order and disruption.

This constructive interplay of negation and affirmation, embracing ontology, dialectics and metaphor is, as I understand it, the defining characteristic of the mediaeval apophatic mystical tradition. It is a tradition of doing theology as such, which is in turn inseparable from the description of the way of life of a Christian. The dialectic is not merely an epistemic discipline practised within the doing of theology, nor are the metaphors of negativity the metaphors of a purely theoretical critique of religious discourse; the dialectic is a practice, most commonly described in the high and later Middle Ages as a practice of detachment, and the metaphors are the metaphors of a way of life, in which the same rhythms of order and disruption are repeated in an apophaticism of selfhood and desire as much as of cognition, in which the patterns of the cataphatic and the apophatic are in exactly the same

---

[15] *ST*, I, q. 2, a. 2, corp.

relations practically as they possess intellectually. There too there
are steps and a ladder, moments of affirmation and moments of
negation, moments of the construction and moments of the deconstruction of experience, whether in worship, private prayer, sacramental or liturgical action. In them God is found in the negation of
experience and in the negation of the negation so that everything is
denied and nothing is abandoned, so that all things lead to a God
who is beyond what they lead to, by means of ways which are the
active practice of the denial of ways.

This mediaeval tradition of 'mysticism' conceived of as the
moment of negativity immanent within the ordinary practice, theoretical and moral, of the Christian life, disappears when the dialectic is detached from the metaphoric, leaving the metaphoric discourse stranded, as it were, in isolation, minus its underpinning
hierarchy of ontology and epistemology. What emerges from the
decline of the apophatic tradition is no longer a true dialectic, but
rather a two-term, anti-intellectualist, experientialist 'voluntarism',
in which the second order is collapsed into the first order and the
metaphors of negativity are reduced to the standing of some mere
first-order negative metaphors.

It is, however, within the dialectics of negativity and in the
metaphors of those dialectics that the common ground between
mediaeval apophatic theology and contemporary intellectual concerns is more likely to be found than either share with the non-
dialectical, 'experientialist' voluntarisms of post-mediaeval 'mysticism'. At any rate as a theory of language, in the mediaeval
apophaticist's obedience to the conditions under which language *as
such* breaks down into disorder, in his subtle sense of the power of
that which is inaccessible to language to determine what language
expresses, therefore in the character of discourse as deconstruction,
there is much to arouse the contemporary mind. And in the project
of a theology done under the conditions of this apophaticism, there
is much to appeal to the contemporary Christian. Whether there is
anything in all this to appeal either to the contemporary student of
'mysticism' or the contemporary practitioner of 'spirituality' I am
rather more inclined to doubt: at any rate they will have little to
gain and much misinterpretation to contribute until such time as
'spiritually' minded Christians and scholars of 'mysticism' alike
equip themselves intellectually so as to understand the coherence
between the many layers of meaning and prescription of Meister

Eckhart's requirement that 'you should love [God] as he is non-God, a nonspirit, a nonperson, a nonimage, but as he is a pure, unmixed, bright "One" separated from all duality; and in that One we should eternally sink down, out of "something" into "nothing"'.[16]

[16] *Sermon* 83, *Renovamini Spiritu,* Colledge and McGinn, *Essential Sermons,* p. 208.

Further reading

THE MAIN AUTHORS DISCUSSED

DENYS THE AREOPAGITE

Pseudo-Dionysius, The Complete Works, trans. Colm Luibheid, New Jersey: Paulist Press, 1987.
A. Louth, *Denys the Areopagite*, London: Chapman, 1989.

AUGUSTINE

Confessiones Libri XIII, ed. L. Verheijen, *Corpus Christianorum, Series Latina*, 27, Tournout: Brepols, 1981. English translation, R. S. Pine-Coffin, Harmondsworth: Penguin Books, 1961.
De Trinitate, ed. W. J. Mountain, *CCSL*, 50 and 51, Tournhout: Brepols, 1968. English translation by A. W. Hadden, in *The Works of Aurelius Augustine*, ed. Marcus Dods, vol. VII, Edinburgh: T & T Clark, 1873.
Gillian Clark, *Augustine, The Confessions*, Cambridge: Cambridge University Press, 1993.

BONAVENTURE

Itinerarium Mentis in Deum, in *The Works of St Bonaventure*, II, eds Philotheus Boehner and M. Frances McLaughlin, New York: The Franciscan Institute, 1956.
J. G. Bougerol, *S. Bonaventura*, II, Grottaferrata: Colegio S. Bonaventura, 1973.

MEISTER ECKHART

The Essential Sermons, Commentaries, Treatises and Defense, trans. and ed. Edmund Colledge and Bernard McGinn, London: SPCK, 1981.

Bernard McGinn, Frank Tobin and Elvira Borgstadt, eds, *Meister Eckhart, Teacher and Preacher*, New Jersey: Paulist Press, 1986.
Oliver Davies, *Meister Eckhart, Mystical Theologian*, London: SPCK, 1991.

ANON

The Cloud of Unknowing and Related Treatises, ed. Phyllis Hodgson, Salzburg: Institut für Anglistik and Amerikanistik, 1982.
Modern translation by Clifton Wolters, *The Cloud of Unknowing and Other Works*, Harmondsworth: Penguin Books, 1978.
Alastair Minnis, 'Affection and Imagination in *The Cloud of Unknowing* and Hilton's *Scale of Perfection*', in *Traditio*, XXXIX (1983), 323–66.

DENYS THE CARTHUSIAN

De Contemplatione, in *Opera Omnia Divi Dionysii Cartusiensis*, 9, Tournai-Parkminster, 1912. There is no English translation, nor any modern introduction to his thought.

JOHN OF THE CROSS

Collected Works, trans. K. Kavanaugh and Otilio Rodriguez, Washington: ICS, 1979.
B. Brenan, *St John of the Cross, His Life and Poetry*, Cambridge: Cambridge University Press, 1973.
Michel de Certeau, *The Mystic Fable, The Sixteenth and Seventeenth Centuries*, Chicago: Chicago University Press, 1992.

GENERAL

Louis Bouyer, *A History of Christian Spirituality*, 3 vols, New York: Seabury, 1982.
A Louth, *The Origins of the Christian Mystical Tradition*, Oxford: Oxford University Press, 1981.
B. McGinn, *The Presence of God: A History of Western Mysticism*, I: *The Foundations of Mysticism*, New York: Crossroad, 1991.
Simon Tugwell O. P., *Ways of Imperfection*, London: Darton, Longman and Todd, 1984.

Index